f my son; to think that so young a lad, only thirteen, should go through so much

iting about his son Ferdinand's behavior during a great te... bus'

f her own brains to save mine." —*British Captain John Smith, reporting the now-legendary mir*

ed up to see if I was sound, by some of the crew . . . When I looked round the shi

on chained together . . . I no longer doubted my own fate." —Olaudah Equiano

*nctly saw the smoke of the field artillery . . . The horrors of battle then presented themselves to m*

*ntal soldier at age fourteen, 1776.* "Shoot me if you dare. I will not tell you." —Dice

l a patriot secret. *"As I looked back on the long line that followed me, I was more proud tha*

had been across the ocean for over a year, had seen whales killed and returned t

home and stowed aboard a whaler at fourteen. *"I found my strong fingers firmly attache*

*uglass, who, as a sixteen-year-old slave, dared to fight his master Edward Covey.* "It is strang

lown off and mangled by the deadly shells, without a shudder." —Susie Kin

*have been burning all around us. We dread tonight because we do not know what moment the*

*f Atlanta.* "I was standing on a bed of snakes, large ones and small ones . . . All

trail, 1860s. *"He returned with unlimited wealth. It filled my mind with the idea that I, too*

*Chew, who sailed from south China to San Francisco in the 1860s after a neighbor returned fror*

oing a man's work, living with men, having men's ideas." —Cowpuncher Tedd

*om my back and burned."* —*Chuka, a Hopi Indian who was forced to go to a white school at th*

ody." —Joseph Miliauskas, nine-year-old coal miner, 1900. *"We ask you to come alon*

*ere."* —*Eighteen-year-old Jennie Curtis to delegates of the American Railway Union, 1893.* "I'n

ionaire than it does to newsboys, and I can't see it." —Kid Blink to a rally of th

*e person and rushed for the boxcar door. I was the first one there."* —*Peggy Eaton, who ran awa*

ge, just to sign my mother's name and tell him I was seventeen." —Calvin Graham

*wire fence by myself and watched the guards walk back and forth, carrying their rifles. Why di*

*he was twelve in 1942, was forced to move with her mother and siblings to an armed camp i*

stitutional right!" —Claudette Colvin, who, at fifteen, refused to surrende

made history by doing the same thing. *"It seemed a kind face and then . . . she spat a*

*calling one person from the mob that tried to prevent her from enrolling on the first day*

ade me a twenty-pound sack. I threw cotton bolls in it until it dragged behind

child and became an organizer for the United Farm Workers during he

*lost siblings. We kids started talking. We decided we liked meeting every month, but w*

*. —Kory Johnson, nine-year-old founder of Children for a Safe Environment, 1990*

# WE WERE THERE, TOO!

YOUNG PEOPLE IN U.S. HISTORY

PHILLIP HOOSE

# WE WERE THERE, TOO!

## YOUNG PEOPLE IN U.S. HISTORY

## PHILLIP HOOSE

MELANIE KROUPA BOOKS
FARRAR STRAUS GIROUX • NEW YORK

*For my mom and dad, with thanks for reading to me and encouraging me to learn*

Text copyright © 2001 by Phillip Hoose
All rights reserved
Distributed in Canada by Douglas & McIntyre Ltd.
Designed by Annemarie Redmond
Maps on pages 34, 61, and 131 by Debra Ziss
The text of this book is set in 11.5-point Minion
Printed and bound in the United States of America
First edition, 2001
1 3 5 7 9 10 8 6 4 2

Library of Congress Cataloging-in-Publication Data
Hoose, Phillip M., date.
    We were there, too! : young people in US history / by Phillip M. Hoose.— 1st ed.
        p. cm.
    "Melanie Kroupa books."
    Includes bibliographical references and index.
    Summary: Biographies of dozens of young people who made a mark in American
history, including explorers, planters, spies, cowpunchers, sweatshop workers, and civil
rights workers.
    ISBN 0-374-38252-2
    1. United States—History—Anecdotes—Juvenile literature.  2. United
States—Biography—Anecdotes—Juvenile literature.  3. Children—United
States—Biography—Anecdotes—Juvenile literature.  4. Youth—United
States—Biography—Anecdotes—Juvenile literature.  [1. Children—Biography.
2. Youth—Biography.  3. United States—History.]  I. Title.

E178.3 .H74 2000
973—dc21
                                                                99-89052

Grateful acknowledgment is made for permission to reprint lines from
"SO LONG It's Been Good to Know Yuh (Dusty Old Dust)," Words and Music by Woody Guthrie, TRO © Copyright 1940 (Renewed)
1950 (Renewed) 1963 (Renewed) Folkways Music Publishers, Inc., New York, NY. Used by Permission.

# Contents

# Introduction

The idea to write this book started with a comment made by Sarah Rosen, a girl I interviewed for a book about young social activists entitled *It's Our World, Too!* Her school had staged a reenactment of the Constitutional Convention of 1787 without allowing girls to participate. Her teacher had explained that since women hadn't taken part then, girls couldn't take part now. Sarah responded by taking over the halls with chanting, poster-carrying girls and organizing a counterconvention. Later, talking to me about her U.S. history class, she remarked, "We're not taught about younger people who have made a difference. Studying history almost makes you feel like you're not a real person."

It made me think about my own education. I couldn't remember having read about anyone my age in my history classes either. I started combing through U.S. history textbooks and found that Sarah was right. A very few young people seemed to have survived in the pages—Pocahontas and Sacagawea, to name two. But for the most part, to become historically *real*, to be remembered in a U.S. history book, you had to be an adult.

It's easy to see why. Adults were more likely to have written journals and diaries. They were also more likely to have accomplished the kinds of things that usually get remembered as historical events. Presidents and generals were adults. But as I began to do research for this book, I found that if you scratch any major event in U.S. history, young people are everywhere. Often they're right in the middle of the action.

The story of Columbus's journey to the New World in 1492 is a good example. Nearly a quarter of the crew members on the *Niña*, the *Pinta*, and the *Santa María* were teenagers and younger boys. According to anthropologists, more than half the Taino Indians they met were fifteen years of age or younger. Several of the Indians that the Spaniards kidnapped and carried back to Spain as trophies for King Ferdinand and Queen Isabella were children. One Spanish boy's misfortune resulted in an early European settlement in the New World. And more than half the sailors on Columbus's fourth and final voyage west in 1502 were boys in their teens or younger.

Young people have acted boldly from the very beginning. A fifteen-year-old Shoshone girl guided white explorers from the prairies to the Rocky Mountains, all the while caring for her baby. Another teenager, Jennie Curtis, sparked a national railroad strike with a single speech. A thirteen-year-old boy was the first undercover agent in the English Colonies. Hundreds of newsboys, tired of being cheated, banded together and nearly brought the nation's presses to a halt until their lost wages were restored. Martin Luther King, Jr., credited young people with much of the success of the civil rights movement. "The blanket of fear was lifted by Negro youth," he said. "When they took their struggle to the streets, a new spirit of resistance was born."

This book is a collection of stories of young people who were a part of U.S. history between 1492 and the present. All of the stories are of real people. Some, like Anna Green Winslow and Carrie Berry, kept diaries while they were young, and their writing has survived. More, like Frederick Douglass and Chuka, wrote about their youth once they got older. Still others became visible through the writings of those who met them. We know Pocahontas mainly through the journals of John Smith, and Sacagawea mainly through the writings of Lewis and Clark. When I reached the twentieth century, I was able to interview living people and hear them tell their own stories.

There are many more stories beyond those that I chose. It's worth researching and interviewing to know them. Why? Because stories of caring and courageous people from history are inspiring. And because we're less likely to repeat mistakes of the past if we know about historical blunders. And because no single person's story, even that of a president, tells enough about a historical event or time. There are always other perspectives worth understanding. The American Revolution means one thing if you see it through the eyes of white men in powdered wigs with the weight of a new nation on their shoulders. But it's something different when you can imagine yourself as a girl in a sunny sewing room, racing your cousin to see who can turn out more homespun cloth for liberty. Or as an apprentice, itching to fight the redcoats, convinced that freedom from Britain will also mean independence from your master. Or as a Haitian slave boy in Georgia fighting alongside French and Continental soldiers to win somebody else's freedom.

All these new voices can be challenging. I kept expecting each new diary or journal or interview to give me the final answer about some part of our country's history. But instead of closing doors, each new voice seemed to raise fresh questions and present new mysteries. Every book or article or Web site seemed to make me want to keep—rather than stop—reading.

Though their surroundings and circumstances may be very different from ours, the basic needs of the young people in these pages should seem familiar. Some were out to get rich, while others needed to feed their families. They wanted adventure, love and respect, a change of scenery. They longed for justice, safety, information, and the freedom to make their own decisions. Some sought to answer spiritual questions.

All the people you'll meet here deserve attention not simply because they are "real people" close to your age. They are important because through their sweat, bravery, luck, talent, imagination, and sacrifice—sometimes of their lives—they helped shape our nation.

*Phillip Hoose*

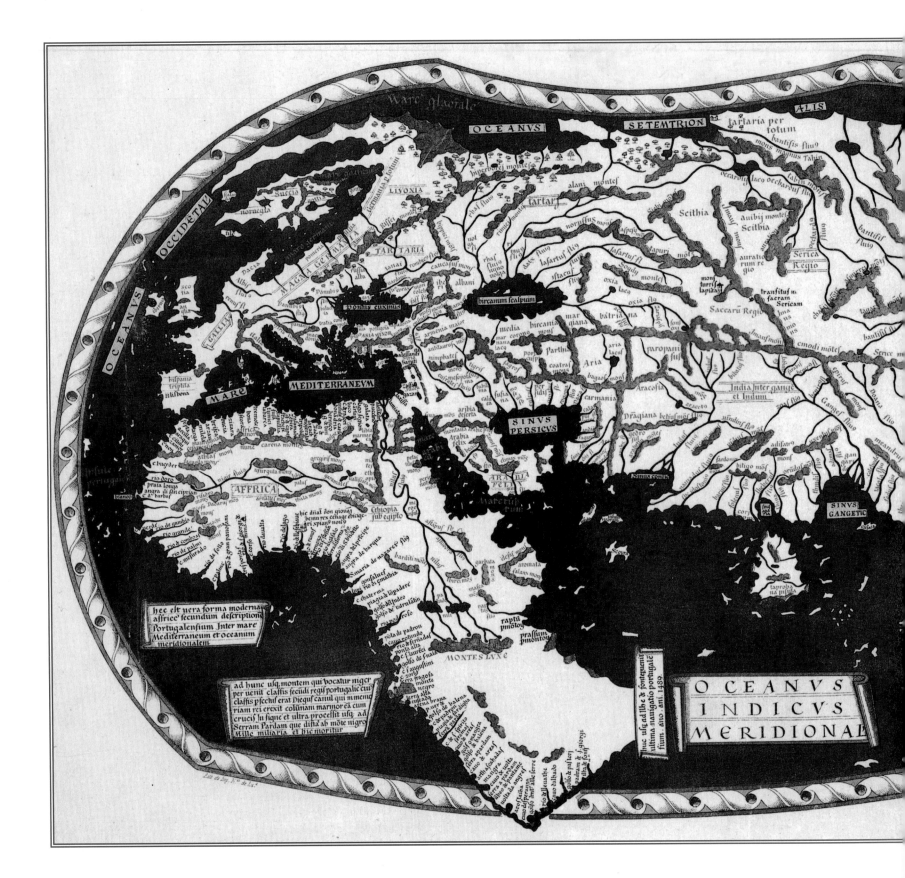

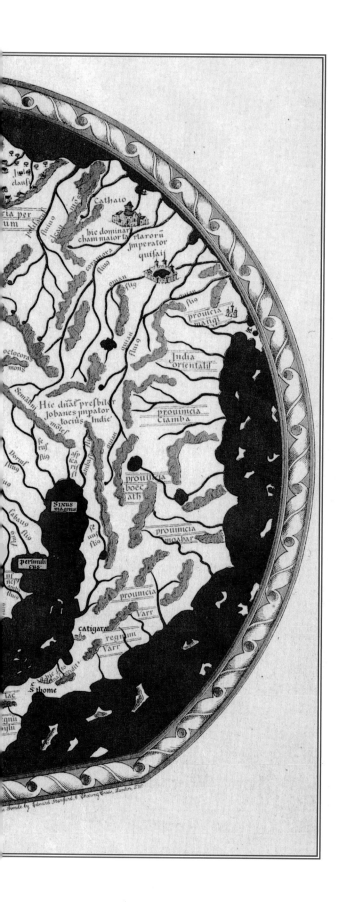

# PART ONE

# "¡*Tierra!*": When Two Worlds Met

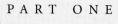

**Y**oung Spaniards living in 1492 knew the world was round, but they thought it was much smaller than it really was. They knew of only three continents—Europe, Asia, and Africa, which were believed to be equally distant from Jerusalem, the center of all Creation. They thought all land was surrounded by one ocean, known as the Ocean Sea, and that the sun, moon, stars, and planets revolved around the earth. Some believed that the lands below the equator were so hot that people trying to reach them by land would burn, while sailors would be boiled alive in the scalding seas.

Meanwhile, a third of the world away from Spain, 75 million people were scattered throughout a chain of continents and islands from Alaska to Chile. They were organized in hundreds of tribes and family groups, each with their own ways of communicating, finding shelter, worshiping, playing, and gathering food. One group of islanders now known as Tainos fished the warm waters of the Caribbean. On October 12, 1492, they met a far greater force even than the hurricanes that sometimes battered their islands. The world would never be the same.

*This map, drawn in 1490 by Henricus Martellus, shows the world as it was known to Europeans just before Columbus's first journey: a single huge continent surrounded by a single ocean.*

*"The first and most unusual of the high points of my life is that I was born in this century in which the whole world became known."*— Girolamo Cardano, an Italian doctor writing of his boyhood in the sixteenth century

# Diego Bermúdez: Sailing into the Unknown

Palos de la Frontera, Spain, 1492

*Twelve-year-old Diego Bermúdez sailed with Columbus aboard the Santa María in 1492. He was one of about twenty boys in their teens or younger who sailed west from Spain to find the Indies and gold. Most were poor boys from small fishing villages along the Spanish coast. Those who made it back to Spain returned with some of the most amazing stories anyone had ever lived to tell.*

## THE INDIES

China, Japan, and the islands of Indonesia were known to Europeans as the Indies. Spaniards and other Europeans had been trading there for many years. The big prizes were gold, silks, and spices like nutmeg and cinnamon that livened up bland-tasting food and masked the horrible taste of spoiled meat. Many, including Columbus, had read a book by the thirteenth-century Italian explorer Marco Polo. He wrote of Japan: "The king of the island hath a mighty palace all roofed with the finest gold . . . The windows are decorated with gold; the floors of the halls and of many chambers are paved with golden plates, each plate a good two fingers thick."

But by 1492, Muslim armies hostile to Christians blocked the old land routes through Asia. So Portugal and Spain were racing to find a new sea route to the Indies. Portugal's idea was to sail around the south of Africa, and it was steadily getting closer to its goal. Columbus convinced Ferdinand and Isabella—king and queen of Spain—that Spain could win by taking the most direct route: straight west across the Ocean Sea to Japan.

Diego Bermúdez probably heard about Columbus's voyage from the booming voice of Martín Alonso Pinzón, leader of the best-known sailing family in the Spanish town of Palos de la Frontera. A crowd gathered around Pinzón as he stood in the dusty town square one afternoon, trying to make himself heard. According to a sailor, this is what Pinzón shouted:

"Friends, come on, make this journey with us, instead of moping around being miserable; make this journey, for with the help of God we will discover land, for according to rumor we will find houses roofed with gold and everyone will become rich and fortunate."

Pinzón was recruiting sailors for a white-haired, Italian-born captain named Cristóbal Colón, known to us as Christopher Columbus. Townspeople listened, though many thought the idea was crazy. Columbus proposed to sail west all the way across the Ocean Sea to Cipango (Japan), Cathay (China), and the Spice Islands, now part of Indonesia. It had never been done before. Columbus was confident the journey would take only about a month. They'd all be back in less than a year, he said.

Diego Bermúdez was part of a large family of sailors, but many of the other boys who sailed with Columbus were homeless orphans who begged for or stole what food they could. Some found work on the boats, scrubbing the decks or repairing ropes. Most couldn't read or write, since there was no public school in Palos. They liked to gather around the docks, listening to sailors tell stories of giant fish, gold, waterspouts, and battles at sea.

*Sailors feared that monsters awaited them in the unexplored Ocean Sea. This sixteenth-century woodcut was called* The Sea of Darkness.

Columbus and Pinzón needed boys for three jobs. Older boys—usually teenagers—would be gromets, or apprentice seamen. They would scramble up the ropes high above the deck to rig and change the sails. They would also repair ropes and row the ships' officers to and from the shore. In storms and heavy seas they'd cling one-armed to the masts, lashing the sails to their wooden frames while the wind tore at their fingers. They had to learn dozens of knots and hitches. Each gromet carried a knife at all times and wore a belt with a supply of rope sections around his waist. Captains hired teenagers partly because they showed little fear and partly because, unlike many of the old sailors, most boys still had both arms and legs.

A few boys, usually from wealthy families, were hired as *criados,* the personal servants of the ships' officers. Columbus's devoted *criado* was sixteen-year-old Pedro de Salcedo. Columbus grew to like him so much that years later he arranged for Pedro to get profits from the sale of all soap in much of the New World.

Younger boys, like Diego Bermúdez, served as pages, the lowest-ranking crew members. Pages kept track of everyone's watch duty and did work that no one else

This woodcut from the illustrated edition of Columbus's 1493 letter to King Ferdinand and Queen Isabella shows a ship similar to the Santa María. The high poop deck, from which pages bellowed their prayers and songs, is seen in the foreground.

### GROMETS, PAGES, AND CRIADOS WHO SAILED WITH COLUMBUS

García Alonso—18, a gromet
Pedro de Arcos—12, a page
Pedro de Salcedo—16, a criado
Diego Leal—a gromet
Diego Bermúdez—12, a page from Palos de la Frontera
Fernando Medel—a gromet
Fernando de Triana—a gromet, probably aboard the Niña
Francisco Medel—a gromet from Huelva
Juan—the servant of Juan Buen Año
Juan Arias—a gromet aboard the Pinta
Juan Quadrado—a gromet aboard the Pinta
Martín de Urtubia—a gromet aboard the Santa María. Died at La Navidad
Miguel de Soria—a gromet and servant of Diego de Lepe
Pedro de Lepe—died at La Navidad
Pedro Tegero—a gromet
Pedro de Terreros—18 or 19. Went on all four of Columbus's voyages
Rodrigo Gallegos—a gromet

wanted to do, like cooking one hot meal per day, washing fire-blackened pots, and scrubbing the decks.

Diego Bermúdez may well have had very mixed feelings about the chance to go on such an adventure. On the one hand, there was the possibility of discovering gold and winning fame. Even if that didn't happen, Columbus had raised enough money to offer every sailor four months' advance pay. This was a fortune to most families of Palos. On the other hand, Diego might well have been worried. Maps of the time showed that huge, dragonlike monsters lurked in the Ocean Sea. Were they really out there? Even if the sailors made it to the Indies, how could they ever get back home against the stiff wind that blew west from the coast of Spain? And how could Columbus and Pinzón really know that you could reach the Indies by sailing west?

Diego signed on aboard the Santa María—with Columbus himself as captain. Early on the morning of August 3, 1492, the whole town gathered to send off the Niña, the Pinta, and the Santa María. Some boys got married just before they sailed, promising their brides that they would return as wealthy husbands.

The ships sailed south to the Canary Islands, where they loaded supplies on board, and then, on September 6, they cast off into the unknown for the West and Cipango. When land disappeared from sight three days later, some sailors burst into tears.

The *Niña* and the *Pinta* were tiny floating universes, each deck about the size of a modern tennis court. The *Santa María* was a little bigger than the other two ships. The *Niña* and the *Pinta* each carried about twenty-five men and boys, the *Santa María* about forty. The crews had to quickly learn to work as a team on the rocking, slippery decks.

Diego, like the other crew members, labored in his bare feet and wore the same clothes every day—a loose-fitting poncho pulled over a shirt, trousers tied with a drawstring, and a red woolen cap jammed onto his head. He bathed by dumping a bucket of seawater over his body. The toilet was a seat called the "garden" that dangled out over the edge of the ship. He slept in his soggy clothes on a thin mattress below deck, where you couldn't stand up without bumping your head. The crew ate small loaves of twice-baked bread called hardtack along with pea stews and salted meat or fish. Even the youngest boys washed their food down with strong white wine.

Diego's most important job was to function as a singing clock. Everyone on ship—even Columbus—had to stand watch for four hours once a day to look out for weather changes or enemy ships. Sailors couldn't wait to get off watch. Every half hour the crew relied on the sound of a page's voice to tell them how much of their shift remained.

Diego and the other pages kept time with a glass called an *ampolleta*, filled with a half hour's supply of sand. When all the sand ran to the bottom, the page on duty turned the glass over and sprinted up to the poop deck—a little landing above the main deck. There he rang a bell, filled his lungs with air, and sang out a prayer loudly enough for everyone to hear. Pages had to memorize sixteen different prayers in all, each for a particular time of day.

They got in trouble if they were caught rubbing the glass between their hands to warm it up and make the sand run faster. That led to the utterance of Columbus's favorite oath, "By San Fernando!" and sometimes a thrashing. Pages also helped measure how fast their ships were going by throwing a piece of wood out onto the water and counting how many seconds it took the object to pass between two marks on the ship's rail.

All in all, it was a hard, busy life for boys at sea, but it wasn't all work. Columbus had to remind his officers to keep the boys from "skylarking"—goofing off. His journal tells of keen-eyed boys who were "posted aloft" to look for land. Once he described a group of boys clustered at the rail of the *Santa María*, laughing and throwing stones from the cooking box at some seabirds near the ship.

> ### PAGE'S PRAYER
> Blessed be the hour God came to earth,
> Holy Mary who gave him birth,
> And St. John who saw his worth.
> The guard is posted,
> The watchglass filling,
> We'll have good voyage,
> If God be willing.
> —The blessing the boys sang
> at the end of the day

The strong westerly wind pushed the ships as far as 180 miles in a single day, but after three weeks at sea with no sight of land, sailors began to panic. In the fourth week, a group of crew members threatened to throw Columbus overboard if he didn't turn back. But three days later a sailor high atop the mast of the *Pinta* cried out, "*¡Tierra!*" He had spotted land. Just as Columbus had said, about a month had passed by. Surely they had reached Cipango.

On the morning of October 12, 1492, the younger boys watched from the rails of the three ships as gromets rowed Columbus and his officers toward the beach of a green, low-lying island. Columbus splashed ashore and jammed a pole bearing Spain's flag into the sand, claiming the land in the name of the Spanish king and queen. A group of about

*In this sixteenth-century engraving Europeans splash ashore in the New World. Of the Tainos who greeted him Columbus wrote, "They . . . believe that I come from heaven."*

thirty naked, painted people watched cautiously from a distance before edging out slowly to inspect—and then greet—the Spaniards.

Columbus and the crew spent a few weeks exploring what are now the Bahamas, Cuba, and an island they called Hispaniola—now the Dominican Republic and Haiti. Columbus wrote that the boys discovered pine trees and other new plants, and that one of them found "certain stones that appear to contain gold."

On Christmas Eve 1492, Columbus returned to the *Santa María* to catch some sleep after three days on shore. He instructed the pilot to steer the boat toward a goldfield the "Indians" (as he had decided to call the people who lived on the islands) had told him about and then stumbled, exhausted, into his cabin. But the pilot was tired, too. He spotted a boy sleeping on deck, shook him awake, and ordered him to take over the ship. That boy may have been Diego Bermúdez, for he was one of the few young boys on the *Santa María*'s crew, but Columbus's journal doesn't name him. Then the pilot, too, fell asleep.

Whoever the boy was, he must have thought he was still dreaming. Everyone knew that boys were strictly forbidden from taking the wheel of any of the ships. Columbus's log tells what happened next:

"The currents carried the ship upon one of these [sand] banks . . . The ship went upon the bank so quietly that it was hardly noticeable. When the boy felt the rudder ground and felt the noise of the sea, he cried out. I jumped up instantly; no one else had yet felt that we were aground. Then the master of the ship, Juan de la Cosa, who was on watch, came out. I ordered him to rouse the crew."

The next day Spaniards and Indians alike tried to free the ship, but it was no use. The only choice was to tear apart the *Santa María* and build a fort with the timbers. They called it *La Navidad*, meaning Christmas. One boy's bad luck had turned into the first Spanish settlement in North America.

## WHAT HAPPENED TO DIEGO BERMÚDEZ?

Little is known. Records show that he made it back to Spain. He did not return to the New World on any of Columbus's other three voyages, but his brother Juan did. In 1515 Juan stopped to explore a group of islands and left behind a few pigs. Later, when British explorers found the islands, they were overrun with the pigs' wild descendants. The Bermuda Islands are named after Diego's brother Juan.

---

### THE BOYS' VOYAGE

Columbus made four voyages to the New World. His final trip could well be called the "boys' voyage," since fifty-six of the ninety-nine crew members were eighteen or younger. Some historians think he took boys and teens because he was tired of stubborn old sailors. Others say that the experienced sailors had been hired on other boats bound for the New World. Among the sailors on the final trip was Columbus's own thirteen-year-old son, Ferdinand. This entry in Columbus's journal, written shortly after they had endured a violent storm, shows clearly that he was very proud of Ferdinand:

"Many old hands whom we looked on as stout fellows lost their courage. What griped me most were the sufferings of my son; to think that so young a lad, only thirteen, should go through so much. But our Lord lent him such courage that he heartened the rest, and he worked as though he had been to sea all his life."

---

*"When you ask for something, they never say no. To the contrary, they offer to share with anyone."*— Christopher Columbus, describing the people he met in the New World

# The Tainos: Discovering Columbus

Guanahaní and Other Islands of the New World, 1492

*The naked people who stared at the pale, armor-clad Spaniards splashing toward them that morning in 1492 repeated the word "Taino," which may have meant "We are the good people." They were farmers and fishers who placed their small villages near fields of corn, sweet potatoes, and manioc. They had lean, olive-tan bodies, decorated with tattoos, necklaces, bracelets, and headdresses. Their weapons were sharpened sticks. While the explorers from Europe convinced themselves that they had reached Cipango—Japan—those who lived there called their island home Guanahaní, which translates to "small upper waters land."*

This sixteenth-century woodcut shows Taino women making cassava bread.

"All those that I saw were young people, none of whom was over thirty years old," wrote Christopher Columbus, describing the first group of people he met in the New World. Indeed, anthropologists conclude that at least half of all Tainos were fifteen or younger.

Taino youth rolled out of their cotton hammocks at dawn and scooped breakfast from a big clay pot, still warm from last night's meal. It was usually leftover "pepper pot" stew, made with the bitter juice of a tall, leafy plant called manioc. After breakfast, girls would go off to help their aunts, cousins, and mothers tend manioc in fields and take care of young children. They peeled and sliced sweet potatoes and rolled manioc into flour to make cassava bread. Girls helped their mothers plant maize, scratching holes into the earth with a pointed stick. Girls also took fiber from cotton and wound it into cords to make hammocks.

| THE SPANISH GAVE THE NEW WORLD: | THE TAINOS GAVE SPAIN: |
|---|---|
| bananas | chili peppers |
| the common cold | corn |
| cows | peanuts |
| ham (the first six pigs) | petunias |
| honeybees | pineapples |
| lettuce | sea island cotton |
| measles | tapioca |
| olives | tobacco (cigars that they |
| onions | smoked through their |
| oranges | noses) |
| stucco houses | |
| wheat | |

Boys hunted and fished with the men. They lowered nets from boats into the ocean, and then hauled in the catch. Sometimes they speared larger fish with bone-tipped harpoons. Tainos made huge canoes by hollowing out the trunks of trees. Some were so large they could hold fifty rowers. When everyone stroked together in rhythm, Taino canoes were faster than Spanish ships.

Taino children roamed the islands with small yellow dogs called *alcos* that couldn't bark and are now extinct. Boys and girls chased down lizards, iguanas, snakes, and birds. They shinnied up trees and caught wild parrots by luring them with tame parrots tied to their hands. They snacked throughout the day, grabbing handfuls of sea grapes and coco plums, snatching birds' eggs from nests, and peeling snails from rocks. Boys and girls practiced a ball game called *batey*—a cross between volleyball and soccer played with a rubber ball. Players sent the ball back and forth through the air, using all parts of their body but their hands. Teams from villages often competed with one another.

When a Taino boy reached twelve or thirteen, he went to live with his mother's brother, who became even more important to him than his father. Taino children grew up to worship two supreme gods, one male and one female. They believed that after a person died, his or her soul would enter a paradise called *coyaba*, where there would be no more hurricanes or hunger or sickness and there would always be plenty of water to drink.

The Spaniards didn't understand much of this. In his journal, Columbus described the Tainos as "people poor in everything." He assumed they would happily believe anything the explorers told them. The Spanish were keenly interested in the small pieces of gold that dangled from Taino ears and nostrils—which, the explorers thought, proved that they had actually reached Japan. The Tainos, fearful of the Spaniards' weapons, were eager to please. The Tainos kept saying yes, there was more gold. And there was, but not much. There were

### EXPANDING THE CHURCH

"They are convinced that we come from the heavens; and they say very quickly any prayer that we tell them to say, and they make the sign of the cross ... Your highnesses ought to resolve to make them Christians: for I believe that if you begin, in a short time you will end up having converted to our Holy Faith a multitude of peoples and acquiring large dominions and great riches for all of the people for Spain."

—Columbus in a letter to Ferdinand and Isabella

no palaces with golden roofs, just nuggets that had washed down to the bottoms of mountain streams in Hispaniola over many years.

The Spaniards grew impatient. On November 11, 1492, they captured five Taino children who paddled their canoe up alongside the *Niña,* perhaps to show off their parrots or trade for trinkets. Columbus wrote that he intended to take them to Spain to learn Spanish and then bring them back to help priests convert Indians to Christianity. A week later the two oldest squirmed free and dived overboard. A furious Columbus watched them splash away.

Three weeks later, a group of girls digging manioc plants in a field glanced up just in time to see eight Spanish sailors creeping up on them. They wheeled and ran for their lives. The Spaniards sprinted after them but soon pulled up gasping in their heavy armor. "The youths were too fast," Columbus noted sourly in that day's journal.

After three months of exploration, the *Niña* and the *Pinta* headed back to Spain with the Tainos they had finally managed to capture. At least six survived the cold, stormy voyage. Others froze or starved, and their bodies were thrown overboard.

When the survivors reached Spain, Columbus marched his Indians through the Spanish countryside, displaying them as if they were creatures from a distant star. The small parade wound hundreds of miles through dirt paths and cobbled streets to Barcelona, where the king and queen had moved the royal court. Whenever they reached a village, people hustled to the roadside to cheer the Spanish sailors and stare at their strange bounty. First in line came the barely clothed Tainos, probably cold, frightened, and confused by the attention. Many villagers reached out to touch them. Next marched the Spanish crew members, holding live parrots aloft in cages or bouncing rubber balls and showing off the golden trinkets and animal specimens they had brought back from the New World. Columbus proudly brought up the rear on horseback.

Ferdinand and Isabella were delighted with Columbus. Surely the gold trinkets meant there was more gold. The six kidnapped Tainos were baptized and given Christian names. The king and queen quickly granted Columbus much more money to return to the New World and establish a Spanish colony.

A few months later, the Tainos who gathered to watch the second group of Spanish ships arrive saw something quite different from those who had seen the first group the year before. This time the Spaniards had come to stay. Now there were seventeen sailing ships carrying twelve hundred men and boys (the first thirty women and girls did not arrive until 1498). A parade of strange creatures spilled out of the boats into the surf: horses, mules, cows, pigs, dogs, cats, chickens, goats, and sheep. All these were new to the western hemisphere. There were sacks of wheat and seeds for garden vegetables and citrus and apple trees to cultivate. There were also cannons, muskets, armor, and attack dogs.

When the Spanish discovered that the fort at La Navidad had been destroyed and all the Spaniards who had stayed behind were dead, it was the beginning of the end for the Tainos. It didn't matter that the Tainos had defended themselves against men who sought to enslave them and capture their women. Now the Spanish cracked down. In 1495, armed men rounded up fifteen hundred Taino men, women, and children and shipped five hundred of the healthiest-looking back to Spain as slaves. In what is now Haiti, the Spaniards ordered each Taino male over the age of fourteen to give the Spaniards enough gold dust to fill a small copper bell every three months—or be put to death. No matter how hard they worked, there wasn't enough gold. Some Taino parents killed their children to keep them from facing a hopeless future.

Even more Tainos began to die of new diseases carried by the Spaniards, especially smallpox. When there were too few Tainos to mine gold and harvest sugarcane, Spaniards began to capture or buy slaves from Africa. Fifty years after the first Spanish men and boys appeared, there were only sixty Tainos left in all of Puerto Rico. The civilization of hammocks, silent yellow dogs, and games of *batey* was gone, never to return.

*Sixteenth-century European view of Tainos panning for gold*

# PART TWO

# Strangers in Paradise:
# The British Colonies

◆━◆━◆━◆

After Columbus, Spanish adventurers swept on through Central and South America, Mexico, and the Caribbean. The spears and poisoned arrows of native peoples proved no match for Spanish muskets, horses, cannons, and—most deadly of all— smallpox germs. In 1565, the Spanish made the first permanent European settlement in North America in what is now St. Augustine, Florida.

England defeated the Spanish navy in 1588, clearing the way for British settlement in the New World. But British attempts to start a colony sputtered until, in 1607, three shiploads of men and boys reached Chesapeake Bay in the land they called Virginia. Described as a paradise by the few who had seen it, coastal Virginia was also the heart of a mighty Indian nation. Settlers were immediately set upon by aggressive warriors quite unlike the gentle Tainos.

But the stubborn Europeans had superior weapons. Within a few decades there was a necklace of British and French colonies along the Atlantic coast of North America. A tide of young people—some orphans, others stolen from or sold by their families—sailed from Europe and Africa to develop the new land with their elders.

*In the sixteenth century, Londoners imagined Virginia as the Garden of Eden, where game was so plentiful that one had only to step forward and pick it up.*

*"Had it not been for Pocahontas, Virginia might lie to this day as it was on our first arrival."*—John Smith, in a letter to Queen Anne of England, 1616

# Pocahontas: Peacemaker, Cartwheeler, Princess

Werowocomoco, 1607

*Pocahontas is usually described as the brave daughter of an Indian chief, a girl who fell in love with the English adventurer John Smith and helped the British get started in the New World. It has been difficult for historians to know what she was really like, partly because most information about her comes from the writings of Smith himself. Her father, Powhatan, was a mighty ruler. He united thirty-one separate tribes into a great nation stretching from Virginia through the Carolinas. He had no use for white colonizers. Twice he drove Spanish settlers away, and his warriors may have destroyed a British attempt to start a colony in North Carolina. He didn't welcome the three new English ships that appeared in Chesapeake Bay in 1607. In that same year Pocahontas's carefree childhood came to an end.*

The year the ships arrived, Pocahontas was eleven or twelve years old. Her real name was Matoaka, or "Little Snow Feather," but because her tribe believed that to reveal one's true name to outsiders gave away power, she also had a second name, Pocahontas, which meant "playful one."

It was easy to be playful in her village, Werowocomoco, where Powhatan children were given a long time to grow up. They built scarecrow houses in the middle of their cornfields and hid inside, throwing stones out at the animals that came to nibble the crops. Boys and girls played running games, some with sticks or balls. They ran almost naked in warm weather and wrapped themselves in deerskin coats and feathered cloaks when the weather turned cold.

Pocahontas's father was the most powerful ruler in the world they knew. Cloaked in a raccoon robe, Chief Powhatan (his real name was Wahunsonacock, but he was called Powhatan as the chief of the Powhatan nation) seated himself high above his subjects on a throne twelve mats thick. It was well known that Pocahontas was his favorite among his twenty-seven children. She often sat beside him, and he respected her insight even though she was young.

---

### "LOVE YOU NOT ME?"

"Kekaten Pokahontas patiaquagh niugh tanks manotyens mawokick."

Translation: "Bid Pocahontas bring hither two little baskets and I will give her white beads to make her a chain." It was a sentence Pocahontas taught John Smith to say when he wanted to send her a message.

"Love you not me?"—a sentence the English boys taught Pocahontas to say. They begged her to say it over and over. She in turn taught it to the girls of her tribe.

In April of 1607, news arrived that ships carrying "round-eyes," or white-skinned men, had arrived and that they had built a small wooden fort on a peninsula near the widening of a river. Chief Powhatan was instantly suspicious. Though they were quick to clap their hands over their hearts as a sign of friendship, he suspected that these men and boys were like the whites who had come before: They would want corn and offer nothing of value in return. Barely a week after they landed, Powhatan sent a party of two hundred braves to attack Jamestown. After killing many whites, the braves were driven off by cannon fire. Those cannons interested Powhatan very much.

Late in the summer, Powhatan sent a small party to Jamestown with food to trade. It was mainly a spy mission. Powhatan wanted to know how many whites there were and whether they would trade their muskets and cannons for corn. Their answer was no, and

Powhatan didn't like it. For a few months, a tense, uneasy truce hovered over coastal Virginia. By autumn, the settlers, who did not know how to hunt or plant in this climate, were beginning to starve.

In December, a red-bearded English adventurer named John Smith took a party of nine other settlers to explore what they called the James River. They were after food and gold, and they sought a path to the Pacific Ocean, which they believed was nearby. A large hunting party of Pamunkey Indians surprised the British and captured Smith. They marched him from village to village, where local chiefs questioned him. How many British were there? What were they doing? How long would they stay?

Smith gave little information away. Finally he was taken to Werowocomoco to appear before Powhatan in his great longhouse of arched saplings. After several hours of interrogation, Powhatan abruptly ordered his chiefs to kill Smith. His warriors seized Smith, shoved him forward, and

*In this drawing from John Smith's* General Historie of Virginia, *Pocahontas begs for Smith's life, as Powhatan's braves prepare to end it.*

King Powhatan commands C.Smith to be slayne, his daughter Pokahontas beggs his life his thankfullnes and how he Subiected 39 of their kings reade y history

forced his head down upon two large stones. Braves lifted their stone clubs above their heads and prepared to smash them down onto Smith's skull. Then, according to Smith, a girl rushed forward, placed her own head on top of Smith's, and begged Powhatan to spare Smith's life. Powhatan hesitated, then stopped the execution. Two days later, Powhatan adopted the astonished Smith into the tribe as his own son—and as a chief himself. "You may call me Father," he told Smith. Pocahontas, he said, referring to the girl who had saved Smith, was to be his guardian and sister.

Historians still debate what really happened that day. Smith's description leaves little doubt that Pocahontas really put her head on his. But why? Love? Compassion? One theory is that the whole episode was scripted by Powhatan. If Smith was adopted as a chief, he would have to offer gifts, as other chiefs did. Powhatan wanted those cannons. And if he made Pocahontas Smith's sister, she would have a reason to spend time in Jamestown, where she could spy for Powhatan. Another theory is that Pocahontas was a genuine peacemaker who recognized Smith's leadership and respected him too much to let him die without trying to save him.

Pocahontas shuttled back and forth between Werowocomoco and Jamestown in the winter and spring of 1608. She played with the English boys, challenging them to races, seeing who could jump the highest. They taught her how to do cartwheels, which she learned quickly. Smith wrote that she got so good that she would cartwheel through the dusty clearing at Jamestown, laughing the whole time. She and Smith taught each other words from their languages. A deep friendship grew between them.

Still, the tension deepened between the two sides as the British refused to part with their firearms. One day, when a group of Indians seemed to be surrounding Smith in a cornfield, he whipped out his pistol and took seven of them captive. Pocahontas, acting as her tribe's official ambassador to the British, appeared before the Jamestown ruling council and coolly demanded their release. The settlers let them go.

*Red-haired, short, and feisty, John Smith was a lifelong adventurer. As a boy, he sold his schoolbooks to run away to sea.*

Late in 1608, yet another shipload of British settlers arrived. More guns, more round-eyes hungry for corn, not one of them respecting Powhatan as king. Powhatan told his people not to trade with the British anymore, and he ordered Pocahontas to stay away from Jamestown. This was a deep blow to Pocahontas, for now she was truly living in two worlds. It meant not seeing her "brother," a man who was opening her eyes to a wider world and a new language. And yet she was loyal to her people. Later, when she heard her father and several of his braves plotting to trap and kill Smith, she had to choose. With no time to lose, she slipped away and raced through the woods to warn him, then quickly returned home.

In the fall Smith abruptly left Virginia for England without saying good-bye to Pocahontas. She assumed he was dead, for she could not believe he would simply abandon her. With Smith gone, the Indians surrounded the fort at Jamestown and kept the settlers from getting food. The British later called it the "starving time." Powhatan moved his inner family farther away from Jamestown and kept Pocahontas away from the British for three years.

During that time Pocahontas married a brave named Kocoum. Little is known of him, but the couple was no longer together in 1613 when the British next came upon her. At that time she was living apart from her father in a village near the river, not far from where a British ship was anchored. With the aid of friendly Indians, the British lured her aboard, taking her hostage. They believed Powhatan would do nearly anything, maybe even surrender, to get her back. Day after day Pocahontas expected her father to come to her rescue, but Powhatan never appeared. As the months dragged by, she began to adopt white ways. She traded her soft deerskin garments for stiff, scratchy petticoats and began to walk with small steps instead of long strides. She perfected her English. She attended Bible classes and, as always, learned quickly. She was baptized as a Christian and given the name Rebecca.

When she was eighteen, Pocahontas married John Rolfe, a twenty-eight-year-old English tobacco planter whose first wife had died on the voyage from London to Virginia.

*A portrait of Pocahontas, painted in England when she was about twenty and the talk of London society*

It was the first official interracial marriage in America. Rolfe gained permission from British authorities by convincing them that Pocahontas offered valuable, living proof that the Indians of Virginia could be civilized.

In 1616, Pocahontas and Rolfe sailed for London to show off their new baby, Thomas, and to raise money for the Jamestown settlement. Sponsors of the Jamestown Colony were eager to show Rolfe's Indian bride to Londoners. They hoped that the elegant, English-speaking princess would prove to potential investors that Virginia was indeed a safe place for British money.

When Pocahontas first caught sight of the hundreds of tall ships in Plymouth Harbor and saw London's bustling streets and impressive buildings, perhaps she finally understood the power of the round-eyes and the hopelessness of her tribe's situation in Virginia.

In the next weeks, Pocahontas was presented to London society at a series of balls and dinners. Dressed in gowns and petticoats, she became a sensation, a celebrity. At one such reception, the great English playwright Ben Jonson is said to have simply stared at her, unable to speak for forty-five minutes. John Smith was also in London, but he didn't contact Pocahontas until he learned that she had become gravely ill. The two had a painful reunion of several hours. Unable to forgive him, she turned her back to him and addressed him impersonally as "Father." The visit seemed to sadden her deeply.

While Pocahontas was in London, a British artist was hired to paint her portrait. The finished canvas shows a poised young woman in a feathered top hat and lace collar, looking straight back at the painter with large, clear eyes that reveal little of her feelings. Ever since Columbus, boys and girls of Europe had heard stories of the naked, bloodthirsty savages who waited across the ocean to fill Europeans' bodies with arrows. But here was a princess, a young mother who dressed elegantly and spoke perfect English. Pocahontas gave Europeans an Indian with a human face, a soul, and a conscience.

## WHAT HAPPENED TO POCAHONTAS?

She died in 1617 at the age of twenty-two while preparing to sail back to Virginia. When Powhatan learned that Pocahontas was dead, he gave up his throne and went to live among the neighboring Patomics. He died a year later. Pocahontas's son, Thomas, went to Virginia in 1635 and became a successful planter.

*"Wee marched to the King [Powhatan], who, after his old manner kindly received him, especially a boy of thirteen years old called Thomas Savage."*
—John Smith, *A True Relation of Virginia Since the First Planting of That Colony*

## Tom Savage: Living Two Lives

Jamestown, Virginia, 1608

*Early in 1608, a second group of English settlers arrived in Jamestown to reinforce the first group, who were starving and under attack from Powhatans, part of the Algonquian nation. Only one boy came with the second group. He was thirteen-year-old Thomas Savage, who left England looking for adventure. He became the first British spy in the New World, and he got all the adventure he could handle.*

Unlike most of the first English children in America, Tom Savage was probably not an orphan. More likely he was the son of people who owned land in the city of Chester, near Liverpool. Though he didn't write about his early life, historians think Tom ran away to London because he was determined to see Virginia.

Many Britishers were thinking about Virginia in 1608. The Virginia Company, sponsor of the colony at Jamestown, tried to attract investors and settlers to the colony by describing Virginia as a paradise. It was advertised as a land of "fair meadowes and goodly tall trees" where colonists snacked on strawberries big enough to choke them, hunted raccoons the size of foxes, and plucked grapes from vines as big around as a man's thigh. Supposedly, it was almost impossible not to find gold.

Once he got to London, Tom made his way to the docks and introduced himself to a one-armed ship captain named

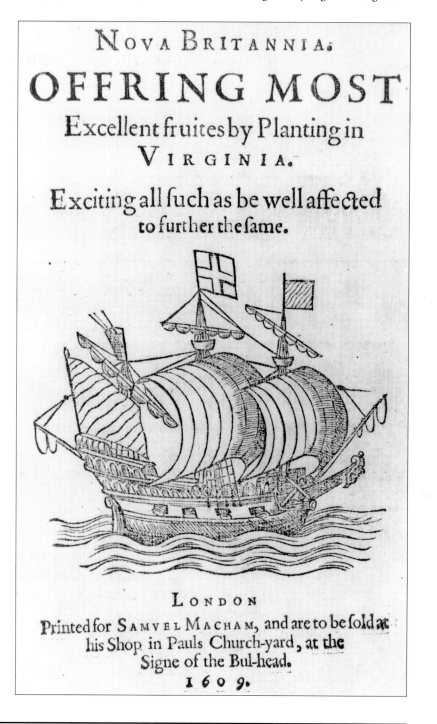

*Advertisements promising the riches of the New World encouraged many English to emigrate.*

Christopher Newport, the very man who had taken the first group of colonists to Virginia. Now he was back for more colonists and fresh supplies. Captain Newport must have liked what he saw of this eager boy. He offered Tom a free trip to Virginia if Tom would agree to become Newport's personal indentured servant. At sea, Tom would cook, rig sails, and scrub decks. Once they got to Virginia, he would become a field hand or Newport's household servant. After seven years, the contract would run out and Tom would be free to seek his fortune.

Had Tom known what Virginia was really like, he might not have been so eager. Jamestown was hardly a paradise. Settlers had to work hard to find food and clear the wilderness, and the Indians were unfriendly and aggressive. Most of the settlers in Jamestown were lazy investors from London who were out to find gold quickly and then sail back home to spend it. These city men who had never hunted or farmed spent their afternoons stumbling along riverbanks, panning for gold in their silk breeches.

By the time Tom arrived at Jamestown with the second group of settlers, in January of 1608, about two-thirds of the Englishmen were dying from starvation, malaria, and pneumonia. Others had been killed by Powhatan's warriors. One of the four original younkers (see sidebar) had already taken an arrow in the heart.

John Smith, the leader of the Jamestown Colony, desperately wanted to know more about the Indians he faced. How many were there? Where were their villages? Which tribes, if any, would trade corn for beads—not guns—and teach the English settlers to plant it? He needed a spy.

Smith learned that tribes sometimes traded children so that the entire Powhatan confederacy could learn from the exchanges. He came up with an idea: Why not offer Powhatan a British boy in exchange for an Indian boy who could be given a chance to sail to England? Powhatan surely had the same questions about the British that Smith did about Powhatan's tribes. And once the Indian boy saw London, he would surely report back that the Indians had no chance to succeed against the powerful British.

Smith convinced Captain Newport to give up his servant for the good of the colony. He offered the boy a deal: If Tom would go live among the Indians for a time and report back with information when he could, he would be granted freedom from his indenture early. Tom agreed. In proposing the exchange, the British told Indian messengers that

Captain Newport was the colony's ruler and that they were offering Powhatan Newport's only son. Powhatan sent a return message saying he wanted to see the boy first.

A few days later Tom, dressed as a gentleman, hiked off with a party of British settlers through the forest to Powhatan's village of Werowocomoco. The group was led by a trumpeter who played flourishes as if he were announcing a king. After formal greetings,

*John Smith's map of Virginia, drawn in 1612. He hoped and believed that the Pacific Ocean was just to the west.*

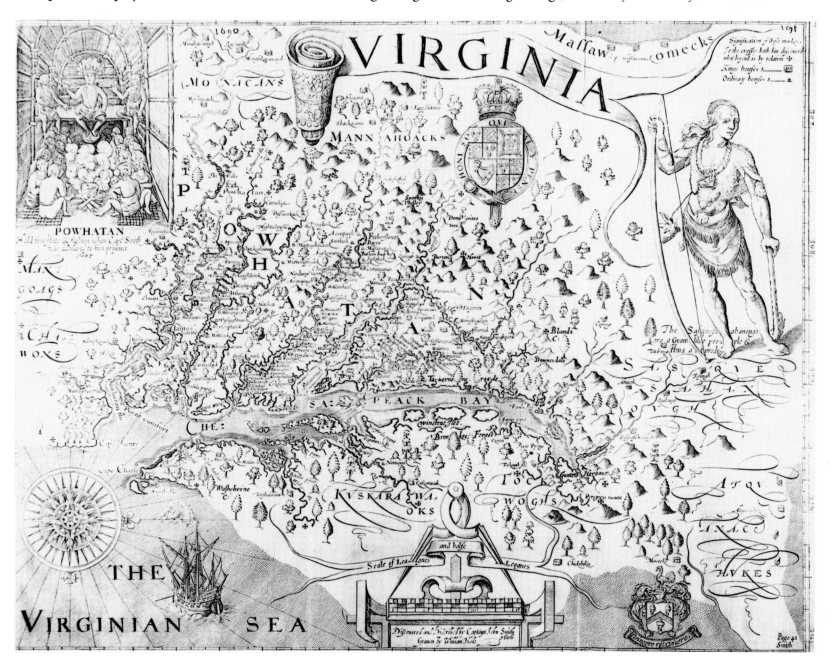

Newport presented his "son," Thomas. The great chief inspected Tom carefully, then accepted him and gave the British a young brave named Namontack. Of course, Namontack was a spy, too, with orders to go to England and report back with information on the round-eyes' strength.

After the colonists left, Tom dropped his London clothes and tied a fringed deerskin cloth around his waist. Algonquian boys painted his chest and back with the juice of the pocan plant to protect him from spirits of the forest. They taught him to stalk deer on all fours with a bow slung over his shoulders. Just a year before, Tom had lived in crowded England. Now he was living in a village of huts held together by woven fibers and sleeping in Chief Powhatan's longhouse, surrounded by warriors.

Tom lived the razor-edged life of an undercover agent. He was forbidden from going to Jamestown by himself, though at least once he was able to warn the colonists of an attack. When British colonists learned that the Indian boy, Namontack, had been killed in a quarrel at sea, Tom's situation became even more dangerous. If Powhatan found out, he might take revenge by killing Tom. As months and then years went by with no word from Namontack, the secret got harder and harder for the British to keep.

After three years, Powhatan finally let Tom visit Jamestown on his own. This time the British decided he would not return, even if Powhatan's warriors came after him. With John Smith back in England, Tom was now the colonist who knew Algonquian words, customs, and leaders the best. At sixteen, he had become one of the most important figures in the Jamestown Colony and was given his freedom from indenture. To reward his courage, the British granted the teenager the military rank of ensign and declared him Interpreter for the Colonies.

## WHAT HAPPENED TO TOM SAVAGE?

In 1619, after Powhatan died, a new chief named Debeavon gave Tom nine thousand acres on a peninsula on the Eastern Shore of Virginia. Tom became the first white settler in that area, which today is known as Savage Neck. He married a British settler named Anna Tying in 1624. They had one child, a son. Tom Savage died in 1627.

*"[Boys and girls of] twelve or fourteen yeers of age, or under may bee kept from idlenesse, in making of a thousand kindes of trifling things, which wil be good merchandize for that country."*—Richard Hakluyt of London, explaining why he favored sending children to the New World

# Orphans and Tobacco Brides: Feeding England's Newest Habit

London and Virginia, 1619

*Though Britain's King James declared smoking ugly to look at, nasty to smell, bad for the brain, and awful for the lungs, the British loved to smoke, and they adored John Rolfe's new Virginia blend. The Jamestown Colony suddenly needed more land to grow it on and workers to plant and harvest the crop. To satisfy the smokers of London and bankroll the colony, Virginians turned to a great, cheap labor supply: English children.*

The seventeenth century was an unsettling time for the youth of England. In the countryside, peasant farmers were driven off their land by landlords who wanted it for raising sheep. Many large families were broken apart, and thousands of children ran away to live in the streets of England's rapidly growing cities.

City officials had responsibility under England's Poor Law to take care of orphans and abandoned children. The usual practice was to "bind them out" to families who would take in more children. But suddenly there were way too many children. When John Rolfe's Virginia blend of tobacco began to take off in London, a logical solution arose: Why not ship England's orphans to Jamestown's tobacco fields?

In 1619, the Virginia Company wrote to the London Privy Council:

"We pray your Lordship to furnish us with one hundred [children] for next spring. Our desire is that we may have them of twelve years old and upward with allowance of three pounds apiece for their transportation and forty shillings apiece for their apparel . . . They shall be apprentices the boys till they come to twenty-one years of age the girls till like age or till they be married."

The request was granted and one hundred children sailed to Virginia. The next year the company went even further. They asked London's leaders for permission to *make* children

### A COLONY FOR SMOKERS

Though the king railed against "the black stinking fumes," London coffee shops grew ever smokier with Virginia tobacco. About twenty-five hundred pounds were exported to England in 1616. Two years later, the figure was fifty thousand pounds, and by the Revolutionary War it was one million pounds—and tobacco ruled Virginia.

## NEW HELP

In 1619, the Virginia Company offered two other new sources of help to Jamestown besides boys. It sent a shipload of "young, handsome and honestly educated maids" from England to be wives to the male settlers. These were poor women and teenage girls who wanted something better than homelessness in London but had no money to pay their fare. When the boat arrived in Jamestown, men clustered eagerly at the dock to see the women. The price of a wife was 120 pounds of tobacco to the company. The women were called "tobacco brides."

And in late summer, there was a second new source of labor. John Rolfe wrote in his journal: "About the last of August came in a Dutch man of warre that sold us twenty negars." These twenty Africans were the first of a great wave of men, women, and children from Africa who came to America's shores in chains. One was a baby named William, the first black child born in Colonial America.

They worked in the tobacco fields with white indentured servants. At first, the British gave the African servants freedom after several years of work. But in 1662, a law was passed in the Virginia colony that said children were slaves if their mother was a slave, and free if she was not. By then, almost all African-American adult women were slaves, so of course nearly all black children became part of their white master's property, just like his furniture and livestock and tobacco and land.

go to Virginia, and, once they were there, for permission to "imprison, punish or dispose" of children who didn't follow their orders. In making this request, they described Virginia's tobacco fields as an ideal reform school and asked the city for one hundred children "of whome the City is especially desireous to be disburdened, and in Virginia under severe masters they may be brought to goodness." Again, permission was granted.

Soon there was a thriving market for children. Investors in the Virginia colony hired people to lure children aboard ships with scraps of food and tales of adventure. Some children were offered indentures, contracts that provided a free trip to Virginia in exchange for years of labor. Others were simply kidnapped or "spirited" away. One boy, rescued from a ship about to sail for Virginia, testified in court that he had been snatched from his parents and forced onto a ship full of crying children on the river Thames. He said he could see his parents from the ship but they didn't have enough money to buy him back from his captors. A London girl testified that a "spirit" named Sarah Sharpe was guilty of "violently assaulting her, tearing her by the hair of the head, and biting of the arm" and for being "a common taker up of children into ships."

Laws were passed to protect children against spirits, but they stayed in business until large numbers of families immigrated to the New World, bringing their own children with them.

*This trading card from 1750 advertised a brand of Virginia tobacco to English smokers. Tobacco from the New World turned out to be far more valuable than gold.*

*"I will make them conform or I will harry them out of the land."*—King James I

# Saints and Strangers: Bound by Hope

London and Plymouth, Massachusetts, 1620

*Two groups of English families crossed the Atlantic together on the* Mayflower *in 1620 to start the second permanent English colony in America. The groups weren't natural allies. One sought fortune in a new world free of rules. The other wanted to practice its religion without being hunted down by the king's men and thrown in jail. The youth of both groups had at least one thing in common: Many of them buried their parents soon after they reached America.*

*The official seal of the Massachusetts Bay Colony in 1629. A smiling Indian invites Europeans to "Come over and help us."*

The people we know as Pilgrims called themselves Saints. Most British called them Separatists because they had separated from the Church of England—the only church allowed in England—and started their own outlaw church. When King James I ordered his men to arrest them as traitors, the Separatists fled to Holland, where they were promised free worship in exchange for their labor.

But after a few years the English children were speaking Dutch, fighting in the Dutch army, and marrying into Dutch families. Elders worried about the future of their church. One elder, William Bradford, wrote that "many of [the English] children . . . were drawne away by evill examples into extravagante and dangerous courses, getting the rains off their neks, and departing from their parents . . . tending to dissolutnes and the danger of their soules, to thee great greefe of their parents and dishonour of God."

The elders thought about moving to South America but finally arranged with the Plymouth Company (Council of New England) to start a settlement near the mouth of the Hudson River, at the northern part of the Virginia colony. Here they would work for seven years in exchange for a free voyage and tools for building and planting. In September of 1620, forty-one Saints carried their belongings aboard a small sailing ship named the *Speedwell* in Southampton. About half the group were teenagers and children. Most of the girls were left behind because, as William Bradford wrote, girls had "weak bodies" and wouldn't be able to survive the voyage or take the hard work of starting a colony.

The *Speedwell* began the journey alongside a second ship, the *Mayflower,* carrying sixty-one English passengers who were not Separatists. The two groups wanted little to do

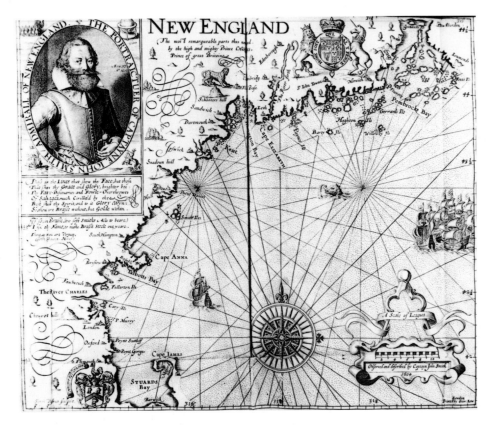

The Pilgrims took this map from John Smith's book about New England with them on their voyage. Smith offered to go along—for pay—but they told him his book was "better cheap" than he.

## PILGRIMS?

If the voyagers who started in Holland called themselves Saints and others called them Separatists, why does history remember them as Pilgrims? William Bradford may have started it all when he wrote that "they knew they were Pilgrims" when they left Holland. The word means "religious travelers." To make it even more confusing, Americans called them founders or forefathers until about 1800, when Pilgrims became the most popular term.

with each other. Some aboard the *Mayflower* enjoyed mocking the worshipful Saints. For their part, the Saints simply called the others Strangers.

But the two groups weren't strangers for long. The *Speedwell* leaked so badly that the ships had to return twice for repairs. Finally the *Speedwell* was abandoned, and passengers from both ships crowded aboard the *Mayflower* for a third and final try. Families staked out living space in the ship's cargo compartment. Each adult was allowed seven feet by two and a half feet—barely room to stretch out. Children got even less. Heavy Atlantic storms sent the ship rising up and skidding down monstrous waves throughout the trip. Everyone but the crew stayed below deck for most of the two-month-long jouney. Food quickly ran low and many got seasick.

Some children accepted the discomfort. Elizabeth Tilley and Mary Chilton were Saints and Constance Hopkins a Stranger, but in violent seas it didn't matter. They were all taking care of family members. Constance had her three-year-old sister to keep track of. Her mother, about to give birth, could offer little help; mostly she struggled just to brace herself as the ship tossed in the water. The three girls were bound by their work and, like the others, by hunger, danger, and hope.

But some young voyagers seemed to go stir-crazy. John and Francis Billington, fourteen and twelve, were the sons of an irreverent London merchant who took great pleasure in mocking the devout Saints. The Billington boys hated being cooped up below deck, where the smell of vomit was so bad that it came as a relief when a barrel of wine accidentally spilled all over the floor.

By the time they spotted land in November, many passengers were dying. The ship had been blown far off course to what is now Provincetown on Cape Cod. It was colder than they expected and they were too late to plant crops for the spring. The men rowed off to explore the coast while women and children remained on board the *Mayflower*, anchored

*This 1877 painting shows young Mary Chilton stepping onto Plymouth Rock. Many believe she was the first British female to do so. Both her parents died in the first winter.*

in Cape Cod Bay. The confinement was too much for Francis Billington to take. One freezing day he decided to try to make a long-tailed firecracker called a squib. When he had it packed just right, he set it off by shooting his father's gun near a barrel of gunpowder in the ship's cabin. The explosion shattered the winter silence. The deck burst into flames, and Saints and Strangers alike raced to the deck to douse the fire. "By God's Mercy," wrote Bradford, "no harm done." Francis was made to scrub the deck.

In December, the men found a place for the colony at what is now Plymouth Harbor. They sent for the *Mayflower,* which sailed across Cape Cod Bay on December 26, 1620. Legend has it that the first female ashore at Plymouth was fifteen-year-old Mary Chilton.

Fewer than half the colonists survived the first brutal winter. Young people proved hardier than their elders, and girls turned out to be the toughest of all. All seven girls aboard the *Mayflower* survived the voyage, as did ten of thirteen boys, including both Billingtons. All but two of the girls made it through the first winter.

When spring arrived, both Saints and Strangers began to lay out streets and frame buildings. With much help from the Wampanoag Indians, they were able to turn their attention to making their settlement work.

The Billington boys continued to find trouble. Late one afternoon John hiked off into the woods and lost sight of the shore. For five days he wandered, totally lost. He survived on berries and slept in trees until a party of Nauset Indians discovered him and took him to their village. An English search party went out looking for him, but by then John was far away from Plymouth. Finally an Indian named Squanto, who was friendly to the settlers, found him. His captors refused to release John until Squanto informed them that the English had signed a peace treaty with a much stronger chief. It would be wise, he said, to return this boy unharmed and right away.

The next day nearly one hundred Nausets paraded John Billington home. When the gates of Plymouth came in view, one of the braves hoisted John up on his shoulders and carried the grinning boy into the settlement. He was wearing a necklace of beads. History doesn't tell us whether or not John was punished.

## WHAT HAPPENED TO SOME OF THE YOUNG PILGRIMS?

Constance Hopkins stayed in the settlement, married, and became the mother of twelve children. Elizabeth Tilley stayed and married a man named John Howland, but only because Howland's first choice, Desire Mintner, decided she liked Holland better and left. Mary Chilton stayed in the colony and became the mother of ten children. John Billington died in 1630 at the age of twenty-four. Francis Billington married, had eight children, and lived to be an old man. Though he had his share of problems in the colony, he is remembered for climbing a tree when he was thirteen and spying a beautiful lake, which turned out to be full of fish. In his honor, the colonists named it the Billington Sea.

*"Their arms, necks, and backs were turned this way and that, and returned again, so as it was impossible for them to do of themeselves and beyond the power of any epileptic's fit or natural disease."*— One who saw Betty Parris, Abigail Williams, and their friends in 1692

# Betty Parris and Abigail Williams: Bewitched or Bored?

Salem Village, Massachusetts, 1692

*In 1630, more than a thousand Puritans came to what was now called the Massachusetts Bay Colony. Instead of starting their own church, Puritans wanted to "purify" the Church of England by taking power from priests and letting the members of the church run it themselves. King James I didn't like that idea. In the next decade twenty thousand more British settlers arrived in New England with tools and weapons, clearing fields and pushing back the wilderness—and the Indians—bit by bit. Salem Village—now Danvers—was about twenty miles north of Boston and just inland from the seaport of Salem. It was there that two girls started an unforgettable episode that is still a mystery today.*

*Four women are hanged as witches in this seventeenth-century English woodcut. The man on the far right is a "witch finder," paid for every "witch" he turns in. Prime suspects include women with moles and pimples, understood to be marks of Satan.*

**B**etty Parris and her cousin Abigail Williams grew up in the parish house on Andover Street in Salem Village, a short walk across the common from the meetinghouse where Betty's father, the Reverend Samuel Parris, preached each Sunday. Betty was frail and sickly, but Abigail was a sturdy blond-haired girl who had been taken in as an orphan by the Parris family. Betty was often excused from chores, but Abigail worked hard to earn her keep.

The seating arrangement for Sunday services at the meetinghouse was like a social blueprint of the whole town. The richest people, church officials, and military officers—addressed as "master" and "mistress"—sat proudly in front, men on one side of the central aisle and women on the other. Behind them were the adults of the middle class, called goodman and goodwife. Poorer people, called only by their given names, arranged themselves in the rear pews. Children sat in the very back with slaves and servants. In the winter it got so cold that some children brought their dogs along so they could bury their hands and feet in warm fur.

Each Sunday, Betty and Abigail listened to Betty's father set forth the rules of Puritan conduct. He warned worshipers against "unnecessary gazings to and fro, or useless whisperings, much less noddings and nappings." He reminded the children that "Jesus was full of business for his heavenly Father but yet he neglected not obedience to his Parents." And he warned: "Wise parents won't suffer children to play with their food." Disobedience, he said, should be answered with "strokes issuing from parental love."

During the winter of 1691, when Betty was nine and Abigail eleven, they sometimes invited friends over to sit by the kitchen fire and listen to Tituba, the family's slave, tell stories. Tituba was a wrinkled, brown-skinned woman, bent from a lifetime of hard work. Reverend Parris had purchased her on the island of Barbados and brought her to Salem with her husband and small son. Tituba told the girls the stories she had heard from the older slaves she had grown up with. Some may have been stories from her ancestral Africa, stories of animals that could talk with human voices and, perhaps, evil demons that preyed on children.

That winter the girls liked to play a game called the Venus glass. They dropped an egg white into a glass of water and watched it dissolve into patterns. Supposedly, a girl could predict what kind of job her future husband would have by the way the egg broke up. One night Abigail dropped her egg and peered into the glass. What she saw didn't remind her of any job at all: Abigail thought she saw a coffin.

Soon after, Abigail and Betty began to act strangely. Their parents sometimes discovered them crouched under tables, twisting their bodies in strange ways and howling like animals. They swore that someone was pinching them all over. Their behavior became the talk of Salem Village. Most Puritans believed that Satan could convince ordinary people to serve him. His men were called wizards and his women witches. Nearly everyone remembered that just a few years before, the Goodwin children of Boston had behaved the same way. Boston doctors had examined them and diagnosed "hellish Witchcraft." A Boston woman had been identified as a witch and hanged in public.

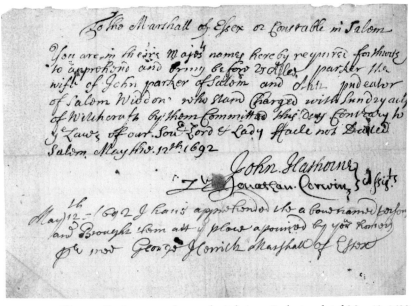

Warrant for the arrest of accused witch Anne Pudeator, dated May 12, 1692

This nineteenth-century engraving shows a dramatic moment in the trial of an accused witch.

Suddenly, Abigail Williams and Betty Parris were the center of the town's attention. Their previously chore-filled lives had become exciting, though in a terrifying way. Soon other Salem girls began to show the same signs. One day in church, twelve-year-old Anne Putnam screamed out loud that there was a yellow bird on Betty's father's head. Most agreed only Satan could have made her do such a thing.

By February of 1692, Betty and Abigail's symptoms worsened. Now they said they could see the shadowy forms of people hitting and pinching them. A doctor pronounced them "under an evil hand." The whole community began to fast and pray for the girls. Town leaders gathered in the Parris home to pressure the girls into naming the witch who had afflicted them. "Who is it that you see?" they demanded. "Who is doing this to you?"

No one knows what Betty and Abigail were thinking. Maybe they really believed they were bewitched, or maybe they started out trying to get some attention and then lost control of the situation. Or maybe both. If they were acting, it would have taken real courage for them to back down and face the scorn of everyone in town and probably receive severe punishments. But they didn't back down. Instead, Betty, Abigail, Anne Putnam, and their friend Elizabeth Hubbard named their witch: Tituba. And then they "cried out upon" two other village women: Sarah Good and Sarah Osburn.

On March 1, 1692, an excited crowd packed the meetinghouse for a public hearing. The three women were accused of witchcraft. While Sarah Osburn and Sarah Good denied every charge, eight girls sat in front, sometimes rolling on the floor and babbling in strange tongues. Then it was Tituba's turn. Amazingly, she confessed. She said the other two accused women were also witches who rode with her on broomsticks and had made her hurt Betty and Abigail. The three women were sent to jail in Boston. Sarah Osburn died in prison and Sarah Good was hanged in public. Tituba was released and sold to another family.

Soon more and more girls and young women began to have fits. Order broke down in the town as it became infected with witch fever. Reverend Parris's group prayer meetings only seemed to make things worse. Neighbors began to accuse one another of working for the Devil.

Terrified people were bullied into false confessions. No one felt safe. Many were thrown into prison, even Sarah Good's five-year-old daughter, Dorcas, who was chained to her mother's leg.

Probably no one will ever know for sure what really caused the girls of Salem to act as they did. Years later, a few gave some clues. One Sunday in 1706, Anne Putnam rose from her pew at the Salem Village meetinghouse and begged forgiveness. "It was a great delusion of Satan that deceived me in that sad time," she explained. Another admitted that it had been a game to her. "It was for sport," she said. "I must have some sport."

If so, it was a very deadly game. In all, more than one hundred residents of Salem were tried as witches. Nineteen people and even two dogs were hanged, and another person was tortured to death. Hundreds of lives were ruined before witch fever finally subsided and people were able to return their attention to fields and families.

## WHAT HAPPENED TO BETTY PARRIS AND ABIGAIL WILLIAMS?

Abigail's story is lost to history. Betty Parris regained her health once she moved away from home to live with relatives. Her mother died in 1696, and her father was driven out of Salem Village shortly after. Betty joined her father, moving from town to town until she married a land trader when she was twenty-seven. She died a respectable New England countrywoman at the age of seventy-eight in 1760.

*"Jaghte oghte." (Maybe not.)*

# Eunice Williams: Captive

Deerfield, Massachusetts, 1704

*Many white children grew up among Indians in the Colonial years. Most were trapped in a bitter struggle between Britain and France for the control of North America, in which Indian tribes took sides. Canada was then called New France, and the northern part of the British colonies was known as New England. Both nations claimed the same territory, both built forts, and both tried to recruit Indian allies. British colonists were predominantly Protestants, while the French insisted that all inhabitants of New France, including Indians, be Catholic. Those who lived in settlements near the border were in mortal danger.*

*One of the most dangerous places to live in those days was the remote British outpost at Deerfield, Massachusetts. Deerfield was raided and burned six times in the 1690s alone. An especially brutal attack took place on the morning of February 29, 1704. Striking at dawn, Abenaki and Mohawk warriors and their French allies swept down upon the town, massacring families in their sleep. They captured more than one hundred prisoners and marched them through the snow all the way to Canada. The hostages included a well-known Puritan minister named John Williams, his wife, and five of their children. Reverend Williams's youngest daughter, Eunice, was seven years old on the night the raiders came.*

*In this woodcut from* The Deerfield Captive, *published in 1832, the Reverend John Williams rises to defend his family from attack.*

Eunice Williams was born into a family of famous Puritan church leaders. Her uncle and cousin were the great Boston ministers Increase and Cotton Mather. Her father, the Reverend John Williams, was the most respected man in Deerfield. By the time the raiders stormed over the Deerfield fence, Eunice had already made great progress in reading her Bible, and she knew her catechism by heart.

But on that horrible day, her life changed by the hour. By noontime, when Eunice and the other shivering captives turned back to look at Deerfield from a high hill, they

## PELT WARS

Part of the fight between the French and British was for control of beaver skins, called pelts. The fur was extremely valuable, especially after Britain's King Charles I decreed in 1638 that all hats made in the colonies had to contain beaver fur. But French trappers had been in beaver country before the British, and, of course, Native Americans before that. Many battles were fought for control of the valuable pelts, with the big losers being the beavers themselves. The Hudson's Bay Company sold 26,750 beaver pelts in *one day* in 1743. It took only a few decades to push beavers to the brink of extinction (from which they have since recovered).

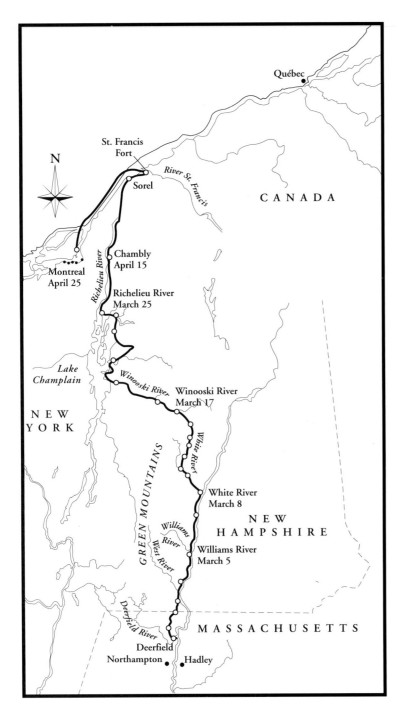

*The route of Eunice Williams's two-month-long journey—most of it taken on the back of a Mohawk warrior—from Deerfield to Montreal*

saw that their town had been destroyed. Her two younger brothers were dead. And now she and her family were prisoners.

The next morning they began to trek single file through the snow toward Canada. Anyone who couldn't keep up was killed to save time and energy. Early in the journey Eunice's mother, still weak from having just given birth, broke through the ice and soon could barely move her frozen feet. She was quickly murdered. Partway through the journey, the French and Indian captors separated Eunice from her father, sister, and three brothers. Bundled in a blanket, Eunice was hoisted up onto the back of a brave who carried her hundreds of miles to Kahnawake, a Mohawk settlement near Montreal.

Eunice didn't see her father again until the following spring, when French Jesuit priests and Mohawk leaders gave them two brief chances to talk. She was healthy, she told him, but scared. She reported that her captors mocked her religion and forced her to say prayers in Latin—the language of the Roman Catholic Church. John Williams, furious, told her to cling to her catechism and the prayers she had learned, and she would be all right. And then he was led away.

Reverend Williams did everything he could to reunite what was left of his family. Within two years he was able to enlist British diplomats to secure his own release and to win the freedom of all his children except Eunice. For some maddening, mysterious reason, the Mohawks refused all proposals to trade hostages for her. They wouldn't even let anyone see her. Year by year, John Williams became more desperate, and the strange story of Eunice Williams spread throughout the land. Each Sunday, in meetinghouses all over New England and New York, worshipers prayed that God would enter the hearts of the "savages" who held Reverend Williams's daughter.

No Englishman saw Eunice again until 1713, the year she turned sixteen. That May, an English diplomat named John Schuyler was allowed to visit her at the home of a priest in

Montreal. Eunice sat down on the dirt floor in the center of the room and gazed directly at Schuyler. He was amazed by her appearance: Eunice's leggings were fringed with moose hair and bound together with porcupine quills. Her hair was heavily greased and pulled back with a ribbon of eelskin. There were spots of red paint on her cheeks and forehead. A man sat silently behind her. The priest introduced the man as Eunice's husband, Arosen, or "squirrel" in Mohawk. And Eunice, who could no longer speak English, wasn't even Eunice anymore. Now she had a Catholic name, Marguerite. She seemed happy and settled. She didn't want to leave.

She remained silent for two hours as the Englishman begged her to return home. Finally, through a translator, she said her only words of the visit: "Maybe not." Schuyler described her on that day as "bashful in the face, but . . . harder than Steel in her breast."

Word of the encounter raced through New England meetinghouses. It didn't make sense: How could Eunice Williams willingly turn her back on her great family to live with savages? They must have taken over her mind. No one could accept that she could have chosen to live among the Indians.

In 1740, when she was forty-three, Eunice finally returned to Massachusetts as a visitor. Her father was dead, but her brothers Stephen and Eleazer were still alive. Rather than staying with her original family, she camped out with Arosen in an orchard. Wrapped in blankets, she attended a church service, during which worshipers offered impassioned prayers for her soul. Those who had known her as Eunice Williams prayed that God would help her come to her senses and remain among them. She listened respectfully, and greeted those who approached her with courtesy. And then, when she felt it was time, she went home.

## WHAT HAPPENED TO EUNICE WILLIAMS?

Eunice made several more visits and formed a warm relationship with her brothers—who never gave up hope—but she always returned to her home in New France. She and Arosen had two daughters and a son. She died peacefully in her village of Kahnawake at the age of eighty-nine.

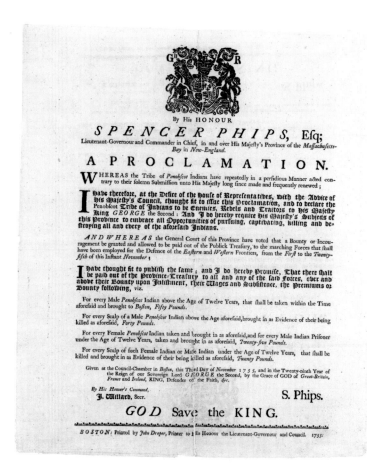

*British authorities didn't take kindly to Native Americans who sided with the French against the British in the Massachusetts Bay Colony. This proclamation offers a reward to anyone who kills a Penobscot Indian. A dead male twelve years or older brought fifty pounds, while his scalp alone brought forty pounds. Adult females and boys under twelve were worth twenty-five pounds, and girls under twelve, twenty pounds.*

*"The longer time we are awake the longer we live . . . Thus I have the advantage over the sleepers in point of long life."*

# Eliza Lucas: Indigo Planter

Wappo Plantation, South Carolina, 1740

*As the British fought France for control of New England, they were also battling Spain for the West Indies and the southern part of North America. Spain controlled Florida, while Britain maintained a very shaky upper hand in Georgia and the Carolinas. Colonel George Lucas commanded British naval forces at the Caribbean island of Antigua. Like many officers, Colonel Lucas was also a wealthy planter. When his wife fell ill during a break in the fighting, he moved his family to the British colony of South Carolina, which had a milder climate. He bought a house in Charleston, three rice plantations, slaves, horses, seed, and farm equipment and set about life as a rice planter. But then fighting resumed in the Caribbean, and Lucas was quickly summoned back to Antigua. His wife was too ill to accompany him, so he left everything—the plantations, the house, twenty slaves, and the care of his wife and younger daughter—to his sixteen-year-old daughter. Colonel Lucas had only one comforting thought: If any girl on earth could handle such responsibility, it was Eliza Lucas.*

Shortly after her father sailed away, Eliza Lucas wrote in her journal that she "could have been moped," but she wasn't the moping kind. She was a doer. First she moved her mother and sister, Polly, out of Charleston and into a house in the country, where she could be close to the fields and away from gossipy society. Then she began to learn the life of a planter. Within a matter of weeks she wrote to her ex-teacher in London:

"I have the business of three plantations to transact, which requires much writing and more business and fatigue of other sorts than you can imagine. But lest you should imagine it too burdensome to a girl at my early time of life, I think myself happy that I can be useful to so good a father, and by rising very early I find that I can go through much business."

Ignoring the elegant plantation balls and porch parties of the Carolina rice country, Eliza filled her journal with daily tributes to oak trees, flowers, and mockingbirds. She

## YOUNG SLAVEOWNERS

Eliza Lucas was one of many young people growing up on plantations who inherited slaves or became responsible for directing their work. George Washington inherited his first slaves at eleven, Thomas Jefferson at fourteen. Eliza Lucas accepted slavery and treated her slaves as well as her time and place allowed. She taught two slave girls to read, and then assigned them to teach the others in a school she started for slaves in her area. In 1745, she wrote this vow to herself:

"I am resolved to make a good Mistress to my servants, to treat them with humanity and good nature; to give them sufficient and comfortable clothing and provisions, and all things necessary for them. To be careful and tender of them in their sickness, to reprove them for their faults, to encourage them when they do well, and pass over small faults; not to be tyrannical, peavish or impatient towards them, but to make their lives as comfortable as I can."

planted orchards and flowers and fig groves. Soon her neighbors were full of curious gossip about the pretty, highly eligible young girl who dared to live out in the country with no man to protect her from Spanish soldiers or rebellious slaves. Eliza offered this description of her life in a letter to an inquisitive neighbor lady:

"In general I rise at five o'clock in the morning, read till seven—then take a walk in the garden or fields, see that the Servants are at their respective business, then to breakfast. The first hour after breakfast is spent in music, then . . . [learning] French or shorthand. After that, I devote the rest of the time until I dress for dinner to our little Polly and two black girls who I teach to read . . . The first hour after dinner is at music, then in needlework till candle light, and from that time to bed time I read or write. Thursdays the whole day is spent in writing, either on the business of the plantations or on letters to my friends. [Also] I have planted a large fig orchard, with design to dry them and export them."

Word traveled fast. Another neighbor warned Eliza that she could spoil her good looks by getting up so early. Her reply came quickly:

"Whatever contributes to the health and pleasure of mind must also contribute to good looks . . . and if I should look older by [rising early], I really am so; for the longer time we are awake the longer we live . . . Thus I have the advantage over the sleepers in point of long life."

The prolonged conflict between Britain and Spain crippled South Carolina's economy. When a Spanish naval blockade prevented South Carolina rice from reaching the West Indies, Carolina families began to suffer. The colony depended too much on rice and desperately needed new crops to sell. Here was just the kind of challenge that triggered Eliza's passion for experimentation. Using seeds her father sent her, Eliza had her slaves plant indigo, ginger, cotton, lucerne, and cassava. Soon

*An indigo plant*

*Slaves haul freshly cut indigo plants to be processed into dye on a South Carolina indigo plantation. The leaves were soaked in vats until they released their dark blue dye, which hardened and was sold in the form of dry cakes.*

she focused her attention on indigo, a bushy plant that produces a dark blue dye. British families used the dye to brighten wool and cotton. With no other supplier, Britain was forced to buy all its indigo from rival France. Eliza set out to make South Carolina Britain's main supplier instead.

It wasn't easy. Her first crop froze. Worms ruined the second crop, and the third season produced only a hundred plants. Colonel Lucas tried to help, sending his daughter more slaves and an overseer to manage them. Then he sent a dye maker, a sour man who deliberately ruined a whole year's crop.

Colonel Lucas tried to send Eliza a husband, too. In 1740, he volunteered to match her with an elderly man who, he said, would be perfect for her. He could come as soon as she gave the word. Eliza replied respectfully:

"A single life is my only Choice and if it were not that I am yet but Eighteen, I hope you will put aside the thoughts for my marrying two or three years at least."

Colonel Lucas wrote back with a second candidate. Now Eliza was firmer:

"[I] beg leave to say to you that the riches of Peru and Chile if he could put them together could not purchase sufficient esteem for him to make him my husband."

When Eliza finally produced a successful indigo crop in 1744, she offered free seeds to all neighbors who would agree to plant indigo the following year. Most accepted. Within a few years, South Carolina's planters were raising so much indigo that Britain no longer needed French supplies. With the crop in good shape, Eliza turned her attention elsewhere. She married a man of her own choosing, a neighboring planter about twice her age named Charles Pinckney who had helped her develop the indigo crop.

## What Happened to Eliza Lucas?

She became the mother of three children and later became a well-known patriot when the colonies fought for their independence from Britain. Two of her sons were Revolutionary War heroes. When Eliza Lucas Pinckney died in 1793, George Washington helped to carry her coffin.

*"I was now persuaded that I had got into a world of bad spirits,
and that they were going to kill me."*

# Olaudah Equiano: Kidnapped into Slavery

Benin, Africa, 1756

*Olaudah Equiano was the youngest boy in a family of seven children in the
African kingdom of Benin (now part of Nigeria). His village was called Essaka
and his language and tribe Ibo. In 1756, the year he turned eleven, Olaudah
and his sister were kidnapped from their village, tied up, separated from each
other, and marched to slave ships anchored off the Atlantic coast. There they
were delivered to white merchants who carried them across the Atlantic
Ocean and sold them into slavery. Later, after Olaudah learned to read and
write, he told the story of his capture.*

*The frontispiece of Olaudah Equiano's
autobiography,* The Interesting Narrative of
Olaudah Equiano, *first published in 1789*

In Ibo, his name meant "good fortune," and how could Olaudah not feel
lucky? His father's forehead bore the crescent-shaped mark of a tribal
leader. His mother was a kind and beautiful woman who took Olaudah with
her to the marketplace. There they would barter for the things they needed most:
firearms, gunpowder, hats, beads, and—greatest of all delicacies in a land with no
lakes or big rivers—dried fish. Olaudah was proud to live in a village of great dancers,
musicians, and artists.

Early in the morning the adults and older children of Olaudah's tribe rose and hiked to a
distant field where they farmed corn, cotton, tobacco, spices, and peppers. Along with their
tools, they carried weapons to protect themselves against attacks by rival tribes who sometimes
sought to capture them and sell them to slave merchants.

The younger children of Essaka remained under guard in the village. The best young
climbers shinnied up into the treetops to watch for strangers. One day, when he was ten,
Olaudah was peering out from the uppermost branches of a tree in his yard when he spotted a man who was not from his tribe, moving furtively below. He later wrote:

"I saw one of those people come into the yard of our next neighbor . . . Immediately
I gave the alarm and he was surrounded by the stoutest [of our young people], who

## HUMAN GOLD

Between 1500 and 1900, about twelve million Africans were kidnapped and shipped to the Americas as slaves. During those centuries, Africa's population stayed about the same while slave labor helped Europe and much of the Western Hemisphere become rich and well populated.

Slavery had long existed in Africa, too. For many centuries, losers in tribal battles had sometimes been enslaved, and sometimes villages punished criminals by forcing them to work. But in the 1600s things changed. With labor needed in the New World, human bodies became as valuable as gold. Now rival tribes were paid by merchants—often in guns, cloth, metal goods, and liquor—to capture one another. Children were valued as future investments who would soon grow strong. William Ellery, a merchant, instructed Pollipus Hammond, captain of a slave ship, to bring back children in 1756:

"If you have a good trade for Negroes [you] may purchase forty or fifty Negroes. Get most of them mere Boys and Girls, some Men, let them be Young . . . If you cannot get home some time in October next [you] may go to Barbados and Dispose of your Negroes, reserving Eight likely boys to bring home."

entangled him with cords so that he could not escape till some of the grown people came and secured him."

But it wasn't long before Olaudah's luck ran out: "One day, when all our people were gone out to their works as usual, and only I and my sister were left to mind the house, two men and a woman got over our walls, and in a moment seized us both; and without giving us time to cry out or to make any resistance, they stopped our mouths and ran off with us into the nearest wood. Here they tied our hands, and continued to carry us as far as they could till night came on."

On the second day, Olaudah saw someone in the distance and cried out for help. His captors quickly gagged his mouth and stuffed him into a sack. That night, they separated Olaudah and his sister, though they clung so hard to each other that their captors had to tear them apart. They never saw each other again.

Day after day, Olaudah and the other captives hiked until they reached a great river, probably the Niger. There they were handed over to people who spoke a language Olaudah had never heard. The next morning they boarded canoes and set off down the river. Finally, the water widened until it had no end: It was the Atlantic Ocean.

"The first object which saluted my eyes when I arrived on the coast was the sea, and a slave ship, which was then riding at anchor and waiting for its cargo. These filled me with astonishment, which was soon converted into terror when I was carried on board. I was immediately handled, and tossed up to see if I was sound, by some of the crew; and I was now persuaded that I had got into a world of bad spirits, and that they were going to kill me . . . When I looked round the ship and saw a large furnace boiling and a multitude of black people of every description chained together . . . I no longer doubted my own fate; and, quite overpowered with horror and anguish, I fell motionless on the deck and fainted."

Olaudah was flung below deck. The odor of so many people living in their own waste was so bad that he couldn't eat. When he refused food he was tied down and beaten. He couldn't understand what was happening to him or why until he met several men chained together who spoke the language of his tribe:

"I asked them if these people had no country, but lived in this hollow place [the ship]. They told me they did not, but came from a distant one . . . I then asked where were their women? Had they any like themselves? I was told they had. 'And why,' said I, 'do we not see them?' They answered because they were left behind. I asked how the vessel could go? They told me they could not tell; but that there was cloth put upon the masts by the help of ropes I saw, and then the vessel went on; and the white men had some spell or magic they put in the water, when they liked, in order to stop the vessel. I was exceedingly amazed at this account, and really thought they were spirits."

His countrymen told him he was being taken to the white men's country to work: "I feared I should be put to death, the white people looked and acted, as I thought, in so savage a manner; for I had never seen among any people such instances of brutal cruelty; and this is not only shown toward us blacks, but also to some of the whites themselves. One white man in particular I saw, when we were permitted to be on deck, flogged so unmercifully with a large rope near the foremast, that he died in consequence of it; and they tossed him over the side as they would have done a brute. This made me fear these people the more; and I expected nothing less than to be treated in the same manner . . . One day, when we had a smooth sea and moderate wind, two of my wearied countrymen, who were chained together (I was near them at the time), preferring death to such a life of misery, somehow made through the nettings, and jumped into the sea."

Weeks later, the ship arrived at the island of Barbados, in the West Indies. Slave buyers rushed aboard to inspect the Africans.

"They put us in separate parcels and examined us . . . They also made us jump and pointed to the land, signifying we were to go there. We thought by this we should be eaten by these ugly men . . . We were conducted to the merchant's yard, where we were all pent up like sheep in a fold without regard to sex or age . . . We were not many days in the merchant's custody before we were sold . . . On a signal given (as the beat of a drum) the buyers rushed at once into the yard where the slaves were confined, and made choice of the parcel they liked best. I remember in the vessel in which I was brought over, in the men's

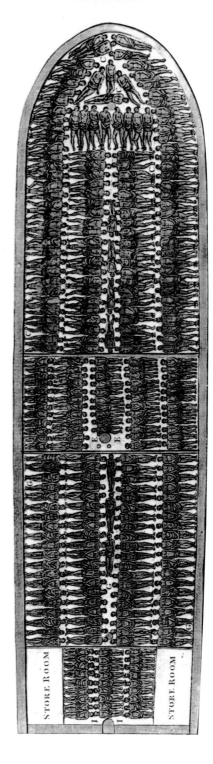

*Slave traders sought to maximize profits by packing captives like sardines in a can into the ships' filthy holds. Historians estimate that about one in six captives died during the Atlantic crossing.*

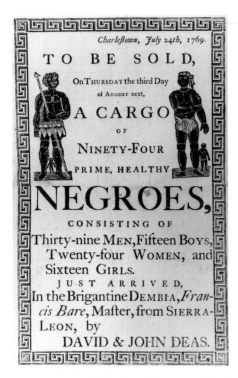

*Charleflown, July 24th, 1769.*

## TO BE SOLD,

On Thursday the third Day
of August next,

## A CARGO

OF

NINETY-FOUR

PRIME, HEALTHY

# NEGROES,

CONSISTING OF

Thirty-nine Men, Fifteen Boys,
Twenty-four Women, and
Sixteen Girls.

JUST ARRIVED,

In the Brigantine Dembia, *Francis Bare*, Mafter, from Sierra-
Leon, by

DAVID & JOHN DEAS.

*Negroes captured in Sierra Leone are offered for sale to South Carolina rice planters. In the 1750s, an African child under ten years old sold in Charleston for approximately one hundred pounds, about one-third the price of a healthy young man.*

### A FAST LEARNER

"Without any assistance from the school of education, and by only what she was taught in her family, she, in sixteen months time from her arrival, attained the English language, to which she was an utter stranger before, to such a degree as to read any of the most difficult parts of the Sacred writings, to the astonishment of all who heard her."

—John Wheatley

apartment there were several brothers who, in the sale, were sold in different lots; and it was very moving to see and hear their cries at parting."

## WHAT HAPPENED TO OLAUDAH EQUIANO?

He was taken to Barbados, in the West Indies, and then to Virginia. There he was sold to a British naval officer who insisted on changing his name to the European Gustavus Vassa. When Olaudah refused to answer to that name, he was beaten. He spent the next ten years at sea, during which he learned to read, write, and speak English. At the age of twenty-one he bought his freedom and began to write his autobiography. It was finally published in 1789, when Olaudah was about forty. One of the first books ever written by an African in English, Olaudah's personal account of being captured, sold, and enslaved became a best-seller in Europe and America. He devoted his life to ridding the world of slavery.

———◆◆◆———

*"Among the blacks is misery enough, God knows, but no poetry . . . Religion, indeed, has produced a Phyllis Whately [sic]; but it could not produce a poet."*
—Thomas Jefferson, 1784

# Phillis Wheatley: The Impossible Poet

Boston, Massachusetts, 1773

*Only a very few slaves got a chance to develop their talents. Most who did were servants of liberal masters in the North, or slaves who had a special skill that whites found entertaining or worth money. A blind boy from Georgia known as Blind Tom showed such amazing talent as a composer and pianist that he was able to play his way to fame. Tom Molineaux, born a slave on a Virginia plantation, became a champion boxer. Onesimus, a slave owned by the Puritan minister Cotton Mather, helped find an inoculation against smallpox.*

*Phillis Wheatley was a slim, shy, deeply religious girl. Born in Africa, she grew up in the home of wealthy Bostonians who taught her to read and encouraged her to write. In 1773, a collection of her poems, most written while she was in her teens, became the first book of poetry ever published by a black American. Many whites didn't believe a slave girl could have written it. The poems spurred a hot debate about whether Negroes were actually capable of writing poetry at all.*

Phillis Wheatley's real name is lost to history. She was born in 1753, probably near the Gambia River in the Senegal-Gambia region of Africa. Later she said that on the day she was captured, her "mother poured out water before the sun at his rising." This may have meant that her people were Muslims, who pray when the sun rises. She was seven years old on the day she was taken from her family and village. Ships' records show that her front baby teeth were missing.

After a march to the sea, the girl was probably chained and packed tightly into the hold of the schooner *Phillis* for a voyage to America. It is known that survivors reached Boston on July 11, 1761. Dressed only in a scrap of a rug, she climbed onto an auction block to be examined by buyers. She was bought by Susannah Wheatley, the wife of a rich Boston merchant, who wanted a girl to work in her house. When Mrs. Wheatley asked her name, the slave dealer answered with the name of his boat. The Wheatleys took Phillis to live in the servants' quarters of their elegant home on King Street in Boston.

One day, not long after, Susannah and her eighteen-year-old daughter Mary came upon Phillis, her face screwed up in fierce concentration, marking the kitchen wall with a piece of chalk. They watched her silently for a while and finally realized she was trying to draw letters. Instead of punishing her, Mary Wheatley showed Phillis how to make them the right way and then began to teach her English. Phillis picked up the language with astonishing speed. A year later she could read

Should you, my lord, while you peruse my song,
Wonder from whence my love of freedom sprung,
Whence flow these wishes from the common good,
By feeling hearts alone best understood,—
I, young in life, by seeming cruel fate
Was snatched from Afric's fancied happy seat:
What pangs, excruciating must molest,
What sorrows labor in my parent's breast!
Steeled was that soul, and by no misery moved,
That from a father seized his babe beloved:
Such, such my case. And can I then but pray
Others may never feel tyrannic sway?
　　—Phillis Wheatley, 1772, from an untitled poem
addressed to Britain's William Legge, Earl of Dartmouth

*With her own room, light duties, and the encouragement of her owners, Phillis Wheatley had a better chance to learn than many white colonial girls. But she still was not free, and her poems reflect her situation.*

*Like Phillis Wheatley, a sightless Georgia slave boy named Thomas Greene Bethune was given a chance to show his talent. An amazing pianist and on-the-spot composer, Thomas played his way to fame—and the fortune of a promoter who advertised him as "Blind Tom."*

the hardest passages in the Bible. By the time she was ten, Phillis was well on her way to mastering Latin and English literature.

The more Phillis learned, the more books and lessons the Wheatleys gave her. They let her read books by the great English poets of the time. Her favorite was Alexander Pope. The Wheatleys excused her from some chores to study and write. They even gave her a room of her own with a fireplace and a kerosene lamp by her pillow. She kept a pen and ink pot near her bed so she could write at night. Though she was a slave, Phillis was actually receiving a better chance to learn than most free children in Boston.

One night when Phillis was twelve, the Wheatleys invited a large group of friends over for dinner. As she served the guests, Phillis overheard two men recounting their adventure about having nearly drowned in a storm at sea off Cape Cod. After she cleared the table, Phillis rushed to her room, took her pen, and began to write the story in poetic verse. When she was finished, she showed it to Susannah Wheatley, who was so impressed that she got it published in a magazine.

After that, the Wheatleys began to take Phillis around to their friends to show her off. She lived in two worlds, not fully a part of either. She slept in a room of her own apart from the other slaves, so she had few black friends. Her life wasn't hard, but she *was* still a slave; she wasn't free. She recited poetry at the fine homes of wealthy white Bostonians, yet she wasn't comfortable enough to eat at the main table with her hosts. She was baptized in the Wheatleys' Congregational church, but she sat back in the gallery with other slaves during services. Her name was the same as the Wheatleys', but her own family was in Africa, if they were still alive. There were mixed signals everywhere.

Phillis kept writing throughout her teens until she had composed thirty-nine poems—enough to make a book. Written in the style of great English poets, her poems were about freedom, faith, God, the growing tension between the colonists and Britain, and, sometimes, the death of children.

The Wheatleys took Phillis's poems to publishers they knew, but no one would publish them because they didn't believe that Phillis could have written them. In 1773, the Wheatleys persuaded eighteen leading Bostonians—including John Hancock, who later signed the Declaration of Independence and would become the governor of Massachusetts—to write a letter to "the world" stating that they believed Phillis had written the poems. That was enough. Later that year her book, *Poems on Various Subjects, Religious and Moral,* was published. The book sold well on both sides of the Atlantic.

But her poems made Phillis controversial. Thomas Jefferson refused to meet Phillis and called her poems "below the dignity of criticism." On the other hand, George Washington visited with her for a half hour in 1776 and praised a poem Phillis had written about him. The problem was that poetry was considered the highest expression of the human imagination. Only superior people were supposed to be able to write poems good enough to be published. But Phillis was black, young, and African-born. She wrote most of her published poems as a teenager, a few when she was only twelve. Her elegant verses especially threatened slave-owning whites like Jefferson, who justified slavery by convincing themselves that blacks were inferior, maybe not even totally human. Jefferson argued that blacks couldn't experience love in ways that inspired the imagination, and therefore couldn't write poetry. But then here was this book—how could one explain Phillis Wheatley?

Phillis sailed with the Wheatleys to England, where publishers and critics praised her poems and pressured the Wheatleys to free Phillis. But soon the American Revolution against British rule destroyed the market for her poetry, especially in England. This cut off her income. Finally, in 1778, both Wheatleys died and Phillis was freed.

To those who opposed slavery, Phillis Wheatley's poems proved that enormous talent, thought, and imagination were wasted by keeping Negroes from reading and writing. Though it was dangerous for Phillis to criticize slavery directly, she revealed her inner feelings in a few poems, such as the untitled poem on page 43, in which she imagines the pain her father must have felt when she was taken from him.

## WHAT HAPPENED TO PHILLIS WHEATLEY?

She married a man named John Peters. They had three children, who all died as babies. After her unhappy marriage ended, Phillis spent her final days in poverty, living in a boarding-house and working as a maid. She died alone at the age of thirty-one. Even a hundred years after her death, Phillis Wheatley was still known as the "mother of black literature in America." She was an important model for white female poets, too, since she used her own name when many other women writers of her time used men's names in order to be published.

### A LETTER TO DOUBTERS

"We whose Names are under-written do assure the World that the Poems specified in the following Page were (as we verily believe) written by PHILLIS, a young Negro Girl, who was but a few Years since, brought an uncultivated Barbarian from Africa, and has ever since been, and now is, under the Disadvantage of serving as a Slave in a family in this Town. She has been examined by some of the best judges, and is thought qualified to write them."
—Eighteen prominent Bostonians, including the governor and lieutenant governor

### USING PHILLIS WHEATLEY TO SCOLD THE COLONIES

"We are much concerned to find that this ingenious young woman as yet a slave. The people of Boston boast themselves chiefly on their principles of liberty. One such act as the purchase of her freedom, would, in our opinion, have done them more honor than hanging a thousand trees with ribbons and emblems."
—*The Monthly Review of London,* December 1773

*We have an old mother that peevish is grown*

*She snubs us like children that scarce walk alone*

*She forgets we're grown up and have sense of our own*

*Which nobody can deny, deny*

*Which nobody can deny.*

*If we don't obey orders, whatever the case*

*She frowns, and she chides and she loses all patience*

*And sometimes she hits us a slap in the face*

*Which nobody can deny, deny*

*Which nobody can deny.*

—Benjamin Franklin

PART THREE

# Breaking Away: The American Revolution

The French and Indian War settled the long struggle in North America between Britain and France. When it ended in 1763, after many years of fighting, Britain was the clear winner. British forces controlled the most important rivers, commanded the key forts, and held the best seaports. But Britain was broke. The war had left a national debt of 133 million pounds, and King George III wanted even more money to put new British "peacekeeping" forces in North America.

He decided that the American colonists should pay for their "defence." Beginning in 1764, British authorities imposed taxes on tea, glass, lead, paints, paper, and other items. The idea backfired: It made many colonists rethink their relationship with Britain. Why were they being treated like children? Why should they be taxed if they had no votes in the British Parliament? Now that the French and Spanish were weak, and now that the colonists outnumbered the Indians nearly twenty to one, why did they need British soldiers to protect them? Hadn't they cleared the wilderness, built their own homes, and organized their own cities? In short, they asked themselves, wasn't this really their land to govern?

*Patriots pulling down a statue of King George III in New York City*

*Anna Green Winslow*

*Young ladies in town, and those that live round,*
*Let a friend at this season advise you:*
*Since money's so scarce, and times growing worse*
*Strange things may soon hap and surprize you:*
*First then, throw aside your high top knots of pride*
*Wear none but your own country linnen;*
*Of Oeconomy boast, let your pride be the most*
*To show cloths of your own make and spinning.*
—A popular song in Boston in 1767

# Anna Green Winslow and Charity Clark: Spinning for Liberty

Rhode Island and Massachusetts, late 1760s

*The thirteen colonies acted together for the first time by vowing not to import goods from England until the hated taxes were dropped. Sadly, that meant no English tea in the afternoon. It also meant colonists now had to make all the goods they used to get from England.*

On a chilly evening in 1766, seventeen girls and women rapped at the door of a large white house in Providence, Rhode Island. Each walked in with all the wool or yarn she could gather. They quickly sat down and began to spin and weave. They were there to protest the British taxes by making their own cloth so they wouldn't have to import it from England.

Whether they meant to or not, they started a movement. Word spread so fast that they had to move their second meeting to a courthouse. Soon there were "patriotic sewing circles" all over New England. Four hundred spinning wheels were built in Boston alone in 1769. One patriot boasted that "some towns have more looms than houses." Soon fashionable Boston girls wouldn't be seen in British brocades or anything fancy-looking at all. In 1768, the entire Harvard graduating class proudly got their diplomas in plain white homespun. The students at Brown did the same the next year.

Girls blazed away at their looms. They knew their strong, nimble fingers were as important to liberty as the male fingers that would soon pull triggers. Charity Clark,

### LIBERTY TEA

The British tea that patriots refused to drink and finally threw into Boston Harbor was a blend that England imported from India (you can still get it from its original shipper, Davison Newman of London). Instead, Bostonians switched to tea made with a local herb called Labrador or else drank hot chocolate or coffee.

fifteen, spun wool for "stockens" in her home in New York City. She wrote to her cousin in England, "Heroines may not distinguish themselves at the head of an Army, but freedom [will] also be won by a fighting army of amazones [women] . . . armed with spinning wheels."

In 1771, a British military officer sent his twelve-year-old daughter, Anna, to Boston to get an education. Anna Green Winslow got an education, all right—just not the one her father intended. One uncle taught her the difference between Whigs (patriots) and Tories (British sympathizers). Another lectured her about politics and religion. But her aunt gave her the best lesson of all: She took Anna to a sewing circle and showed how she could help the cause of liberty.

The girls and women met at Anna's church each morning. As the sunlight poured in and the minister stood before them reading from the Bible, each sat at a wheel spinning wool as fast as she could. Sometimes they sang together. They raced one another to see who could spin the most. During breaks they refreshed themselves with liberty tea, made from local herbs, instead of British India tea. Soon Anna began to boast of spinning feats in her diary. After a week she wrote, "Another ten knot skane of my yarn was reel'd off today." A few days later, the girl whose diary had just weeks before been full of notes about parties and feathered hats wrote her own declaration of independence in a letter to her father: "As I am (as we say) a daughter of liberty I chuse to wear as much of our own manufactory as pocible."

## WHAT HAPPENED TO ANNA GREEN WINSLOW?

Anna's health was poor throughout her life. She died at a relative's home in Marshfield, Massachusetts, in 1779, at the age of nineteen.

*Colonial girls began to spin yarn and weave cloth when they were very young.*

*"We have been told that our Struggle has loosened the bands of Government every where. That Children and Apprentices were disobedient—that schools and Colledges were grown turbulent—that Indians slighted their guardians and Negroes grew insolent to their Masters."*—John Adams, reporting what he had heard about Boston while he was away in Philadelphia

# Christopher Seider and Samuel Maverick: Martyrs of the Revolution

Boston, Massachusetts, 1770

*Boston was a red-hot volcano in the years leading up to the Revolutionary War, and young people were at the molten core. Whig children (loyal to the colonies) and Tory children (loyal to Britain) confronted one another throughout the city. In a Dorchester church "the boys were so turbulent, the spirit of independence so riotous, that six men had to be appointed to keep order." A fight even broke out in the Harvard College dining hall when Tory students began to noisily slurp English tea. Angry young patriots smashed their teacups against the wall. The patriot boys had to pay for the damages, but no one could bring tea into the dining room anymore.*

*In 1768, Britain sent soldiers to Boston "to keep order." When Americans refused to pay for their food and lodging, the soldiers pitched tents in the middle of town and stayed up nearly all night playing their drums and bugles as loudly as they could. Angry crowds, including many teenage boys, formed near the British army posts and outside customs buildings where British tax collectors worked. It was clear that before long something would erupt.*

On a winter morning in 1770, about 150 Boston schoolchildren gathered outside the shop of Theophilus Lillie, a merchant who had chosen not to boycott British goods. The children were there to make him pay for it. One boy carried a hand-shaped sign with a pointed finger and the word IMPORTER painted on it. Taking a boost from a couple of friends, he shinnied up a signpost and nailed it to the top, aiming the finger at Lillie's door.

A few minutes later Ebenezer Richardson, a British customs inspector who lived in the neighborhood, came around the corner and saw the sign. He rushed toward it and tried to tear it down. Students showered him with stones, opening a gash in his head. Covering his bleeding scalp, Richardson staggered home and grabbed his musket from the wall. He stormed up to the second floor, flung open a window, took aim, and blasted a ball of lead into the crowd. Eleven-year-old Christopher Seider was stooping down to pick up a rock when the shot struck him in the head. He died later the same day.

That shot seemed to unite the whole town against the British. Four days later, six young boys carried Christopher's coffin through downtown Boston to the burial ground. The parade that followed—led by five hundred children—was nearly a mile long.

Two weeks later, on the frosty evening of March 5, 1770, a young barber's apprentice, Edward Garrick, walked past Hugh White, a British soldier standing guard outside the British customhouse, where taxes were paid. The sight of White's red coat brought back the memory of Christopher Seider and reminded Edward that he also had a personal problem with British soldiers: He thought White's captain owed his master money for a haircut.

Edward walked back to White, stood before him, and called White's captain mean, which meant "cheap." A few words later, the two went for each other. White swung his rifle butt at Edward's ear, sending him sprawling to the ground. Edward howled for help and a crowd quickly gathered. Someone sprinted inside and rang the fire bell, and dozens more poured from houses and shops out onto King Street. Soon White stood alone against hundreds ready for his blood. He yelled for reinforcements, and eight armed British soldiers appeared.

Seventeen-year-old Samuel Maverick, an apprentice just home from work, was eating supper when he heard the fire bell. He stuffed down a final mouthful and plunged outside into the angry mob. Working his way to the front, he found himself pressed against British muskets. The soldiers were nervously dodging heavy chunks of ice thrown at them from the back of the crowd. People were calling them lobsterbacks and redcoats. A few were daring them to shoot.

## APPRENTICES

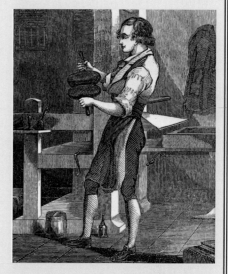

Apprentices were in the thick of the fight for independence—from Britain and from their masters. They were boys who signed a contract with a craftsman to learn a trade. The master was supposed to provide food and a decent place to live, and to teach the trade while the apprentice worked for free for up to seven years. Most apprentices hated the arrangement. Besides getting no pay, they were often fed badly and kept apart from the master's family. Frequently the master waited until the very end of the contract to teach the trade, so the apprentice would not run away early.

Apprentices looked up to Revolutionary leaders who had once been apprentices themselves. They all knew that Tom Paine and Ben Franklin had run away from their masters—Franklin's autobiography was a favorite book. Ebenezer Fox, a fifteen-year-old apprentice to a Boston wigmaker, expected a better deal for apprentices after the war. In 1779, he wrote: "I and other boys situated similarly to myself, thought we had wrongs to be redressed; rights to be maintained . . . We made a direct application of the doctrines we daily heard, in relation to the oppression of our mother country, to our own circumstances . . . I was doing myself a great injustice by remaining in bondage, when I ought to go free; and that the time was come when I should liberate myself."

But the better deal didn't come. After the war, new laws were passed that gave apprentices even *less* freedom. In New York, apprentices caught running away from their masters had to serve *double* time. Some apprentices organized and walked out of their shops, but things didn't really change until years later when factories replaced shops.

This famous engraving by Paul Revere, depicting well-disciplined British troops calmly firing into a peaceful gathering of Boston citizens, heated anti-British passions to a boil. It hardly mattered that the scene was inaccurate.

Then someone threw a club and struck a British soldier in the head. The soldier fell, then scrambled to his feet and fired into the crowd. Samuel Maverick turned and tried to push back through the wall of people. There was another shot, and another. Samuel was covered with blood. He crawled home and died in his mother's arms.

The British kept firing. When it was over, five Bostonians were dead and six more wounded. Two of the wounded were seventeen-year-old apprentices, like Samuel Maverick. The British soldiers were arrested and tried for murder. Paul Revere, an engraver and silversmith (who later became famous for his midnight ride), drew a picture of the shootings and etched it into a piece of copper so that it could be reproduced again and again. It showed—inaccurately—an even row of British soldiers calmly shooting at unarmed and peaceful citizens. Revere's patriot friend Sam Adams dubbed the event the "Boston Massacre." The picture and the story spread like fire throughout the colonies. And helped ignite a war.

———◆✴◆———

*"The smell of war began to be pretty strong."*

# Joseph Plumb Martin: "And Now I Was a Soldier"

Milford, Connecticut, 1775

*Joseph Plumb Martin was a tall, strong, hardworking boy who grew up on his grandparents' farm in Connecticut. Though he never went to school, he managed to write one of the best diaries of the Revolutionary War.*

Joseph Martin forced the metal plow deep down into the stony soil while his grandfather walked alongside, guiding the horse that pulled it. It was a fresh April morning, a perfect planting day. Suddenly the silence was broken by the sound of bells and gunshots in Milford. Joseph dropped the plow and dashed into town, his grandfather following behind as fast as he could.

A crowd was gathered in front of the tavern, where an express rider from New Haven shouted news of three days before: There had been a bloody battle in Concord, Massachusetts.

> ## REGULARS
>
> Unlike militiamen, who volunteered to fight when men were needed, the Continentals—or "regulars"—were professional soldiers who got paid to enlist and fight in the army. Continentals and militiamen often fought together in a battle. Each Continental soldier got assigned to a company of eighty-six men. Eight companies made up a regiment, also called a battalion. The Continental army had twenty-six regiments of foot soldiers, one of riflemen, and one of artillerymen.

Many were dead. Soldiers were needed now. A silver dollar was the reward for anyone who would enlist in the American army and march off to New York to join General Washington.

Joseph was only fourteen, a year too young to enlist. Until that day, his thoughts about soldiering had always been clear: "I felt myself to be a real coward. What—venture my carcass where bullets fly! That will never do for me. Stay at home out of harm's way, thought I."

But now friends his age and even younger were scrawling their names and grabbing up those dollars while adults cheered. Joseph was torn. He hated to stay home while his friends marched off to glory, and the thought of a whole silver dollar made "the seeds of courage begin to sprout," but he needed more time to get used to the idea. Two months later, he was ready. On June 25, 1776, Joseph slipped away from his grandparents' house and hiked into town, his mind made up to enlist for six months, the shortest term possible. When a group of boys he knew saw him coming toward the tavern, they began to taunt him:

" 'Come, if you will enlist, I will,' says one.

" 'You have long been talking about it,' says another. 'Come, now is the time.'

"Thinks I to myself, I will not be laughed into it or out of it. I will act my own pleasure after all . . . So seating myself at the table, enlisting orders were immediately presented to me. I took up the pen, loaded it with the fatal charge, made several mimic imitations of writing my name, but took especial care not to touch the paper with the pen until an unlucky [friend] who was leaning over my shoulder gave my hand a strike which caused the pen to make a woeful scratch on the paper. 'O, he has enlisted,' said he . . . Well, thought I, I may as well go through with the business now as not. So I wrote my name fairly upon the indentures. And now I was a soldier, in name at least."

His grandparents were unhappy, but they "fit him out" with clothing, a musket, and powder. His grandmother gave him cheese and cake and stuffed his Bible into his knapsack. He sailed to New York City to join a Connecticut company. For more than a month all they did was march in parades and

Besides money, this recruitment notice for the Continental army promises good clothing, ample rations, and "the opportunity of spending a few happy years in viewing the different parts of this beautiful continent."

TO ALL BRAVE, HEALTHY, ABLE BODIED, AND WELL DISPOSED YOUNG MEN,
IN THIS NEIGHBOURHOOD, WHO HAVE ANY INCLINATION TO JOIN THE TROOPS, NOW RAISING UNDER
GENERAL WASHINGTON,
FOR THE DEFENCE OF THE
LIBERTIES AND INDEPENDENCE
OF THE UNITED STATES,
Against the hostile designs of foreign enemies,

TAKE NOTICE,

practice battle drills. Joseph's biggest problem was getting used to the food—salt pork or boiled beef, hard bread, and turnips or boiled potatoes.

But even as they practiced, hundreds of British warships were arriving at nearby Staten Island, unloading 32,000 redcoated soldiers. Late in August, Joseph's company was ordered to Long Island to stop British forces from taking New York City. Just before they marched off, Joseph climbed onto the roof of a house and squinted in the direction of the battlefield: "I distinctly saw the smoke of the field artillery, but the distance and the unfavorableness of the wind prevented my hearing their report, at least but faintly. The horrors of battle then presented themselves to my mind in all their hideousness. I must come to it now, thought I."

They took a ferry across the East River to Brooklyn and marched toward a field, the shots growing louder and louder with each step until they boomed like thunder. "We now

*With his mother at his side, a young boy summons his courage and prepares to sign the enlistment roster that will make him a soldier in the Continental army.*

began to meet the wounded men, another sight I was unacquainted with, some with broken arms, some with broken legs, and some with broken heads. The sight of these a little daunted me, and made me think of home."

And then all at once he was fighting, too. "Our officers . . . pressed forward towards a creek, where a large party of Americans and British were engaged. By the time we arrived, the enemy had driven our men into the creek . . . where such as could swim got across. Those that could not swim, and could not procure anything to buoy them up, sunk."

On the opposite bank of Gowanus Creek he could make out a long row of British soldiers—professional warriors from what was then the best army in the world. They stood straight and tall in red jackets as they fired on command at the retreating Americans. The creek was filling up with American bodies. Joseph's company shot back furiously, trying to provide cover for those still thrashing through the water.

Then they marched on to a part of Manhattan called Kip's Bay and readied themselves for another battle. One night they camped so close to a British warship that Joseph could overhear soldiers on board mocking the Americans. Early on a Sunday morning, Joseph slipped into an unlocked warehouse for a rare moment of privacy and peace. He was seated on a stool, reading some papers he'd discovered, when "all of a sudden there came such a peal of thunder from the British shipping that I thought my head would go with the sound. I made a frog's leap for the ditch and lay as still as I possibly could and began to consider which part of my carcass would go first." They were soon dashing for their lives, leaping over the bodies of their friends. As Joseph put it, "The demons of fear and disorder seemed to take full possession of all and everything that day."

Joseph was still alive when October came and cool weather set in, and life got even more uncomfortable: "To have to lie, as I did almost every night on the cold and often wet ground without a blanket and with nothing but thin summer clothing was tedious . . . In the morning, the ground [often was] as white as snow with hoar frost. Or perhaps it would rain all night like a flood. All that could be done in that case was to lie down, take our musket in our arms and packe the lock between our thighs and 'weather it out.' "

When Joseph was discharged from the Continental army on Christmas Day, 1776, he felt older than fifteen. A battle-tested patriot, he was proud that he had stood his ground against the British. He set off for home, fifty-two miles away, with four shillings of discharge pay in his pocket and enough stories to get him through the winter and more. He

## RECRUITING FOR THE CONTINENTAL ARMY

After the wave of enthusiasm that gripped Joseph Plumb Martin and his friends in 1775, recruiting for the army got harder each year. Part of the problem was that the Continental soldiers faced the well-equipped British forces in ragged uniforms that they had to provide for themselves. Often they fought with muskets that lacked bayonets. Food was scarce and soldiers were not always paid on time, if at all. Not that it mattered much— privates got only about seven dollars a month. Some soldiers deserted, but many more remained out of a desire for independence and a respect for General George Washington.

farmed for a year, got bored, and reenlisted. When the war ended six years later, he was still a soldier. And he was also a free citizen of a new nation.

## What Happened to Joseph Plumb Martin?

He moved to Maine in 1794 and began to farm. He married and became the father of five children. He loved to write, tell stories, and draw pictures of birds. When he was seventy, his Revolutionary War account was published. He died in Maine at the age of ninety.

———◆✖◆———

*"This child . . . learned more French in a day than I could learn in a week with all my books."*—John Adams about his son, John Quincy

# John Quincy Adams: Translating for the Revolution

America, France, and Russia, 1770s and early 1780s

*John Quincy Adams—"Johnny" to his family—was born to be a patriot. Both his parents, John and Abigail Adams, were leaders of the American Revolution. Johnny had an amazing talent for learning languages. He was so good that as a boy he traveled the world with his father, seeking money and support for the American cause. By the time he reached his early teens, he was one of America's most experienced statesmen.*

One afternoon when Johnny Adams was eight, a sound like thunder rocked his family's farm. His mother grabbed his hand and pulled him to the top of Penn's Hill, the highest point on their property. Looking north toward Boston Harbor, he could see a British warship launching cannonballs at the village of Charlestown. Pillars of smoke rose toward the clouds, and houses were in flames. He looked up at his mother and knew the war had started. "I witnessed the tears of my mother and mingled them with my own," he wrote later. Soon four thousand English soldiers

*Dutch artist Isaak Schmidt drew this portrait of John Quincy Adams at age sixteen. Adams didn't like it.*

marched into Boston, and city people fled to the countryside. Before long it seemed that everyone the Adamses knew—and some they didn't—were living at their farm.

Johnny's father rode off for Philadelphia to represent Massachusetts in the Continental Congress, to decide how the colonies would organize an army and unite as a nation. He told Johnny to "fix your attention on great and glorious objects" while he was gone. Johnny tried, but the most glorious objects around the farm seemed to be potatoes, peas, and chickens. After his ninth birthday Johnny became a post rider, carrying mail on horseback along the rutted road between his farm and Boston. The detailed letters from his father to his mother alone would have been valuable to the British, but Johnny managed to make the eleven-mile trip home safely each time.

Johnny yearned to make his heroic parents proud of him. He studied for hours each day and volunteered for just about every task. He worried that he was too lazy, while his parents worried that he was too serious. At the age of nine, Johnny wrote this letter to this father in Philadelphia:

> *Dear Sir,*
>
> *I love to receive letters very well, much better than I love to write them. I make but a poor figure at composition. My head is much too fickle. My thoughts are running after bird's eggs, play and trifles, till I get vexed with myself. Mamma has a troublesome task to keep me a studying . . . I wish, sir, you would give me in writing some instructions with regard to the use of my time, and advise me how to proportion my studies and play, and I will keep them by me, and endeavor to follow them.*
>
> *With the present determination of growing better, I am, dear sir, your son*
> *John Quincy Adams*

After the colonies declared independence from England in 1776, the Continental Congress dispatched John Adams to France to persuade King Louis XVI to join the American cause. Eleven-year-old Johnny begged to go along. On February 13, 1778, shortly after father and son boarded the *Boston* and set sail, a British warship spotted the vessel and fired a signal to stop. Instead, the crew let out more sail and raced for the open ocean. A two-day chase ended when a gale overwhelmed both ships. Mammoth waves crashed over the deck and hurled passengers against the cabin walls. A bolt of lightning split the mast, killing four sailors. When at last the sky brightened, the crew found themselves looking at yet another British ship with cannons pointed right at them. Tired of running, they opened fire, captured the ship, and continued on to France.

Johnny loved Paris and had a wonderful ear for French. The king readily agreed to send a French ambassador back to America, but he selected a man who could barely sputter a word of greeting in English. Johnny became his tutor, standing at the ship's rail and patiently giving the ambassador vocabulary drills and explaining how verbs worked, until the man could communicate in English.

The more Johnny helped, the more people asked him to do. At age fourteen he went to Russia to help America's new ambassador, Robert Dana. French was the language spoken in the Russian court, and Johnny was fluent. He didn't really want to go, but he couldn't bring himself to say no when so many American boys were fighting. He found Russia to be a dark, cold, and impoverished land. "There is nobody here but slaves and princes," he wrote his mother. He worked all day long and found few friends his own age.

After two years, he and an Italian teenager departed for France. For months they journeyed by sled over the frozen rivers and snowfields of Sweden, Denmark, and Germany until they reached Paris. On April 20, 1783, Johnny finally got to hug his joyous father. Soon after, he watched as John Adams, Benjamin Franklin, and John Jay signed a peace treaty with Britain, ending the Revolutionary War. Back home, his proud father described Johnny Adams as "a son who is the greatest traveller of his age, and . . . as promising and manly a youth as in the whole world."

## WHAT HAPPENED TO JOHN QUINCY ADAMS?

He returned to Boston at eighteen to study law at Harvard. That year he wrote: "In America I can live independent and free; and rather than live otherwise I would wish to die." And he kept studying languages. He married Louisa Catherine Johnson and became the father of three children. By the time John Quincy Adams was inaugurated as the sixth president of the United States in 1825, it was said that he was so learned that he could write English with one hand and translate Greek with the other.

---

### ANOTHER YOUNG REVOLUTIONARY

Young people from many nations fought in our Revolutionary War, most on the side of the colonists. In 1779, a regiment of 550 slaves sailed from Haiti to Savannah, Georgia, to help the French—who controlled Haiti—fight against their mortal enemies, the British. One of the Haitians was eleven-year-old Henri Christophe, a bright, quick-tempered boy who was glad to get out of the kitchen where he worked. He saw little action in Savannah, but thought hard about the mix of black and white soldiers from several countries who were fighting to overthrow a colonial ruler. Later, he and other young Savannah veterans led a successful revolution of Haitian slaves against their French masters. Henri Christophe later became king of Haiti.

*"The British are burning Danbury! Muster at Ludington's!"*

# Sybil Ludington: Outdistancing Paul Revere

Fredericksburg, New York, April 26, 1777

*Nearly everyone has heard of the midnight ride of Paul Revere. That's mainly because Henry Wadsworth Longfellow wrote a poem about it soon after it happened. But far fewer people know that two years later a sixteen-year-old girl rode much farther over rougher roads. Alone and unarmed, Sybil Ludington raced through the night for freedom.*

Just after dark on the rainy evening of April 26, 1777, Colonel Henry Ludington, commander of a regiment of militiamen near the New York–Connecticut border, heard a rap at his door. Outside stood a saluting messenger, rain streaming from his cape. His words came fast. British soldiers had just torched the warehouse in Danbury, Connecticut. Food, guns, and liquor belonging to the Continental army were being destroyed. Drunken soldiers were burning homes, too. Could Colonel Ludington round up his men right away?

It was easier said than done. Colonel Ludington's militiamen were farmers and woodsmen whose homes were scattered throughout the countryside. Someone would have to go get them while the colonel stayed behind to organize them once they arrived. But who? Who besides he himself knew where they all lived and could cover so many miles on horseback in the dead of night? Deep in thought, he heard his daughter Sybil's voice. She was saying that she wanted to go.

For Sybil Ludington it was an unexpected chance to help the war effort. As the oldest of eight children, her days were filled with chores and responsibilities. Still, each week when her father's men drilled in their pasture, she paused from her work to watch them. She wished she could fight. People kept saying she was doing her part for liberty at home, but she wanted to do more. Suddenly, with this emergency on a rainy night, she had a chance.

In 1975, the U.S. Postal Service issued a Sybil Ludington stamp to mark the American Bicentennial.

Her father looked at her. How could he let her take such a risk? The whole countryside was full of armed men. There were skinners and cowboys who stole cattle for the British, soldiers from both sides, and deserters trying to get back home under cover of darkness. But Sybil was right: She knew every soldier in her father's unit and she was a fine rider. Rebecca, her next oldest sister, could mind the children. Most of them were already asleep anyway.

Colonel Ludington walked with Sybil out to the barn and held a lantern while she threw a saddle over her yearling colt, Star. Together father and daughter went over the names of his men and where they lived. Then the colonel watched Sybil disappear into the darkness.

It was raining hard. Sybil put away thoughts of who might appear in the roadway and concentrated on the road map in her head. With no time to lose, she had to reach all the men, taking the most efficient route possible. She picked up a long stick to bang on doors. That way she wouldn't have to waste time dismounting and getting back on Star. One by one, hearing the rap of the stick, the sleepy farmers cracked their doors open, some poking muskets out into the darkness. Sybil said the same thing to all: "The British are burning Danbury! Muster at Ludington's!" Once she knew they understood, she galloped off, refusing all offers of rest and refreshment.

It took her till dawn to get back home. She was soaked and sore, but as she rode up to her farm she could hear the sounds of drums and bugles. Many of her father's men were already there, getting ready to march. Soon her father's militia set off to join five hundred other Colonial soldiers. They missed the British at Danbury but finally fought and defeated them at Ridgefield, Connecticut, a few weeks later.

## WHAT HAPPENED TO SYBIL LUDINGTON?

Word of Sybil's night ride got around. George Washington thanked her personally, and Alexander Hamilton wrote her a letter of appreciation. When she was twenty-three, Sybil married her childhood sweetheart, Edmond Ogden, and became the mother of four sons and two daughters. Sybil died in New York at the age of seventy-seven. There is a bronze statue of Sybil Ludington atop Star at Lake Gleneida in Carmel, New York. In 1975, an eight-cent U.S. postage stamp was issued in her honor.

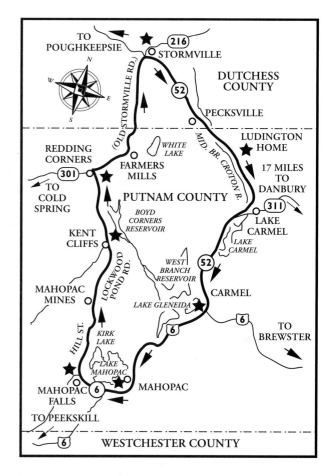

*The route of Sybil Ludington's night ride through the New York countryside*

### SYBIL RODE FARTHER

On April 18, 1775, Paul Revere raced from Boston to Lexington to warn American rebel leaders, "The British are coming!" He rode fourteen miles on good roads for some two hours, while Sybil Ludington rode all night—nearly forty miles over cart tracks and rutted fields in the blackness of rural farm country.

*"Shoot me if you dare. I will not tell you."*—Dicey Langston to a gun-pointing loyalist demanding that she reveal a patriot secret

# Mary Redmond, John Darragh, and Dicey Langston: Spies

Pennsylvania and South Carolina, 1777–1783

*Young people made excellent spies during the American Revolution. Often overlooked by adults, they heard and saw plenty. Secrets were everywhere, encoded even in the way laundry was hung on the line to dry. Patriots and loyalists lived together and spoke the same language. Sometimes you couldn't help but overhear.*

## NEW JOBS FOR LIBERTY

With men away and women doing double duty, young colonists took on many new jobs throughout the Revolutionary War. One amazed observer saw Massachusetts children "making cartridges, running bullets, making Wallets, and baking biscuit."

In 1777, British troops invaded Philadelphia and took over the city. Many colonists fled, but some stubbornly stayed in their homes, even when British soldiers moved in. With enemies living just walls apart, Philadelphia became a city of secrets. The British didn't know whom they could trust. Armed redcoats patrolled the streets and set up guard posts around the town. Colonists had to show passes and state their business before they could even go to the marketplace.

The city was honeycombed with spies, many of them children. Some worked in teams. One girl named Mary Redmond worked with a boy who carried messages into Philadelphia from Continental soldiers camped in the surrounding countryside. The messages were stitched into the back of his coat. The public market was the handoff place.

Mary's job was to watch the British soldiers closely as the boy approached the market. If it ever looked as if the British were on to him, she was supposed to flash a signal to nearby contacts. One morning, though, there was no time to signal. Mary saw two British soldiers eyeing her partner as he neared the market. Both men started toward him. With no time to signal for help, Mary took off running across the square as fast as she could and, pretending to be playing, drove her shoulder hard into the boy's legs in a flying tackle. He went down in a heap. As they rolled in the dust she threw her shawl over his back, ripped the message from his coat back, and stuffed it in her dress. Then, laughing, she skipped away from both the boy and the puzzled soldiers and went on to deliver the message. Later

British forces often communicated through "masked" messages. This 1777 letter from one British officer to another contained misleading information, but when an hourglass-shaped mask was placed over the letter, the real message was revealed.

she liked to recall that her loyalist relatives enjoyed chuckling over "our little black-eyed rebel." She doesn't say if they ever found out that their little rebel was a spy.

Elsewhere in Philadelphia, a group of British officers took over a large room in the home of Lydia Darragh, a pleasant Quaker woman. Normally, Quakers stayed out of wars, but Lydia's son Charles had enlisted in the Continental army and was now a lieutenant. The British tenants used the room as a "council chamber," to make war plans. As they schemed, Mr. and Mrs. Darragh and their fourteen-year-old son, John, lay flat on the floor above them, ears pressed hard against a crack between two boards. Whenever they heard important information, Mr. Darragh wrote it down in code on small scraps of paper. Mrs. Darragh sewed the messages inside large cloth-covered buttons and fastened them to John's coat.

Then it was all up to John. If the British caught him delivering military secrets, he could be jailed or even executed. Looking as casual as he could, he would wander out the door, through the city, and to the road that led from town, presenting his pass to British soldiers at each checkpoint. Sometimes they questioned him roughly and shook him down, but they never thought to inspect his coat buttons. Once past the guard, he would fade into the trees at the edge of the city and go to meet his brother, who would cut off his buttons and send them straight to George Washington.

Farther south, fifteen-year-old Dicey Langston lived in peril. The southern colonies had more loyalists than those up north. Many country people resented the wealthy planters along the coast and didn't mind a bit if the British put them in their place. Dicey lived among loyalists near Spartanburg, South Carolina, but her father and brothers were patriots. Neighbors distrusted her, and with good reason. They knew her brothers were militiamen, scattered in secret places in the woods nearby.

As she did her chores, Dicey often overheard her neighbors and loyalist uncles talking about troop movements. Whenever she heard anything of interest, she hiked off to inform her brothers' militia unit, camped across the Enoree River. But one night she stayed away too long and returned to face a group of men shining lanterns in her eyes and asking pointed questions about where she had been. After that, her father made Dicey promise to stop sneaking away. She did, until she overheard one secret she couldn't keep. A company of loyalist soldiers called the Bloody Scout knew exactly where her brother's militia was headquartered. They were planning to wipe it out.

With no time to lose, Dicey slipped into the woods after dark and ran until she came to the edge of the Tyger River. Heavy rains had raised the angry water almost to the banks and washed out the footbridges. Dicey steeled herself and plunged in. In an instant the water was up to her neck and the current was carrying her rapidly away. She was far downstream by the time she struggled to the opposite bank. Shivering, she retraced her steps and found her brothers' camp.

After that, life became terrifying for the Langston family. One night armed soldiers rode up to their house with orders to kill every Langston man. Only Dicey's father, Solomon Langston, frail and elderly, was still there. A soldier dismounted from his horse, took out a pistol, and shoved the barrel against the old man's chest. Dicey sprang between her father and the gun. The soldier threatened to kill her father if she didn't move, but she stood her ground and said he'd have to kill her first. The soldier hesitated, then reholstered his pistol and ordered his men to depart.

## WHAT HAPPENED TO DICEY LANGSTON?

She lived to be an old woman in South Carolina. At the time of her death she liked to boast that she had thirty-two sons and grandsons willing to bear arms for their country.

---

### SPY VERSUS SPY

British and Colonial forces each used spies and had a number of techniques for coding messages. Both sides liked to use invisible ink, a colorless fluid that could be read by heating the paper or treating it with a chemical. But they had to make sure not to get the paper damp, because moisture spread the chemical around and blurred the message. Both sides compiled small dictionaries of coded words, which spies used to write messages. Both sides made codes by numbering the letters of the alphabet. For example, in one British message, the letter A was number 51, B was 52, and so on to Z. A few numbers were scrambled and skipped. Both armies used code names for cities and generals. In messages from British general Sir Henry Clinton, Philadelphia was Jerusalem, Detroit was Alexandria, and General Washington was called James. Congress was known as the Synagogue.

*"I shall never prove a traitor to my country."*

# James Forten: Saved by a Game of Marbles

Philadelphia, Pennsylvania, 1780

*In 1776, the year the Declaration of Independence was signed, one of every six Americans was of African ancestry. Ninety-nine percent of them were slaves. James Forten was one of about two hundred free blacks living in Philadelphia. He was fourteen years old in 1780.*

Whenever an American privateer captured a British ship, practically everyone in Philadelphia lined the docks along the Delaware River to cheer the American sailors as they led the defeated vessel into harbor. Then the crowd surged to the London Coffee House, where the ship's cargo was auctioned off and the proceeds divided among the American crew. When there was gold aboard, even boys—powder monkeys and cabin boys—soon had pockets sagging with heavy coins. Like many boys in Philadelphia, James Forten wanted to sail aboard a privateer more than anything in the world.

It wasn't just the money. James wanted to fight for American freedom. He believed the American cause offered a better chance for his people than that of the British, who ran an enormous slave empire in the West Indies. James owed his freedom to his grandfather, an African-born slave who had somehow scraped together enough money to buy freedom for himself and his wife. All their children, including James's father, had been born free. James had even been lucky enough to go to a school run by a Quaker teacher opposed to slavery. James knew the sweetness of freedom, and he wanted it for everyone.

At first James's mother was dead set against his going to sea. James's father had died and James was her only son. She needed him. But he had a powerful argument: The family was living in rags, without even enough money for new shoes. He reminded his mother that a

*James Forten, who owed his freedom to his grandfather's labor, devoted his life to the abolition of slavery and lived to see his sons and grandsons become leaders in the anti-slavery movement.*

privateer's wages—four dollars a month—could make ends meet for the family even if there wasn't any prize money. And if there was, they could breathe much easier. When she nodded her head, James was in heaven.

He signed on as a powder monkey for the *Royal Louis,* the best-known privateer in Philadelphia. It had been built by the Pennsylvania Commonwealth to protect American vessels from British warships that threatened their harbor. Captained by Stephen Decatur, the *Royal Louis* captured more British ships than any other privateer, and the crew earned more prizes. Best of all, the crew was racially integrated—James would be one of twenty Negroes on board.

James's main job was to keep the cannons on deck supplied with gunpowder, which was stored below in a dry room called the magazine. Powder monkeys had to be fast, brave, and cool in battle. Usually they were small, too, but James was already nearly six feet tall. But if it didn't bother Captain Decatur, it didn't bother James.

James's courage was tested on his very first voyage, when the *Royal Louis* met the British ship *Active* and quickly traded cannon shots. James tucked bags of flammable gunpowder inside his jacket to shield it from flying sparks and sprinted up and down stairs as the ship rocked from cannon blasts. Shells exploded all around. Men screamed in pain and officers shouted to make their orders heard. The ships drew closer and closer until they collided. Americans swarmed aboard the *Active,* where sailors fought hand to hand. James's coat was drenched in blood when the British sailors finally gave up.

After a rousing welcome in Philadelphia, the sailors split up the money and headed back to sea. But this time their luck ran out. The *Royal Louis* went hard after a British ship that led them into a trap. Soon the Americans were surrounded by three British warships and forced to surrender. James was in serious trouble. He had been free in Philadelphia, but now he was a British prisoner. He knew that the British often sold black captives to British sugar plantations in the West Indies. Was he about to become a slave?

James and others were taken aboard a British ship. The British captain, John Beasley, inspected them one by one, moving his way slowly along a line of captives. He stopped when he got to James. His eyes went to a small bag James held in his hand. He asked what was in it. "Marbles," James replied.

The captain brightened. It so happened that his son, Willie, was aboard. Willie was about James's age and loved marbles. A game was quickly arranged and the boys became

The dreaded British prison ship Jersey, anchored off Long Island, where young James Forten was imprisoned for seven months. During the Revolutionary War more than ten thousand American prisoners died in the ship's disease-infested hold.

friends. James had learned to shoot expertly from his father's friends, and, though slavery might be in his future, when it came to marbles, James Forten owned Willie Beasley. Captain Beasley was so impressed that he offered to take James back to England and pay for his education if he would renounce his allegiance to America. James answered without hesitation: "No! I was captured fighting for my country and I will never be a traitor to her."

Instead of shipping him to the West Indies, Captain Beasley sent James to the *Jersey*, a prison ship in New York Harbor. It was more like a death ship. James spent seven months in an airless space below deck and nearly starved. When he was finally traded for another prisoner, his hair had fallen out and he looked like a skeleton. But he was free. "Thus," James Forten wrote later, "did a game of marbles keep me from a life of West Indian servitude."

## WHAT HAPPENED TO JAMES FORTEN?

He grew up to be a wealthy and well-known sailmaker and an outspoken opponent of slavery. He hired both blacks and whites at his Philadelphia sailmaking business. He strongly supported women's rights. Respected by all, he was offered the chance to become president of Liberia, in Africa, but chose to remain in America.

### PRIVATEERS

Privateers were privately owned ships allowed by the American government to chase British vessels and keep anything of value they captured. The American navy was very small, but there were more than one thousand privateers that fought in the Revolutionary War, capturing more than six hundred British ships. There was money to be made: In 1779, one fourteen-year-old cabin boy made $700, one ton of sugar, thirty-five gallons of rum, and twenty pounds each of cotton, ginger, logwood, and allspice. But many privateering sailors were killed or captured, and the British treated them harshly.

# Private Deborah Sampson: Alias Robert Shirtliffe

Massachusetts and New York, 1779–1782

*The war was supposed to be fought by men, but at least one young woman put on—and altered—the uniform of the Continental army. She served for three years in a fighting regiment.*

Deborah Sampson was born into a large, poor family in Plymouth, Massachusetts. One day when she was little, her father walked away, leaving her mother with too many children to feed. Deborah was sent to live with a neighbor, and then to the Thomas family, farmers who needed an indentured servant.

In a way, Deborah thought, it wasn't so bad. She liked hard outdoor work, and the Thomases treated her well enough. But they wouldn't let her go to school because, they kept saying, school meant too much time away from chores.

Deborah was determined to learn anyway. Some afternoons she slipped down to the road in front of her house and convinced the schoolchildren who passed by to lend her their books overnight. She fell asleep trying to make sense of the words and numbers, but she hustled down to the road the next morning to return the books and ask the students to help her understand what she couldn't figure out. They did their best to help her, but it wasn't like having a real teacher.

When Deborah turned sixteen, in 1776, she went to live with another farm family who agreed to give her half a day free to go to school. She was the oldest student, and far behind the others, but she outworked everyone until she caught up. Soon she was assisting the teacher.

Meanwhile the Revolutionary War stormed through New England. Liberty had a special meaning to Deborah, since people had been telling her where to live and what to do all her life. She volunteered to do farmwork for families whose men had gone off to war, but she never felt that she was doing enough. She considered becoming a nurse or a bandage supplier, but she really wanted to fight. It seemed unfair that females

## BETTY ZANE

Though perhaps only Deborah Sampson fought in uniform, many girls and women saw action in the Revolutionary War. In 1782, sixteen-year-old Betty Zane saved the lives of many American soldiers during the siege of Fort Henry, West Virginia. With the fort surrounded by Indians who were fighting on the British side, the Americans ran out of gunpowder. Betty said she knew of a stash of powder in a nearby house. She dashed out of the fort, made it to the house, and emptied a barrel of powder onto a tablecloth. Then she bundled it up and hauled it back to the fort through a hail of bullets, enabling the soldiers to survive.

couldn't enlist. Years of farmwork had made Deborah as strong as most men, and she knew how to handle heavy equipment.

As she worked, a daydream formed and soon began to harden into a plan. She knew she couldn't join the local militia, where people would recognize her. But soldiers were needed in the Continental army to fight in New York and Pennsylvania. No one knew her there. With money she earned teaching school in the summer, she bought several yards of coarse fabric and sewed a suit of men's clothing. She hid each piece in a haystack until the whole outfit was finished. Then she told her family that she was leaving to find better wages and hiked off with her clothes tied in a bundle. Once out of sight, she slipped inside a grove of trees, cut her hair, put on her disguise, and walked to Medway, Massachusetts, where a company was forming. She introduced herself to the commander as "Robert Shirtliffe." Captain Thayer invited young Shirtliffe to live with his family until the company was complete and ready to join the main army. He issued the new soldier a uniform, which didn't quite fit. Mrs. Thayer was amazed to see Shirtliffe take out a needle and scissors and alter it expertly. The young soldier explained that he had grown up in a family without girls and his mother had made him learn to sew.

DEBORAH SAMPSON.
Published by H. Mann, 1797.

*Deborah Sampson, also known as Robert Shirtliffe, from the cover of her biography*

When the company was formed, Deborah was assigned to West Point, New York. Action came swiftly. Heading toward Tarrytown, New York, the Continental soldiers

*Deborah Sampson's "muster certificate," proving to all that she had indeed served as a soldier in the Revolutionary War. By 1791, the date of this document, she was using her married name, Gannet.*

were surprised by a fast-moving Hessian cavalry unit. Deborah took her position with her unit and fired again and again. Only when the battle was over did she notice the two bullet holes through her coat and one in her cap. The soldier positioned next to her lay dead. Somehow, Deborah wasn't seriously hurt.

For three years she fought the British and managed both to stay alive and to keep her secret. Most of the time it wasn't so hard. Soldiers rarely bathed and they slept in their uniforms. She kept her hair short. A few noticed that she never seemed to shave and called her Molly, but she felt no need to respond. No one could fault her as a soldier. She was as good as anyone in her company with a musket or bayonet. Often she volunteered to scout possible enemy positions and never backed down in a fight. Twice she was wounded, first by a British sword that slashed the left side of her head and later by a bullet that passed through her shoulder. Both times she was treated with her uniform on.

But in 1782, as the war was winding down, Deborah fell ill. Feverish and unconscious, she was taken on horseback to a field hospital, where the nurse on duty could not detect her pulse. "Poor Bob is gone," she reported to the doctor. The doctor felt for a heartbeat and discovered a bandage wrapped tightly around the soldier's chest. Removing it, he got the shock of his career. He kept Deborah's secret and took her to his own home, where his family took care of her until she recovered. Only then did he inform her company commander.

Without explanation, Deborah was given an honorable discharge from the army. She went back to Plymouth to help her mother. Word about what Deborah Sampson had done soon spread through her town. Some treated her as a criminal who had deceived her country for three years. She was expelled from her church. At first she was ashamed to have caused problems, but the more she thought about it, the less apologetic she felt. What was there to be ashamed of? She had fought at least as well as the men in her company. She came to feel proud that she had risked her life again and again for her nation and that she had acted boldly for the cause of liberty.

## WHAT HAPPENED TO DEBORAH SAMPSON?

She married and became a schoolteacher. One day, years later, she received a letter addressed to "Robert Shirtliffe, or rather Mrs. Gannet." It was from George Washington, now president of the United States, inviting her to visit the capital. There, Congress awarded her a pension, land, and a letter thanking her for remarkable service to her country. Later she traveled throughout New York and Massachusetts, telling war stories and showing amazed audiences how well she could handle guns and swords. "I burst the tyrant bonds which held my sex in awe," she said, "and grasped an opportunity which custom and the world seemed to deny as a natural privilege."

---

### LIVING IN A LARGE FAMILY

During her military life, Deborah wrote to her mother, artfully concealing her true job. In one letter she said, "I am in a large but well-regulated family. My employment is agreeable though it is somewhat different and more intense than it was at home."

# PART FOUR

# Learning to Be a Nation

◆❖◆

Independence from Britain gave America a chance to try to succeed as a nation but didn't guarantee success. For the states, the hard work of learning to govern together came at a time when the whole continent seemed to be seething with energy and motion. Thousands of British soldiers remained around the western and northern perimeters like wolves, spoiling for another fight. Westward-pushing settlers and Native Americans struggled to control land and resources. Every effort to start a new state seemed to touch off a furious debate—would it be slave or free? And thousands of slaves risked their lives to escape northward to freedom.

Even the very nature of work changed. The shop gave way to the factory. Apprentices learned to pull levers. New water-powered looms spun cotton into yarn much faster than could be done by hand. Children went to work in mines and mills, and many didn't come home, sleeping instead in company-owned boardinghouses. An inventor named John Baxter advertised that his new six-spindle loom "could easily be turned by children five to ten years of age," and his twelve-spindle model by "girls from ten to twenty." The new cloth-making machines ate up raw cotton, making slave labor more important than ever to cotton planters.

The Constitution, ratified in 1788, reflected the new nation's unrest. It began with the words "We the People," but left out more than three-fourths of all Americans: women, Native Americans, almost all African Americans, and young people. Like the new nation itself, it was clearly a work in progress.

*The enormous flag that inspired Francis Scott Key's "Star-Spangled Banner"*
*on display in 1873 in the Charlestown, Massachusetts, navy yard*

# Smith Wilkinson: The Same Thing Over and Over

Pawtucket, Rhode Island, 1790

*The first factory workers in American history were boys and girls who happened to live near an old warehouse on a river in Rhode Island. On the morning they first stood stiffly at their machines, they had no idea that they were pioneers. They did not know that the work they were about to begin would doom the apprentice's shop or that the struggle to pass a law regulating child labor would last another 148 years.*

## SAM SLATER'S SECRET

The man who built America's first spinning mill was little more than a boy himself, but a very serious one and a great schemer. Samuel Slater grew up in England and was apprenticed at age fourteen to the factory master of a cotton mill. In the 1780s, English manufacturers knew how to use water power to drive machinery that spun cotton into yarn. America was still spinning yarn by hand on small wheels. This secret gave the English a huge economic advantage, and they were determined to hold on to it. Britain passed laws that kept anyone who knew how to build spinning machines from leaving the country, and also forbade the export of parts used in the mills. American manufacturers were offering big rewards for anyone who could design an English-style cotton mill.

Sam Slater kept his mouth shut and his eyes open. He memorized everything he could about how the machines worked. Then, without telling even his mother, he took off for America in disguise. He arrived in New York knowing no one. He was so naïve that a pair of street hustlers easily sold him socks without bottoms. But soon he hooked up with some Rhode Island businessmen who put up the money for a mill in Pawtucket. With the help of child laborers, Samuel Slater's mill worked. Not yet twenty-one, he had smuggled the Industrial Revolution across the Atlantic in his head. He died a millionaire.

Early on a Monday morning in December 1790, four small boys ducked through the frame door of an old furniture factory in Pawtucket, Rhode Island, and stepped into a gloomy room full of strange-looking machinery. It was still dark and so cold that the factory owner, Mr. Slater, told them to wait while he crawled out onto the ice-covered Blackstone River and smashed the ice with a stone. When water began to run freely over a great wheel, the machines groaned slowly to life. Shouting to be heard over the grinding gears and pounding wooden frames, Slater told ten-year-old Smith Wilkinson what to do. First, he said, take up a handful of cotton and pull it apart with both hands. Then put it all into your right hand. Then feed the cotton into your machine by moving your hand back and forth over the frame that sorts the cotton. That's it. Just keep doing it.

And that's what Smith did, except for two short breaks, until 7:30 that night. A few days later three more boys and then two girls joined the crew. The oldest was twelve and the youngest seven. Those nine children were the first factory workers in American history.

Ten years later there were one hundred children in that room. The youngest were only four years old. There were so many machines that the sound of clashing gears made hearing nearly impossible. The air was stuffy and filled with floating fibers of lint that got in their eyes and lodged fast in their lungs. As foremen inspected their work, children spread cleaned cotton onto a machine to be combed, and then passed it on to other children who operated a machine that turned the cotton into loose balls. They in turn passed it to more children who operated a machine that spun the cotton into yarn, arraying it onto dozens of spindles. The littlest children removed full bobbins, attached empty ones, and picked up and knotted broken threads. Sometimes when they got tired and slowed down or quit, they were beaten.

Now that water-driven machines could spin cotton into yarn, redbrick textile mills sprang up along swift-moving New England rivers. Suddenly there was a huge demand for cotton to feed the machines, and a second machine soon accelerated the cloth-making process even more. In 1793, a Yale College graduate named Eli Whitney invented a device that let a man and a horse clean the seeds from cotton fifty times faster than by hand. Later, when the cotton "gin" (short for engine) was hitched to a steam engine, it could go twenty times faster than that.

The cotton gin's speed created a huge need for people to pick, bale, clean, and load cotton into barges. Planters feverishly bought up property and turned the South into a money-making land of cotton. Slavery, which had been slowly dying out, roared back like a monster. Within a few years, rivers were churning with steamboats loaded down with

*Young girls called can-tenders were hired to pack cotton rope into cans and replace full cans with empties in a textile mill's "card room."*

## THE FIRST U.S. FACTORY WORKERS

The first nine factory workers in U.S. history were named Smith Wilkinson, Jabez Jenks, Turpin Arnold, Charles Arnold, Eunice Arnold, Otis Borrows, John Jenks, Varnus Jenks, and Ann Arnold. None was older than twelve on the day he or she started. They worked fourteen hours each day, six days a week, turning cotton into yarn. They got paid between 80 cents and $1.40 per week. Even on their day off they went to a Sunday school at the mill but learned little of value. Slater was a strict boss; he sometimes struck the children with a cane if they couldn't keep up. One boy named James Horton explained why he quit: "If Mr. Slater had taught me to work all the different branches I [would still be] with you now. But instead, he kept me always at one thing and I might have stood there until this time and never knew nothing."

cotton bales and headed north to New England's rivers. By 1830, more than a million children worked in textile mills. And throughout the land, Americans put on shirts, dresses, and trousers made of cotton that had been picked by slaves in the South and spun and woven into cloth by women and children in the North.

## WHAT HAPPENED TO SMITH WILKINSON?

He married, became the father of a son and three daughters, and was hired as the superintendent of a large and prosperous cotton mill in Pomfret, Connecticut. One description of him says that he checked the tail of his coat every five minutes to see if his wallet was still there. No wonder—by the time he died at the age of seventy-one, his estate was valued at $128,588.

*"You take the drum and I'll take the fife."*

# Rebecca and Abigail Bates: An Army of Two

Scituate, Massachusetts, 1814

*The British didn't simply disappear after the Revolutionary War. Thirty-five thousand soldiers and loyalists settled just north of the U.S. border in Nova Scotia. Still more British soldiers continued to live in the forts they had captured west of the Appalachian Mountains, helping Indian allies fight against American settlers who wanted tribal land. Resentment grew. Overseas, there were even bigger problems. Britain and France were at war, and both nations captured American ships, jailed American sailors, and blocked the United States from trading with European nations. In 1812, America again declared war against Britain, and the two powers squared off for the second time in forty years. The so-called War of 1812, which didn't end until 1815, settled matters once and for all.*

Rebecca Bates, nineteen, and her sister Abigail, fifteen, were part of a very nervous family in Scituate, Massachusetts. Their father was the lighthouse keeper for Scit-

LEARNING TO BE A NATION

*Rebecca and Abigail Bates ready their fife and drum as the British ship* La Hogue *looms just out of sight in Scituate Harbor.*

uate Harbor, and the Bateses lived in a gray house attached to the lighthouse itself. Unfortunately, that put them closer than anyone else to the British warship *Bulwark,* which had dropped anchor at the mouth of Scituate Harbor in the spring of 1814. For months, whenever they cleaned the lighthouse windows or helped their father keep watch, the girls had to stare at that ship. They prayed their home wouldn't get blown to bits the way the Boston Light House had during the Revolution.

On June 11, the British finally made a move. Several boats full of heavily armed soldiers were lowered to the water, and sailors began to row toward the town wharf, where a crowd of unarmed townspeople gathered to meet them. Soon a redcoated British officer climbed onto the town pier and haughtily demanded that Scituate residents load up the British boats with meat, fresh water, and vegetables. The town parson angrily refused. While some British soldiers trained their rifles on the townspeople, others lit torches and set fire to American barges in the harbor. Then the British seized four boats belonging to townspeople, loaded them up with all the fresh goods they could steal from people's gardens and stores, and rowed the boats back to the *Bulwark.*

Later in the summer, a regiment of American soldiers arrived to chase the *Bulwark* away. Several men moved in with the Bates family to protect the lighthouse, including two musicians—a fife player and a drummer. During the long summer months, the soldiers taught Rebecca and Abigail how to play four tunes on their instruments, including the Revolutionary War anthem "Yankee Doodle." As the summer passed with no further sign of a British ship, the soldiers moved on. The two musicians went with them, but they left their instruments behind.

One day, early in September, when Rebecca and Abigail were alone with their little brother in the lighthouse, another huge British ship suddenly appeared off the coast. "I knew the ship at a glance," Rebecca later recalled. "It was the *La Hogue*. 'O Lord,' says I to my sister . . . 'they'll burn our barges just as they did before.' You see, there were two vessels at the wharf loaded with flour, and we couldn't afford to lose them." Rebecca weighed their options. The American soldiers had left muskets behind, and she knew how to shoot, but she could never take on that many soldiers. "I might have killed one or two, but they would have turned around and fired on the village."

Then Rebecca spotted the fife and drum the soldiers had left behind and she got an idea. "I said to my sister, 'You take the drum and I'll take the fife.' 'What good'll that do?' says she. 'Scare them,' says I. 'All you've got to do is call the roll. I'll scream the fife and we must keep out of sight.' We ran out behind the cedar woods." Just as before, the British dropped rowboats into the water, and soldiers stroked the oars toward shore. When the boats neared the girls' hiding place, Rebecca and Abigail began to play "Yankee Doodle."

After a few verses, they peeked out. "I could see the men in the barges resting on their oars and listening," Rebecca recalled. It seemed as if they were wondering if the Americans were massing for an attack. And then the girls saw a blessed sight: The British boats turned around and began to chop water back to the big ship in a panic. "They turned about so quick a man fell overboard," said Rebecca. "And they picked him up by the back of the neck and disappeared." That night, *La Hogue* left, firing one last shot at the lighthouse that fell far short. The redcoats had been routed by two girls.

## WHAT HAPPENED TO REBECCA AND ABIGAIL BATES?

Neither married, and neither moved from Scituate. They made their living as seamstresses. Magazine articles made them so famous that in their later years they sold autographs to visitors from their front porch—for ten cents apiece.

*"Oh, say does that star-spangled banner yet wave?"*—Francis Scott Key

## Caroline Pickersgill: Stitching the Star-Spangled Banner

Baltimore, Maryland, 1813

*Thirteen-year-old Caroline Pickersgill sewed flags with her mother and grandmother in the sunny front parlor of their redbrick house in Baltimore. The floor was strewn with strips of bright wool bunting and half-used spools of thread. Flagmaking was a tradition in Caroline's family. Her grandmother, Rebecca Young, had made the first flag of the American Revolution. Her mother, Mary Pickersgill, had built up a good business sewing flags and pennants for ships from all over the world that sailed into Baltimore Harbor. During the War of 1812, the Pickersgills were ready for the most important order they ever got.*

In the spring of 1813, Major General George Armistead, commander of Fort McHenry, a star-shaped fort that guarded Baltimore Harbor, called at the Pickersgills' house on Albemarle Street in Baltimore. Caroline Pickersgill, her mother, and her grandmother listened as the general explained that he wanted them to sew the biggest American flag ever made—forty-two feet by thirty. That, they realized, was wider than their whole house. Armistead wanted to raise a giant banner over Fort McHenry so that it would be the first thing the British saw if they ever entered Baltimore Harbor. Such a flag would give his men pride, he said, and let the British know

*Mary and Caroline Pickersgill work on the star-spangled banner in Claggette's Malt House, while a cousin watches and Major General Armistead's soldiers hover impatiently.*

they were attacking a city defended by proud Americans. And one other thing: He needed it right away.

The Pickersgills quickly agreed. It was a good time to take on a big project, since Caroline's cousins Eliza Young, thirteen, and Mary Young, fifteen, had just moved in after the death of their father. As soon as enough wool bunting could be purchased, the three girls and two women put away their other projects and began to cut out red and white stripes that quickly bunched up on the floor in Mary's upstairs bedroom. When it came time to attach the blue field (for the stars) to the stripes, they had run out of space.

They carried the stripes several blocks to a neighborhood brewery and into a large winter malt room that was unused during hot months. After shoving kegs of beer back against the walls, they swept the floor clean and laid out the material. They worked at top speed from dawn till midnight six days a week, often with Major General Armistead's men hovering over them.

In September they finally attached a blue rectangular square to the stripes, and then cut out fifteen stars and stitched them to the flag, spacing them carefully. When the flag was finished, two soldiers folded it, stuffed it into a duffel bag, and hauled it to the fort in a cart. They tied it to a stout pole and raised it aloft as the Pickersgills watched. As it neared the top, the banner unfurled in the wind, forming a colossal symbol of patriotism. The giant flag was visible not only from the harbor but from just about every window in Baltimore.

The British didn't arrive until nearly a year later. In August 1814, they sailed an army into Chesapeake Bay near Washington, D.C., just thirty miles to the south. After easily winning a battle, redcoats torched the president's house and burned down the Capitol. When Baltimoreans heard the news, they worked feverishly to fortify their city. Outside her windows, Caroline could hear the drums and fifes of militiamen drilling on the common. Slaves and masters labored side by side, digging trenches and rolling cannons toward Baltimore Harbor. The great explosions that rocked Caroline's house meant that ships were being sunk in a great semicircle in Baltimore Harbor to form a barrrier against sea invasion. Though many Baltimore families were dragging their belongings into the countryside, the Pickersgills prepared to face the crisis from their home. It wouldn't be long now.

The first British ships arrived around noon on Sunday, September 13, 1814. When officers realized their path to the city was blocked by sunken ships, they attacked Fort

## A WHOPPER OF A FLAG

The flag the Pickersgills made for Fort McHenry was forty-two feet long and thirty feet wide. It had fifteen stripes and fifteen stars, representing the number of states in the Union at the time. When it was finished, the flag weighed two hundred pounds. It was sewn onto four hundred yards of *English* wool bunting, which made the Pickersgills feel good. For a fee of $405.90—including the cost of material—the girls and women sewed 1.7 million stitches. Today the original flag is on display at the National Museum of American History in Washington, D.C. A restoration project, ending in the year 2000, cost over $18 million.

McHenry with powerful cannons that could send shells two miles. The Pickersgills' home shook all night and into the next day. Caroline and her family watched the fireworks from their attic. For a while, they could see their flag from a window, but then heavy rainclouds obscured it and darkness came.

Out in the harbor, an American lawyer named Francis Scott Key was trapped aboard one of the British gunships, where he had been trying to arrange a prisoner exchange between the two sides. Unable to leave, all Key could do was watch the British rockets light up the sky. The most visible object, lit up with each blast, was the Pickersgills' giant flag. But then, deep into the rainy night, the British stopped shelling the fort. There was an eerie silence. What had happened? Was Fort McHenry still standing? Was the flag still there? Key began nervously to make up new lyrics to an old English drinking tune. "Oh, say does that star-spangled banner yet wave?" he wrote.

Dawn came, and there was the flag, tattered and riddled with holes, but still rippling over the fort. Overnight the tide of battle had turned: Now Baltimore's militia was routing the British forces. Soon the Americans had won a decisive victory.

News of the battle of Fort McHenry, of the giant flag, and of the words to Key's new song spread quickly, inspiring Americans all over the country. On December 24, 1814, in Ghent, in what is now Belgium, the British agreed to a peace treaty. It took another six weeks for word to reach the United States from Europe, during which time many more soldiers died. Though they never fired a shot, Caroline Pickersgill and her family had the satisfaction of knowing they had helped secure their new nation's future.

## WHAT HAPPENED TO CAROLINE PICKERSGILL?

At nineteen she married an iron merchant named John Purdy. The couple had no children. Caroline inherited her mother's house in 1857 and sold it seven years later when she needed money. She died in poverty in 1881. Today her home, called the Flag House, is a National Historic Landmark on Albemarle Street in Baltimore.

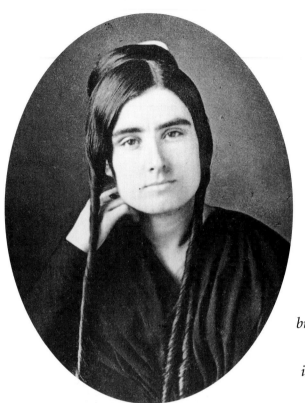

*Strike leader Harriet Hanson at the age of eighteen*

*"Why it is nothing but fun. It is just like play."*
—Lucy Larcom to her family after her first day of work

# Lucy Larcom and Harriet Hanson: Voices of the Mills

Lowell, Massachusetts, 1830s

*Textile mills sprang up along rivers throughout New England, their noisy rooms filled with girls and young women from New England farms. They were hardworking girls who left home to help their families and to find adventure in the city. A mill girl arrived in a factory town clutching a single carpetbag or "hair trunk" and walked down treeless streets lined with brick boardinghouses that all looked alike, searching for the address that had been written on a scrap of paper. Upon arrival she would check in with the mistress, throw her bag on a bed, introduce herself to six or eight new roommates, and try to get some sleep. She would need it.*

Lucy Larcom was eleven when she and her older sister Linda first walked through the gates of the giant mill at Lowell, Massachusetts. Lucy had agreed to apply for a job because she felt guilty that she was another mouth for her mother to feed. Lucy's mother ran a boardinghouse for mill girls and women, but there was never enough money. The mill agent had only one job. He offered it to Lucy because she was taller than Linda and he thought that meant she was older. Both girls kept their mouths shut.

Lucy's aunt had taught her to read and she loved the time she had spent in school. Still, even as a little child, she always expected that she'd wind up in the mill. "As a small child I got the idea that the chief end of woman was to make clothing for mankind," she later wrote. "I supposed I'd have to grow up and have a husband and put all those little stitches in his coats and pantaloons."

But, for the sake of the family, Lucy put aside her dreams and took a job as a "bobbin girl" in the spinning room. The windows were nailed shut and the room was hot and damp. Her wage was a dollar a week. Still, she made up her mind to be happy. "I went to my first day's work in the mill with a light heart," she wrote. "And it really was not so hard, just to change the bobbins on the spinning frames every three-quarters of an hour or so, with half a dozen other girls who were doing the same thing."

## THINKING ON THE JOB

When Lucy was working in the spinning room a relative noticed that books stuck out of her pockets and asked her, "How can you think with all that noise?" "How can anyone live *without* thinking?" was Lucy's reply.

But after a while the fun wore off. Each day started at five in the morning with a bone-rattling blast from the factory whistle. There was barely enough time to splash cold water on her face, stuff breakfast in one pocket and lunch in another, and sprint to the spinning room on the second floor of the mill. Like the others, Lucy pinned her hair up to make sure it didn't get caught in the wheels. Then she faced her machine, reminding herself to be careful about where she put her fingers.

As the days wore on, Lucy pasted poems on the nearest window and tried to will the noise away. "I defied the machinery to make me its slave," she wrote. "Its incessant discourds could not drown the music of my thoughts if I would let them fly high enough." But sometimes it was hard to make thoughts fly so high. "The buzzing and hissing whizzing of pulleys and rollers and spindles and flyers often grew tiresome. I could not see into their complications or feel interested in them . . . When you do the same thing twenty times—a hundred times a day—it is *so dull!*"

Lowell mill girls got a fifteen-minute breakfast break and another thirty minutes for lunch at noon. Most stood all day. The little ones often fell asleep standing up. But the machines never slept. Mill owners convinced themselves that they were helping children build character through hard work. They fired men and replaced them with women and children, who worked for lower wages. Soon whole families began to live off the wages of their exhausted children.

In the 1830s, the mill women and girls began to stand up for themselves, organizing strikes for more pay and shorter hours. Eleven-year-old Harriet Hanson, also the daughter of a rooming-house keeper, was one of fifteen hundred girls who walked out of the Lowell mill in 1836. They were protesting the company's plan to raise the fees the workers had to pay to sleep in a company-owned boardinghouse like the one run by Harriet's mother.

Because the company controlled virtually every part of a mill girl's life, it took a lot of courage to even think about "turning out," as they called striking. For weeks, Harriet listened as girls and women on her floor discussed just that, and then, finally, made up their minds to walk out. When the strike day came and the signal to stop working was passed around, so many workers on the upper floors spilled out chanting into the street that the

[1870]

# 75 Young Women

## From 15 to 35 Years of Age,

### WANTED TO WORK IN THE

# COTTON MILLS!

### IN LOWELL AND CHICOPEE, MASS.

I am authorized by the Agents of said Mills to make the following proposition to persons suitable for their work, viz:—They will be paid $1.00 per week, and board, for the first month. It is presumed they will then be able to go to work at job prices. They will be considered as engaged for one year, cases of sickness excepted. I will pay the expenses of those who have not the means to pay for themselves, and the girls will pay it to the Company by their first labor. All that remain in the employ of the Company eighteen months will have the amount of their expenses to the Mills refunded to them. They will be properly cared for in sickness. It is hoped that none will go except those whose circumstances will admit of their staying at least one year. None but active and healthy girls will be engaged for this work. as it would not be advisable for either the girls or the Company.

I shall be at the Howard Hotel, Burlington, on Monday, July 25th ; at Farnham's, St. Albans, Tuesday forenoon, 26th, at Keyse's, Swanton, in the afternoon; at the Massachusetts' House, Rouses Point, on Wednesday, the 27th, to engage girls,—such as would like a place in the Mills would do well to improve the present opportunity, as new hands will not be wanted late in the season. I shall start with my Company, for the Mills, on Friday morning, the 29th inst., from Rouses Point, at 6 o'clock. Such as do not have an opportunity to see me at the above places, can take the cars and go with me the same as though I had engaged them.

I will be responsible for the safety of all baggage that is marked in care of I. M. BOYNTON, and delivered to my charge.

### I. M. BOYNTON,

Agent for Procuring Help for the Mills.

*Most of the girls who answered this recruiting notice were put to work on a spinning frame. A typical job was to replace empty bobbins of thread with full ones every forty-five minutes or so. "It is so dull!" wrote Lucy Larcom.*

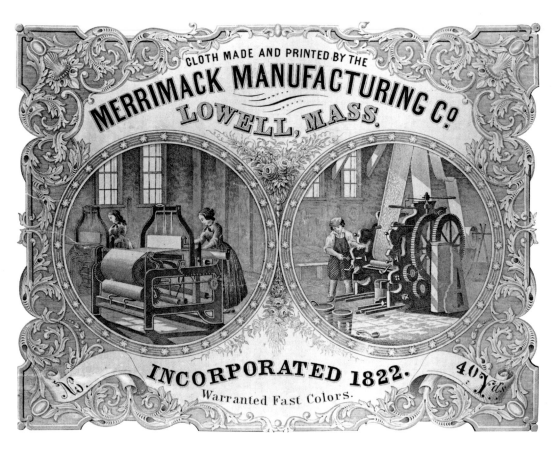

*Lowell, Massachusetts, was America's first large planned industrial community. Its main product was cotton cloth, ranging from plain "negro cloth," which planters bought to clothe their slaves, to the fancy calico prints of the Merrimack Manufacturing Company.*

### I CANNOT BE A SLAVE

These are the words to the song the strikers sang as they marched out of the Lowell mill:

*Oh, isn't it a pity such a pretty girl as I
Should be sent to the factory to pine away and die?
Oh, I cannot be a slave,
I will not be a slave
For I'm so fond of liberty, that I cannot be a slave.*

entire mill was shut down. But the girls in Harriet's spinning room remained frozen in place, glancing nervously at one another and wondering what to do. What if they lost their jobs? What would the company do to them?

Harriet was disgusted. After all their talk about oppression, how could they even think about staying inside? For long minutes they stood indecisively at their looms, whispering among themselves. Finally Harriet faced them. "I don't care what you do," she said firmly. "I am going to turn out whether anyone else does or not."

With that, Harriet marched toward the door, eyes straight ahead. In the next moment she heard a great shuffling of feet. She looked back to see the entire floor lining up behind her. Everyone was turning out. As expected, the company punished Harriet by taking the boardinghouse away from her mother. "Mrs. Hanson," the agent lectured, "you could not prevent the older girls among your boarders from turning out, but your daughter is a child, and *her* you could control."

Harriet never regretted what she did. Many years later she said that leading that walkout was the best moment of her life. "As I looked back on the long line that followed me," she later wrote, "I was more proud than I have ever been since."

## WHAT HAPPENED TO LUCY LARCOM AND HARRIET HANSON?

Lucy left Lowell and went west with her sister and brother-in-law. She never stitched a husband's pantaloons, choosing a life of teaching and writing over marriage. She became a well-known writer and poet. Harriet continued to lead and to fight. She eventually married a newspaper editor, and together they worked to convince people to oppose slavery. In 1882, Harriet became one of the first women to testify before Congress in favor of the right of women to vote.

*"I thought [writing the Cherokee language] would be like catching
a wild animal and taming it."*—Sequoyah

# Anyokah: Teaching Leaves to Talk

Southeastern United States, 1820s and 1830s

*As white settlers crossed the Appalachian Mountains and pushed westward, eastern tribes
tried to stop them from chipping away at their homeland. Shawnees, Seminoles, Creeks, and
other tribes fought valiantly, but they were outnumbered and outgunned. Treaty after treaty
was broken, and Native Americans were pushed back bit by bit.*

*One tribe tried something different. The Cherokees decided to imitate white ways. They took
on white names. Many became Christians. They tore down their stick-and-wattle structures
and learned how to build log cabins and brick houses. Most important, a Cherokee named
Sequoyah (who took the name George Guess) and his young daughter, Anyokah, developed
an alphabet of syllables that gave Cherokees a written language.*

Anyokah was a solitary, dark-haired girl of six when she began to work on the alphabet with her father. She was the only member of the family—and, in fact, the only person at all—who showed even a spark of interest in her father's project. But that wasn't surprising. Despite the difference in their ages, Sequoyah and Anyokah were very much alike: Both were dreamers, both hard workers, and both visionaries. One writer who observed them as they worked together reported that Anyokah simply "seemed to enter into the genius of her father's labor."

Most Cherokees thought Sequoyah was wasting his time trying to "speak at a distance," but he barely noticed their criticism. He and Anyokah were too busy. At first they tried to make a list of all the sounds in the Cherokee language and then to draw a picture of each. Anyokah's hearing was better than Sequoyah's, and she suggested new sounds to add to the vocabulary. When they agreed on a sound, he painted the sound's image onto a wooden shingle. At one point Anyokah's mother became so disgusted with the all-consuming project that she set fire to the piles of shingles. Sequoyah quietly wandered away from the house for a while. Maybe the fire was a blessing, he concluded; the idea wasn't really working anyway.

The next idea was to make a list of all the syllables that were commonly spoken by Cherokees. To make the whole vocabulary easier to learn, they needed the smallest possible

| CHEROKEE WORDS | | |
| --- | --- | --- |
| *English* | *Cherokee* | *Pronunciation* |
| Amen | ℞ᏫᎲ | e-me-nv |
| baby | ᎤᏍᏗᎦ | u-s-di-ga |
| bad | ᎤᏲᎢ | u-yo-i |
| bed | ᎦᏂᏏ | ga-ni-si |
| bird | ᏥᏍᏆ | tsi-s-qua |
| boy | ᎠᏧᏣ | a-tsu-tsa |
| bread | ᎦᏚ | ga-du |
| bridge | ᎠᏒᏥ | a-sv-tsi |
| cat | ᏪᏌ | we-sa |
| chair | ᎦᏍᎩᎶ | ga-s-gi-lo |
| chicken | ᏦᏔᎦ | tsa-ta-ga |
| corn | ᏎᎷ | se-lu |
| day | ᎢᎦ | i-ga |
| dog | ᎩᎵ | gi-li |
| earth | ᎡᎶᎯᏃ | e-lo-hi-no |
| father | ᎡᏙᏓ | e-do-da |
| flower | ᎭᏥᎸᎭ | hu-tsi-lv-ha |
| forest | ᎠᏙᎯ | a-do-hi |
| friend | ᎣᎩᎾᎵᎢ | o-gi-na-li-i |
| girl | ᎠᎨᏳᏣ | a-ge-yu-tsa |
| God | ᎡᏙᏓ | e-do-da |

*Anyokah helping her father, Sequoyah, create the Cherokee syllabic alphabet*

number of syllables. Sequoyah and Anyokah listened constantly as people spoke, barely paying attention to what they were saying but quickly writing down any new syllable they heard. At first there were about two hundred syllables, but Anyokah kept reminding her father that they had heard some of them before. Finally they whittled the list down to eighty-six distinctive syllables, giving each its own symbol, many of which were English letters.

In 1821, Sequoyah and ten-year-old Anyokah mounted horses and rode from Arkansas to New Echota, Georgia, to show the written language to the Cherokee Tribal Council. At first the tribal leaders wouldn't even allow them to demonstrate it. They laughed at the idea that marks on a piece of deerskin could actually carry messages that everyone could read. Sequoyah proposed a test: He would leave the room. They could tell Anyokah anything they wanted and she would write it down. Then Sequoyah would come back, look at the marks on the skin, and tell them what they had said. It worked again and again. The first few times the elders called it luck, but gradually doubt gave way to excitement. Soon thousands of Cherokees wanted to learn how to read. The syllabic alphabet led to the preservation of the Cherokee language and then to the first American Indian newspaper, the *Cherokee Phoenix*. Before long schoolchildren were learning to read in both Cherokee and English. The letters were called talking leaves.

For a while, the ability to read and write helped Cherokees to prosper above all other tribes. They wrote a constitution and built an impressive capital city. Some Cherokees owned huge farms and lived in plantation-style homes. Some owned slaves. They built schools and planted orchards. But not even the power of literacy could keep whites from driving the Cherokees from their land after gold was discovered in a part of Georgia. In the warm May of 1838, the Cherokees went the way of the Choctaws, Chickasaws, Seminoles, and Creeks before them— west. Seven thousand U.S. soldiers were sent to Cherokee country with orders to round up every Cherokee man, woman, and child and drive them from the land. Men were ordered at gunpoint from their plows and women from their looms. Children at play were motioned into wagons by long steel rifle barrels. They were to leave their things behind and get moving.

The Cherokees were herded into camps and then driven on foot or in wagons eight hundred miles to what is now Oklahoma. Many died before they got there. The journey was called the Trail of Tears. One elder who was five years old on the leaving day recalled that he had been playing in his front yard when the wagon came and the soldiers told him to get in. He gathered up his toys, but the soldiers made him leave them in the dirt. By the time the wagon pulled out, he could see that a white boy had already moved in and was playing with them.

## WHAT HAPPENED TO ANYOKAH?

Little is known of her after she helped her father demonstrate the syllables to the elders. It is not known if she married. If she did, and married a white man, she might have been allowed to remain in the Southeast. If she married an Indian, she would have probably been forced west on the Trail of Tears.

*"Anyone who secretly enters into a ship and is later detected will be put to death."*—Sign posted on the Japanese coast, 1851

# Manjiro: Bringing America to Japan

Japan and Massachusetts, 1840s

*In the nineteenth century, Japan was a feudal society closed to the other nations of the world. Her leaders drew up the Decree of Exclusion, which said, "So long as the sun shall warm the earth, let no Christian dare to come to Japan . . . If he violates this command [he] shall pay for it with his head." Japanese citizens were forbidden from travel and contact with outsiders. Most obeyed without question, and a boy named Manjiro would have, too, if a gust of wind and a whaling ship hadn't delivered him into another world.*

On January 5, 1841, the year of the cow, five Japanese fishermen put out from a tiny port named Usa at the southwest corner of their island. The youngest, Manjiro, was a boy of fourteen. As a peasant child, Manjiro rated only one name and had no hope of

*Manjiro at age twenty-seven*

ever going to school. His father was dead and his mother was too poor even to send him to a Buddhist temple for lessons, so he went to sea with fishing crews to help support his family. On this day, he and his mates were bound for the rich Kuroshio current. They had enough rice, firewood, and fresh water to stay out for several weeks.

But the trip seemed jinxed from the start. For six days the crew hauled in nothing but empty nets, and on the seventh day the sky turned deep purple and gusts of wind whipped the sea in circles. As they struggled for land, they came at last upon a great school of fish. Unable to resist, they stopped rowing and tossed out their nets. But soon mountainous waves washed away all their oars but one. Then the rudder snapped and they were swept onto a rocky, uninhabited island many miles from shore. There they lived by killing albatross and drinking rainwater that had collected in the hollows of rocks.

After six months they spotted a ship far in the distance. While the others hesitated, Manjiro stripped naked and swam toward the vessel. He was spotted by a crew member of the *John Howland,* a whaling ship from Massachusetts. Soon all five Japanese fishermen were safely aboard. A few days later, Manjiro, refreshed, watched from the deck as the *Howland*'s crew chased and killed a sperm whale and then cut the animal up and drained it of oil. He remembered the elders in his village saying that seven ports would thrive with the catch of one whale. He thought that if he could master the whaling techniques of these foreigners, he could feed *seventy* Japanese ports.

The whaler's captain, William Whitfield, was impressed by Manjiro: He was strong, fearless, and eager to learn. He never ran out of questions about how things worked. Once, when they came upon a giant sea turtle, Manjiro dived into the water and killed the creature with a knife. When they reached Hawaii, Whitfield let the other four Japanese off, but he took Manjiro around the tip of South America to his home in Fairhaven, Massachusetts. As they sailed into the American harbor, Manjiro saw wide streets lined with white-framed houses and a towering church steeple. On shore, women walked in bonnets, muslin ruffs, and hoop skirts. At fifteen, Manjiro had become the first Japanese to reach the United States.

Whitfield gave him a new name—John Mung—since, he explained, all Americans had two names. John enrolled in a school—something a peasant couldn't do in Japan—and quickly outshone the other pupils by outworking them. One Sunday, Captain Whitfield proudly took John to church, where they sat together in the captain's front pew. After the service, the deacon informed Captain Whitfield that from then on John would have to sit

## ALONE IN THE WORLD

In the 1630s, Japan's leaders decided to cut off contact with other nations to keep order in Japan. Japan became isolated for more than two hundred years, adopting a rigid form of feudalism. The country was ruled by the emperor and the shogun—a military leader. There were 250 daimyo (lords), many samurai (knights), and then the rest of the people, who were broken up into classes. Everything from your name to your food to your clothes to the way you made your living was determined by the rank of your parents. Manjiro, the son of peasants, was of the lowest class.

with the Negroes in the back. Captain Whitfield changed churches twice until he found a Unitarian minister who would agree to accept John as an equal.

John might have settled in New England, but at heart he was a Japanese patriot with a huge goal: He wanted to bring Japan into the modern world of ideas and machines by showing them American technology. He mastered math and navigation, often staying up all night to study. As an apprentice, he learned to make barrels that held whale oil. He told himself that the more he learned, the more he could do for Japan.

His first problem was to get enough money to go back home. He worked on a whaling ship but earned way too little. Then he traveled to the California goldfields, hoping his luck would change. One day, while panning in a river, John spotted a glittering nugget about the size of an egg. He looked around to make sure no one was watching and then buried it in the ground and sat on it all night. He sold it for six hundred dollars the next day and bought a boat to sail back to Japan.

In January of 1851, after weeks at sea, twenty-four-year-old Manjiro and two others approached the coast of Japan. When they landed, they saw a sign that read: "The sending of ships to any foreign country is hereby forbidden. Anyone who secretly enters into a ship and is later detected will be put to death. Any person who leaves the country to go to another and later returns, then he, too, shall meet with the same fate." Manjiro—a young man from the very bottom level of Japanese society—had clearly broken his country's most sacred law.

The handful of fishermen who first encountered Manjiro and his companions pretended they couldn't understand him. They took Manjiro to a local official, who promptly took him to a higher

*Among his many talents, Manjiro became an accomplished artist. He entitled this brush-and-ink drawing* Cutting-in a Whale.

official. For two years he was questioned by authorities who asked the same things over and over. Again and again he stomped on a picture of Jesus Christ to prove he wasn't a Christian. He was even summoned to tell his story to the shogun. There is no record of their conversation, but some historians think Manjiro influenced officials favorably toward Americans who wanted to trade with Japan. In the next few years the Japanese rulers' curiosity about American technology finally overcame their caution. In 1860, John Mung, as he was now called even in Japan, was permitted to return to America with the first official Japanese trade delegation to the United States.

## WHAT HAPPENED TO MANJIRO?

After two years in Japan, he was finally allowed to return to his village and visit his mother. After greeting him, townspeople took Manjiro to see his own cemetery stone. He stayed in Japan and became an English teacher, instructing high Japanese officials. He also worked as a whaler, shipbuilder, interpreter, and translator.

---

*"In New Bedford, fathers, they say, give whales for dowers to their daughters and portion off their nieces with a few porpoises a-piece."*—Herman Melville

# George Fred Tilton: "Why, Whaling I Suppose"

New Bedford, Massachusetts, 1870s

*When the* Mayflower *reached Plymouth Bay in 1620, the water was so full of whales that some passengers wanted to go chase them before going ashore. Whaling soon turned into a huge industry in the New World. In 1846 alone, 735 whaling ships left from New England ports. At first, whalers stayed close to home, but before long crews were chasing whales around the world and staying away for years. Crews killed an average of one hundred whales every time they went out. Each ship hired at least one or two cabin boys to do the dirty work of the crew. Boys served meals to the officers, swept the deck clean of blood, bone shards, and blubber, and lit the lamps when it got dark. When men were killed at*

## PERFUME, LAMPLIGHT, AND BUGGY WHIPS

Whalers tried to salvage and sell as much of a whale as they could. The oil from whales' heads was used to light the streets and lanterns of America until the 1850s. A substance called ambergris found in whales' intestines helped to preserve perfumes. Whales' flexible bones were fashioned into ladies' corsets and buggy whips.

*sea, boys filled in. Boys who couldn't get their parents' permission sometimes stole aboard whaling vessels. Once such boy was George Fred Tilton, the fourth of ten children from a seafaring family, who finally smuggled himself aboard a whaler the year he turned fourteen.*

*George Fred Tilton at the age of fourteen, a short time before he ran off to sea*

George Fred Tilton's first idea for getting on a whaler was to forge his father's signature on a seaman's contract. When the shipping agent found out and turned him in, George Fred's father guarded him so closely that he even slept in George Fred's room. That just made George Fred more determined. A few weeks later a family member caught him trying to run away to meet a captain who had agreed to take him whaling without a contract. Once again he was returned home. His luck finally changed when he read a notice that the whaler *Union* was scheduled to leave New Bedford, Massachusetts, the next week: "I made up my mind that when the *Union* sailed, George Fred would be among those present, but I kept right on working and being the best behaved boy you ever saw."

The day before the ship was to sail, George Fred ran away to New Bedford and found the *Union* at anchor. When darkness came, George Fred blended in with a crowd of boys playing around the ship and slipped aboard. "I dropped down into the hatchway, then into the lower hold, and worked my way clear up into the 'eye' of the vessel, just as forward as I could get. There I made myself as comfortable as I could, and settled down for the night." Though the smell of sperm oil and human waste made him sick, he willed himself to stay below until the day after the ship left port. Then he hoisted himself up onto the deck to take a look around. "There was no land in sight. My first voyage had really begun." He was quickly discovered by a crew member, who led him to the captain. The captain looked George Fred up and down with distaste and said sternly, "Do you know where you are going?"

"Why, whaling I suppose," George Fred replied.

The captain had no choice but to put him to work and give him a bunk. The crew was a rough bunch of sailors from all over the world. On the seventh night at sea, George Fred's bunk mate, a fifty-year-old Finn, got drunk and slit his own throat. Another sailor enjoyed beating up George Fred—until the boy lay in wait for him one afternoon and smashed him on the head with a club as he was coming up from below deck.

Three weeks later, near Bermuda, they spotted their first sperm whale. Rowboats were lowered to the sea, and the crew leaped in and began churning in pursuit. George Fred was assigned to the mate's boat, at the "stroke" oar, near the stern. "I was the most excited and anxious boy in the world," he wrote. "I don't suppose anyone ever moved faster than I did." As they closed in on the monster, George Fred changed his mind. "I was scared blue. I thought that anyone must be perfectly crazy to attempt to kill such a thing." He began shaking as he strained at his oar. His back was to the whale when the harpooner stood up in the boat and hurled his weapon deep into the creature's flank. Now the crew and the whale, fastened together, held on for a "Nantucket sleigh ride," as the wounded giant towed them

*One company advertised its sperm oil, used to lubricate sewing machines, with a picture of a "Nantucket sleigh ride."*

crashing through the waves. Letting out more and more rope, they hung on for dear life.

When they finally landed the whale, George Fred wrote, "We cut him in, tried him out and stowed the oil below but I hadn't got over my scare enough to learn how it was done." Crew members hooked the thirty-ton corpse tight to the ship while others artfully sliced meat and blubber away from the whale, rolling it over and over. Then the blubber was thrown in a great boiling pot on deck to force out the oil. Finally, the whale's head was cut from its body and hoisted up out of the water. Sperm whales have a great cavity in their heads, filled with a rich oil called spermaceti that burns a

*Whaleboat crew of the* John R. Manta

long time. George Fred watched a seaman tie a bucket to a pole and ladle the oil out of the whale. When the supply got too low, he climbed into the whale's head to get the rest. After a while the entire deck was ankle-deep in oil. They got sixty-five barrels of oil from George Fred's first whale.

George Fred stayed at sea fourteen months, spending his fifteenth birthday on the tropical island of St. Vincent. When he got home, he was sixty-five pounds heavier and thirty-five dollars lighter, since the *Union* crew hadn't killed enough whales to make a profit. A whaling agent paid his debt and bought him a new suit of clothes. He made his way home and walked right into his family's house without knocking. His sister looked up and screamed at the stranger who stood before her. "My mother [recognized me], though," George wrote, "and she was mighty glad to see me. Nobody said one word to me about running away and for two weeks I stayed around home. I felt like considerable of a hero among the folks of the neighborhood. I had been across the ocean for over a year, had seen whales killed and returned to tell the tale. What more could a boy want?"

## WHAT HAPPENED TO GEORGE FRED TILTON?

He became a well-known ship captain. Near the end of his life he wrote a popular book about his life as a whaler.

### AN EXTENDED ABSENCE

Sailors usually couldn't control how long they were on ship. In 1856, fourteen-year-old Daniel Hall boarded the *Condor* in New Bedford, Massachusetts, to put some adventure in his life. He signed on for only a few months. His parents reluctantly allowed him to go. The captain took an instant dislike to him and beat him savagely until he escaped with another boy to the Siberian coast—one of the coldest places in the world. For eight months he survived in the wilderness with the help of the Yakut people. He was rescued the next spring by another whaler and finally made it home—five years after he set out.

# Frederick Douglass: Taking On a Tyrant

Maryland, 1833

*Frederick Douglass, the best-known black leader of the nineteenth century, was a slave until he was twenty. Later, in his widely read autobiography, he wrote about his yearning to know his parents, his struggle to read, and a life-changing wrestling match with his brutal master. He wrote that one thought dominated his boyhood: "Why am I a slave?" Finally, he decided, "I will not stand it. I have only one life to lose. I had as well be killed running as die standing."*

Whenever people on the Lloyd tobacco plantation on the Eastern Shore of Maryland wanted to make Frederick Douglass mad, they told him that his father was really Master Anthony, the plantation overseer. Frederick denied it angrily, but deep down he suspected that maybe they were right.

His mother, whose name was Harriet Bailey, was almost as mysterious to him. She had been sold to another plantation when Frederick was a baby, but sometimes she slipped away at dark and hiked twelve miles through forests and fields just to hold him for a few hours. He never knew when to expect her. "I do not recollect of ever seeing my mother by the light of day," Douglass wrote later. "She was with me in the night. She would lie down with me, and get me to sleep, but long before I waked she was gone." Her last visit came when Frederick was about seven. Only years later did he find out for sure she had died.

At the age of ten Frederick became a gift to a wealthy white boy. He was sent off to Baltimore to be a companion to young Thomas Auld. Life at the Auld house was soft compared to the Lloyd plantation: "Instead of the cold, damp floor of my old master's kitchen, I was on carpets; for the corn bag in winter, I had a good straw bed, furnished with covers." And the work was light, too — all Frederick had to do was run errands and keep Tommy Auld out of trouble.

Best of all, Tommy's mother, Sopha, gave the boys reading lessons every afternoon. Frederick couldn't believe his good luck. "In an incredibly short time I had mastered the alphabet and could spell words of three or four letters." Things were going beautifully until the night that Sopha proudly told her husband how quickly Frederick was learning to read. Hugh Auld exploded. "If he learns to read the Bible," Auld sputtered, "it will forever

## THREE-FIFTHS OF A PERSON

At the Constitutional Convention of 1787, Southern delegates claimed that slaves were not people but property, like cattle, and therefore slaveowners shouldn't have to pay taxes on them. On the other hand, Southerners wanted slaves to count as part of a state's population, since the more people a state had, the more representatives it had in Congress. A compromise was reached: In matters of both taxation and representation, slaves would count as three-fifths of a person.

unfit him to be a slave. He should know nothing but the will of his master, and learn to obey it." The lessons stopped at once.

But it was too late. Frederick had discovered that "knowledge unfits a child to be a slave," and he was determined to be free. But now he had to learn on the sly. "When my mistress left me in charge of the house," he later wrote, "I had a grand time. I got Master Tommy's copy books and a pen and ink, and in the ample spaces between the lines I wrote other lines as nearly like his as possible. I ran the risk of getting a flogging." Late at night, while the Auld family snored, Frederick quietly spread out paper on a flour barrel and copied words from the Bible.

When daylight came, he found white children on the street and traded them bread for reading lessons. To improve his writing he wrote out letters on paper and told them they couldn't write half as well as he could. They always grabbed the pen and wrote with their best handwriting. Then Frederick took the paper home and tried to match it.

The Aulds sent Frederick back to the plantation, where he began teaching other slaves to read and write during Sunday-school classes. Word got around quickly. One Sunday the door burst open and "in rushed a mob . . . who, armed with sticks and other missiles drove us off, and commanded us never to meet for such a purpose again." One man threatened to fill Frederick with bullet holes if he ever caught him teaching a slave to read again.

To tame his spirit, Frederick was sent to live with a

### HOW OLD AM I?

"I do not remember a slave who could tell his birthday. The white children could tell their ages. I could not tell why I ought to be deprived of the same privilege."
—Frederick Douglass

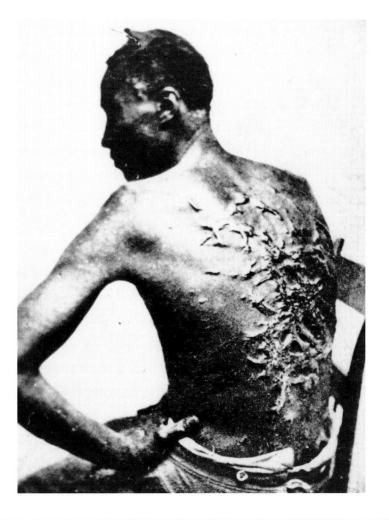

*Frederick Douglass wrote that during his first six months with Edward Covey, he was "whipped either with sticks or cowskins every week." Like the man pictured here, Douglass's back bore the signature of slavery for the rest of his life.*

tough local farmer named Edward Covey. Every slave around knew Covey. He was a poor Methodist minister who rented his land and worked his slaves brutally hard. Lean and tough, Covey prized his reputation as a "slave-breaker." He had all sorts of methods. He worked his field hands from sunup to sundown. He spread plenty of food out before them at break time, but then ordered them back to work before they could finish it. Slaves called him the Snake, because he hid in the bushes and watched them, waiting for someone to stop working so he could spring out and punish them.

But mainly he just beat them. Less than a week into the job, Covey whipped Frederick so hard with a pointed tree branch that he raised welts "as large as my little finger" on Frederick's bloody back.

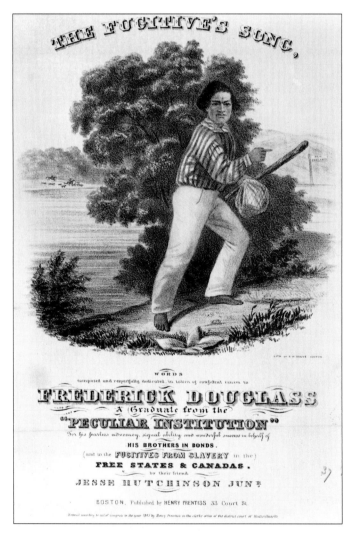

*In 1845, songwriter Jesse Hutchinson, Jr., wrote "The Fugitive's Song" to honor all slaves who had dared bolt for liberty. He dedicated it to Frederick Douglass, and it became a mainstay of antislavery meetings.*

A few weeks later, Frederick passed out while working in a field under a boiling August sun. Covey woke him up with a series of brutal kicks and then smashed him in the head with a hickory stick for good measure.

When he recovered, Frederick fled from the farm and considered his options. None seemed very good. First he went to his old master and asked to be taken back. The man refused. Then he thought about trying to escape north, but he didn't know anyone who could help him. Reluctantly, he decided to go back and stand his ground even if Covey killed him. When Frederick walked into the yard on a Sunday, Covey greeted him with a broad smile. He asked Frederick gently if his head still hurt and gave him extra food. But the next morning Covey slipped up behind him, tripped him, and tried to get a noose around his ankles. Breathing hard, Frederick leaped away and spun around to face Covey. Frederick was only sixteen, but he was tall and strong. It was now or never.

"Whence came my daring spirit I do not know," he later wrote. "The fighting madness had come upon me and I found my strong fingers firmly attached to the throat of my cowardly tormentor . . . as though we were equals before the law. The very color of the man was forgotten. I felt as supple as a cat, and was ready for the snakish creature at every turn. I flung him to the ground several times. I held him so firmly by the throat, that his blood followed my nails. He held me and I held him."

They wrestled nonstop for two hours. At one point, Frederick hurled Covey into a pile of cow manure. The fight finally ended with Covey walking away and pretending he had won. Frederick let him go. They both knew the real score. "The fact was . . . he had not drawn a single drop of blood from me. I had drawn blood from him." Frederick lived with Covey for six more months, but Covey never challenged him again. Frederick always thought it was because Covey didn't want word to get around that a slave had stood up to him. Frederick later called the fight the turning point of his life. "I was nothing before," he wrote. "I am a man now."

## WHAT HAPPENED TO FREDERICK DOUGLASS?

Disguised as a sailor, he escaped to Massachusetts when he was twenty. He opposed slavery in speeches, in his newspaper, the *North Star,* and in a widely read autobiography. In the Civil War, he helped recruit black soldiers for the Union army, including two of his sons. He had the respect, and the ear, of President Lincoln throughout the war.

*"I did not tell him that it was wrong to shoot."*

# Allen Jay: Underground Railroad Conductor

Indiana and Ohio, 1844

*Between about 1820 and 1860 at least one hundred thousand slaves fled from the South into the Northern states and Canada. They were helped by those who organized and lived in a chain of secret houses called the Underground Railroad. There was no map; a runaway slave learned the path one "station" at a time. Sometimes "conductors," both black and white, led slaves from station to station. Owners offered rewards for their capture, and the runaways were tracked by hunters on horseback.*

*Since the bounty hunters paid closest attention to adults, it was frequently the children of families on the Underground Railroad who kept their eyes open for runaway slaves and hid them until it was safe to move on. Allen Jay, thirteen in 1844, was*

Thirteen-year-old Lucinda Wilson grew up in a Quaker family in southern Ohio. One morning she was picking berries in a field near her house when she spotted two teenage runaway slave girls crouched behind bushes. Their bare feet were swollen and bleeding.

She helped them back to her home and began to fix them a meal while they lay down to rest. A heavy knock on the door sent the three girls scrambling up the stairs. Lucinda helped one girl hide inside an empty clothes hamper and pulled her sister's nightclothes over the other. She and Lucinda leaped into Lucinda's bed, with the runaway hiding her dark hair inside a nightcap and burying her face in the pillow.

Bootsteps thundered up the stairs, and the bedroom door burst open. Two bounty hunters, rifles at their sides, filled the door frame, breathing heavily and looking around. All they could see was two girls, one still sleeping soundly, facedown. The men seemed embarrassed. They moved their eyes around the room and backed away quickly, closing the door softly behind them. Months later, Lucinda learned that the two slave girls had reached safety in Canada.

*Like Allen Jay, many children became active in the antislavery movement. Some were influenced by children's books published by abolitionists. This illustration of "Little Lewis: A Slave Boy" appeared in* The Children's Anti-Slavery Book.

*a Quaker farm boy whose home was an Underground Railroad station in southern Ohio. The members of his family avoided speaking directly about the runaways, even among themselves. Allen later recalled one very determined fugitive slave he met.*

"Our family physician had ridden up to our gate, called my father out, and told him that there was a runaway slave out in the woods nearby and that he was being pursued by his master and others. My father turned to me and said, 'I am going out back of the house to work. If any negro comes to the gate thee can take him down in the cornfield and hide him under that big walnut tree, but thee is not to tell me or anyone else.'

"In a little while the poor man came, with his bleeding feet and ragged clothes, looking . . . very much frightened. I went to him and told him I would hide him. When

I told him I was Mr. Jay's son he followed me. I took him down to the walnut tree and told him to remain there until I came after him. He said, 'I am hungry. I want a drink.' When I got back to the house mother was in the kitchen fixing up a dinner in a basket. I knew what that meant without asking any questions. She said, 'Allen, if thee knows anybody who thee thinks is hungry, take this basket to him.'

"I started out with it and a jug of milk. The poor man heard me coming through the corn and had his pistol ready to shoot when I came in sight. The moment he saw me he commenced smiling. I left my load with him and promised that I would come after him about dark.

"During the afternoon, the men who were pursuing him came up to the gate and called. They asked my father if he had seen a 'nigger' going by. Father truthfully said he had not. I kept out of sight. They threatened to search the house. Father told them they were welcome to do so, provided they had the proper authority. After talking roughly for a while, they rode off in a hurry. Then he came into the house and asked me how I would like to go to my grandfather's. Understanding what he meant, I told him I would be very willing to go. He added, 'If thee knows of anybody thee thinks ought to go, thee had better take him along.'

"I went out and closed the door and soon had the negro in the buggy with me. The poor fellow could see that I was a little afraid to be with him alone. He said, 'If you are afraid of me, I will let you carry the pistol.' After we got started he said, 'If anyone comes

## HARRIET TUBMAN

The most famous Underground Railroad conductor of all was only three when she started picking cotton on a Maryland plantation. At seven, Harriet Tubman's mistress caught her stealing a lump of sugar and went after her with a rawhide whip. At thirteen Harriet bravely tried to stop another slave from being whipped. Enraged, the master threw a two-pound weight at the slave, who ducked. The object crashed into Harriet's head. The resulting concussion caused blackouts for the rest of Harriet's life. As an adult Harriet made her own escape on the Underground Railroad, then went back south nineteen times to help others escape. In all, she conducted more than three hundred slaves to freedom. Despite a price on her head that rose to $40,000—a fortune in those days—she was never caught and never lost a passenger. She even freed her own parents. In this photograph Harriet Tubman (left) appears with a family she led to freedom.

to take me, you must give me the pistol. I will get out and you drive on, for I do not want you to be hurt. I am never going to be taken back. They may kill me, but I intend to kill one of them first.' I looked at the poor man and saw his condition. He showed me his lacerated back that had been cut by the whip. I did not tell him that it was wrong to shoot. Neither did I stop to give him a lecture on peace principles.

"About 10 o'clock we reached my grandfather's. I went to the door and told him what was up. He understood. He called on my uncle, Levi Jay, and in about thirty minutes my uncle and the negro were on horses and on their way to Mercer County, where there was another 'station.' We learned afterwards that the negro reached Canada safely."

## WHAT HAPPENED TO ALLEN JAY?

He became an important Quaker leader and scholar, helping to found Earlham College in Richmond, Indiana. He died at the age of seventy-nine, in 1910.

Maria Weems, disguised as a carriage driver

*"Are you the passenger expected from Washington?"*—William Still

# Maria Weems: Escape to Canada

Rockville, Maryland, to Ontario, Canada, 1855

*In 1850, Congress passed the Fugitive Slave Act. The law said that anyone who helped a slave become free or hid a slave could be fined $1,000 or jailed for six months. Suddenly unsafe, thousands of slaves who had escaped to Northern states fled a second time to Canada. And slaves in Southern states now made Canada, a longer journey, their goal.*

*The Pennsylvania Anti-Slavery Society maintained a line of the Underground Railroad. Members raised money to buy slaves from their masters and also arranged for runaways to be conducted safely to Canada. Their leader was William Still, a free African American whose parents had been slaves. It was said that any runaway who could make it to Still's office in Philadelphia was as good as free. Hundreds arrived by foot, boat, and rail—and in one famous case, even in a box. Still kept detailed records of the hundreds of cases he handled. Maria Weems was one of his youngest passengers.*

The year she turned twelve, Maria Weems was sold without warning from the plantation where she had grown up to a quick-tempered slave trader from Rockville, Maryland, named Charles M. Price. Her new home was hellish. Price drank heavily and turned violent when he got drunk. His wife was quick-tempered and rough, too.

Maria clashed with Price from the start. She had free relatives, some of whom had been bought and freed by abolitionists, others who had escaped. She was determined to be free and made no effort to hide her feelings from Price. Her fearless, independent spirit made him just as determined to keep her on his farm. Price even made Maria sleep in the same room with him and his wife to keep her from running away. It was a dangerous place to be, especially when he started drinking. Maria's only thought was escape, but she needed help.

Then Charles Bigelow, a wealthy Quaker lawyer, entered the scene. Bigelow worked out of an office near the stage depot in Washington, D.C., raising money to buy slaves and set them free. When he heard of the girl trapped in a bedroom with the notorious Charles Price, her case became his number one project. He rode out to Maryland and offered to buy her on the spot, but Price just laughed at him. Desperate, Bigelow turned to the Pennsylvania Anti-Slavery Society in Philadelphia. Could they please send someone to Washington at once who could help this girl escape, hide her, and escort her to Canada? Bigelow would pay all expenses.

The committee sent a young man whose code name was Powder Boy to case the Price farm. He returned with grim news: The Prices rarely let Maria out of their sight. There was nothing to do but make a plan with her now, be patient, and wait for a break. Surely Price would drop his guard sometime.

The chance came three weeks later, in October of 1855, when Price finally let Maria sleep with the other slaves for one night. Barefooted, Maria took off running shortly after dark, arriving at the prearranged spot where a committee agent was waiting for her. Under cover of darkness, the two hustled off to Bigelow's office in Washington. Price was furious when he realized Maria was gone. He quickly took out a newspaper advertisement offering a $500 reward for her capture.

---

### A FAVORITE ROUTE

Many of William Still's Philadelphia passengers went first to Burlington, New Jersey. From there they traveled to Bordentown, New Brunswick, Rahway, and Jersey City. Then they were whisked to the Forty-second Street train station in New York City, where they boarded trains for Syracuse. From there it was on to Niagara Falls and the Canadian border.

---

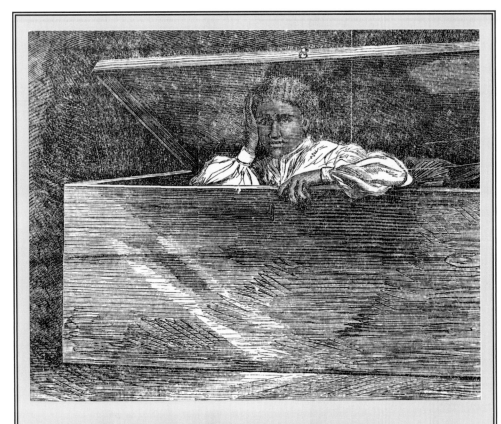

## THE GIRL WHO ESCAPED IN A BOX

In 1855, Lear Green, eighteen, escaped from her Baltimore master in a wooden chest. She was packed away with a quilt, a pillow, a bottle of water, and a little food, then stowed with the other freight aboard a steamship. Her boyfriend's mother, a free woman, accompanied the chest and twice loosened the ropes to give Lear air. After eighteen hours Lear was deposited on a Philadelphia dock and delivered to a house on Barley Street. She was still alive when the chest was opened. Later she married and went to live in Elmira, New York.

Maria hid in Bigelow's office while bounty hunters patrolled the nearby coach depot. She took the identity of Joe Wright and did chores around the office in boy's clothing. Meanwhile, in Philadelphia, the Anti-Slavery Society tried desperately to find a conductor to go to Washington and bring Maria back to William Still's office so that he could move her on to Canada. The only experienced conductor available was Dr. Howard, a college professor who couldn't travel until the Thanksgiving holiday, still six weeks away. They continued to wait.

Just after dawn on November 23, 1855, young "Joe Wright," now dressed in a carriage driver's cap and long coat, cautiously urged Bigelow's team toward the White House, where Dr. Howard's carriage was waiting. As Bigelow greeted Dr. Howard, Maria slipped from his carriage into Dr. Howard's. The horses snorted nervously as she took the reins and whip. Howard said good-bye and gave the command to drive on, which Maria did, for only the second time in her life. Amazingly, the horses obeyed, prancing straight out through Washington and into the suburbs of Maryland. There Dr. Howard took the reins.

To reach Philadelphia they still had to make it through ninety miles of bounty-hunter-infested countryside. They would need to stop at least twice to feed the horses, and they would have to spend one or two nights at a hotel or farmhouse. When darkness fell, Dr. Howard took a chance. He pulled the horses up to the farmhouse of an old friend and rapped on the door. This man was a slaveholder, to be sure, but Dr. Howard thought it unlikely that he would have heard of Maria. His friend was overjoyed to see him. After hours of conversation, Dr. Howard yawned. He explained that "Joe" had to sleep in the same room with him, since he sometimes passed out in the night and needed the boy to help him with his medicine. Soon the doctor was in bed, sleeping soundly, and Maria was wrapped up in a comfortable quilt on the floor.

At four o'clock on Thanksgiving Day, Dr. Howard and Maria arrived at William Still's home in Philadelphia. Dr. Howard dropped her off and disappeared. Still was out, but when he got home, he found a young coachman seated quietly at his table. "Are you the passenger expected from Washington?" Still asked. Without answering, Maria got up and walked outside. Still followed. "Yes," she whispered, "I am the one the doctor went after, but the doctor told me to tell no one but you and there are others inside."

Three days later, Maria, still dressed as a boy, was conducted to the home of Louis Tappan in New York City. The Tappan family hid her in their attic, bought her some girl's clothing, and found a conductor named Reverend Freeman to take her to Canada. Three days later they crossed into safety at Niagara Falls. On the other side, at Chatham, Ontario, they stopped at a boardinghouse, where Reverend Freeman told the proprietor his coachman's story. Reverend Freeman later wrote: "The proprietor seemed greatly surprised and said, 'I will call my wife.' She came, and all the women in the house came with her. They soon disappeared, and 'Joe' with them, who, after being gone awhile, returned and was introduced as Miss Maria Weems. The whole company were on their feet, shook hands, laughed, and rejoiced, saying this beat anything they had ever seen before."

## WHAT HAPPENED TO MARIA WEEMS?

She reunited with other family members who had escaped to freedom in Canada. She went to school at the Buxton Settlement in Canada.

# PART FIVE

# One Nation or Two? The Civil War

The long-rising tension between slave states and free states finally burst into outright rebellion in December 1860, when South Carolina simply left the United States. Within months, ten other Southern states followed. They formed their own nation, the Confederate States of America, named their own president, printed their own currency, and raised an army. The United States insisted they couldn't get away with it: The Constitution said we were one nation, not two. But at 4:30 A.M. on April 12, 1861, Confederate cannons opened fire on Fort Sumter, a federal fort guarding Charleston, South Carolina. The Civil War had begun.

Recruiting officers soon needed soldiers so badly that as many as 20 percent of all soldiers on both sides were younger than eighteen, the official age of enlistment. Many eager boys wrote the number eighteen on a piece of paper and slipped it into their shoe, so that as they stood before a recruiter they could honestly say they were "over eighteen." Townspeople sent them off with parades that made them feel like heroes. Boys who enlisted learned to gamble, suffer, smoke, drink, swear, steal food, kill, and bury their friends. Girls became nurses, farmers, spies, and teachers—and, sometimes, heads of families.

For four years they fought without helmets, using new, powerful weapons. At the war's end, 600,000 soldiers, including one-third of all rebel forces, were dead. Slaves were free but faced an uncertain future in a shattered South. Most survivors who still had both legs walked home. One teenage Confederate veteran wrote: "I found my father and mother working in the garden. Neither knew me at first glance, but when I smiled and spoke to them, mother recognized me and with tears of joy clasped me to her arms."

*The Emancipation Proclamation helped turn slaves like the ragged boy known only as "Contraband" Jackson into a uniformed drummer for the Seventy-ninth U.S. Colored Troops.*

*"The recruiting officer didn't measure my height,
but called me five feet, five inches high."*

# Elisha Stockwell: "Such a Mess As I Was In"

Wisconsin, 1861

*Elisha Stockwell, a farmer's son from Jackson County, Wisconsin, was fifteen when he first tried
to join the Union army. He wrote of his family's reaction and of his early days as a soldier.*

## THE CIVIL WAR SOLDIER

The average soldier was about five feet eight inches tall and weighed 143½ pounds. His average age was twenty-five, which dropped as the war went on. One soldier in ten died of disease, one in ten was wounded, and one in sixty-five died in battle. Most were farmers or farmers' sons. A quarter were born in another nation. Nine of ten Confederate soldiers had never owned a slave.

"In September [1861] I was helping a neighbor sack grain and we heard there was going to be a war meeting at our little log school house." Elisha Stockwell wrote his name down when they called for volunteers, but "my father was there and objected to my going, so they scratched my name out, which humiliated me . . . My sister called me a little snotty boy, which raised my anger . . . I could rake, and bind and keep up with the men, so why couldn't [I] fight like one too?"

Elisha's next chance came when a friend of his father's returned home from the war for a few days on leave. Elisha begged to go back with him: "I told him I was bound to go, and if he wouldn't help me, I would go alone and have to foot it." The soldier reluctantly agreed. Now Elisha had to figure out how to slip away from his dad. An idea came quickly.

He told his father that there was going to be a dance Sunday night and asked if he could take the oxcart. His unsuspecting father agreed. "I drove up to my brother-in-law's, tied the oxen to the fence, and went in and saw my sister a few minutes. I told her I had to go down town. She said, 'Hurry back, for dinner will soon be ready.' I didn't get back for two years."

There was one last hurdle. He had to convince the company captain and the recruiting officer that he was old enough to serve. That turned out to be a cinch. The captain, happy to see any eager recruit, told the recruiting officer that Elisha was clearly old enough. Then the recruiter asked Elisha to state his age. "I [said] I didn't know just how old I was but thought I was eighteen. He didn't measure my height, but called me five feet, five inches high. I wasn't that tall until two years later when I re-enlisted."

Southern boys were doing the same thing. Just after the shelling of Fort Sumter, sixteen-year-old Mississippian George Gibbs excitedly began stuffing clothes into his sack, planning to go off to a recruiting center. George barely listened as his parents pleaded with

him not to go. Finally they gave in, helped him sign up, and went with him to join his company. When the unit lined up to board the train that would take him off to war, George turned to look back at his parents. They were still there, sad-eyed and waving. He stepped out of line, hid from his mates, and burst into tears. "This seemed to help me," he said, "and I felt better about leaving home."

Some parents pushed their sons to enlist. Another Mississippian, fifteen-year-old Ned Hunter, was dismissed by a recruiting officer who could see that the boy was obviously too young. Ned's father stepped forward, put his hands squarely on the table, and glared down at the recruiter. "He can work as steady as any man," Mr. Hunter said, "and he can shoot as straight as any who has been signed today." The officer shrugged and handed Ned the pen.

## B.C. HARDTACK

One of the hardest things for new soldiers to get used to was army food. The main course was hardtack, or twice-cooked biscuits that looked like crackers, often eaten with small white soup beans. William Bircher, a teenaged diarist from Minnesota, wrote: "Our hardtack was very hard. We could scarcely break it with our teeth . . . We had fifteen different ways of preparing it. On the march it was eaten raw . . . A thin slice of nice fat pork was cut down and laid on the cracker, and a spoonful of good brown sugar put on top of the pork. If there was time for frying, we either dropped the dry crackers into the fat and did them brown to a turn . . . or pounded them into a powder, mixed it with boiled rice and made griddle cakes and honey . . . minus the honey." Bircher also figured out how to make hardtack pudding, hardtack stew, and fricasseed hardtack. The letters "B.C." were stamped on all the unit's cracker boxes. The boys in Bircher's unit were sure that meant their hardtack had been first baked "before Christ."

Fresh young recruits were often tested in camp by the older men. Elisha Stockwell encountered a bully right away: "One of [our] company was known as Curley. He was a big husky man and quite handy with his fists. He said he had to try all the recruits to see if they could fight, and proceeded to cuff me around until I got quite enough of that play. I told him I didn't enlist to fight that way, but if he would get his gun and go outside of the camp, we would stand thirty or forty rods apart, and I thought I could convince him that I could shoot as well as he could. He turned it off as a joke and said he guessed I would pass. I never liked him after that, but he never bothered me again."

Sometimes it went further. One Confederate boy of fifteen, tired of being teased by an older soldier about how badly his uniform fit, went after his tormentor with a cocked pistol, demanding an apology. The older man grabbed his own rifle and shot the boy dead.

If camp life didn't toughen boys, the first taste of real battle usually did. Elisha Stockwell's unit joined the battle of Shiloh in the spring of 1862. After spending the first night standing in a soaking rain, they advanced to the front at dawn. As Elisha was walking, he nearly stumbled over a bulky object. He looked down. "[It was] the first dead man we saw ... He was leaning back against a big tree as if asleep, but his intestines were all over his legs and several times their natural size. I didn't look at him the second time as it made me deathly sick."

Elisha's unit silently formed a battle line and then flattened themselves against the ground, hearts pounding with fear. On command, they leaped up and sprinted screaming downhill toward rebel soldiers who waited in the bushes. The air quickly filled with smoke and thunder. As he was running, Elisha felt something sharp hit him in the

*A shoeless fourteen-year-old Confederate soldier lies dead after having taken a bayonet thrust to the heart.*

back of the head. It was a bayonet from one of his own men, who had been shot dead and had fallen forward onto Elisha. He kept running, his vision bouncing up and down, shooting his gun at bushes he could barely see. He felt the hot sting of a ball of lead in his arm, but he kept running and shooting until he heard a call to retreat. The battle had been a disaster: Nearly half of Elisha's unit was dead or badly wounded. His arm had been injured. And they had lost the camp they were trying to defend.

That night, when he had time to think about his first day of battle, Elisha remembered how he felt when he was waiting on his belly in the grass for the command to charge: "As we lay there . . . my thoughts went back to my home, and I thought what a foolish boy I was to run away to get into such a mess as I was in. I would have been glad to see my father coming after me."

## EMMA SANSOM

Though few put on uniforms, many girls saw action during the Civil War. When her six brothers enlisted in the Confederate army, Emma Sansom took over the family's Alabama farm with her mother and sister. One spring morning in 1863, sixteen-year-old Emma was working a field when a mounted company of Union soldiers thundered past and raced across the wooden bridge that spanned rain-swollen Black Creek. Once all had crossed, they set the bridge ablaze and waited. When the Confederates pursuing them arrived, the Yankees stood up and opened full fire. Confederate general Nathan Forrest spotted Emma near the gate and sprinted up to ask her if there was anywhere else to cross the creek. She told him of a nearby cattle trail and offered to lead him to the crossing. Under heavy fire, she leaped bareback behind Forrest and guided him and his troops across the stream. Once across, General Forrest's troops intercepted Yankee forces and kept them from destroying more railroad bridges. The Confederate Congress gave Emma a gold medal for her help, and later a statue of her was erected near the creek. Emma Sansom High School in Gadsden, Alabama, is named in her honor.

## WHAT HAPPENED TO ELISHA STOCKWELL?

When the war ended, he was marching with his unit toward Montgomery, Alabama. They celebrated for a day and then Elisha started walking back to Wisconsin. When he got home, he found that of the thirty-two men and boys from his town who had left with him to fight, only he and two others were still alive. He went back to life as a farmer in Wisconsin.

*"The Yanks have to send their babies to fight."*—A rebel soldier's assessment of Johnny Clem

# Johnny Clem: Poster Boy of the North

Battlefields, 1861–1864

*If you were too young to be a soldier but really wanted a taste of war, your best bet was to find a drum and some sticks and start practicing. Drummers and buglers were classified as noncombatants, so boys were allowed to join. Some were still little boys. At least twenty-five drummers during the Civil War were ten years old or younger. Many more were in their early teens. John Clem, a tiny, tough young drummer, became one of the most famous figures of the conflict.*

Nine-year-old John Clem ran away from his Ohio farm to try to join the Third Ohio Regiment of the Union army in the spring of 1861. He knew no one would mistake him for a man—he was small even for his age—but he also knew that he could usually find some way

to get just about anything he really wanted. The captain of the regiment waved him back home, but instead John slipped inside the baggage compartment of the train carrying the soldiers to camp at Lexington, Kentucky. Once there, John hopped out and presented himself to the men of the Twenty-second Michigan Regiment. They were charmed by the eager, round-faced boy. They agreed to take him on as a drummer and even chipped in their wages to pay him a salary of thirteen dollars a month. They made him a tiny uniform and sawed off a shotgun so he could have a weapon. A warrior at last, he was in heaven.

*This studio portrait, taken after the battle of Shiloh, was used to turn Johnny Clem into "Johnny Shiloh," child-hero of the North.*

Johnny saw his first action in 1862, in the battle of Shiloh, a furious clash during which huge cannons traded massive fire. It was the first real battle for many soldiers. The shelling was so horrible that thousands of soldiers simply ran away and hid. Not John Clem. When a cannonball fragment glanced off a tree and shattered his drum, he stayed at his commander's side. When the fight was over, he carried the pieces back to camp and proudly showed them to the survivors in his unit. They made him a sergeant, raised his pay, and set up a photo session for him. He became the Union's poster child, proof that even Northern boys who were years away from their first shave were eager to fight. People took to calling him Johnny Shiloh.

Then, in 1863, he found himself in the battle of Chicamauga, Georgia. It was another massive struggle, this time to see which side could control a railroad depot near Chattanooga, Tennessee. During the smoke-filled action John got lost behind enemy lines. When he could finally see, he was looking at a Confederate officer, who ordered him to surrender. Johnny dropped to the ground, pretending to give up, and then killed the man with his tiny shotgun. He crawled off and lay among a pile of dead bodies until it got dark enough to steal away to the Union side.

Once again, the survivors in his regiment were proud of him. They made him a lance corporal and gave him another raise. He was now eleven and didn't quite weigh sixty pounds, but soon he was famous in both armies as the "drummer boy of Chicamauga."

## YOU'RE A FINE COOK, AIN'T YOU?

Drummers rarely rested. When they weren't practicing or fighting, they hauled water and gathered wood, rubbed down the horses, dug trenches, and built roads. A few cut hair. They helped surgeons amputate and stack up limbs. Many were made to cook for the men, who had to be patient while the boys learned. It didn't always work out. One boy, William Bircher, was ordered to cook a chicken for an officer named Stalcup, whose favorite part was the gizzard— a sac full of tiny stones that chickens use to help digest their food. "Not being an expert at cooking," wrote Bircher in his diary, "I forgot to cut the gizzard open and cleanse it from all its foreign substances. I simply put it in whole to cook. At noon I pronounced the dinner ready . . . Stalcup plunged his fork into the dish and took it in one mouthful. But [then] he began to curse like a sea captain as he spit about a pint of gravel stones and said, 'You're a fine cook, ain't you?' Next time I cook a chicken, you bet I will not forget to dissect the gizzard."

The next year he was caught once again behind Confederate lines. This time rebel soldiers recognized him and held him until the North agreed to trade him for a high-ranking Confederate officer. When they let him go, one rebel cracked that the only thing John Clem proved was that "the Yanks have to send their babies to fight."

## WHAT HAPPENED TO JOHNNY CLEM?

He was finally discharged on September 19, 1864. He was four feet tall and had spent three years in the deadliest war in U.S. history. He reenlisted in the army after the Civil War and became a career officer, retiring in 1916 with the rank of major general. He died at eighty-five in 1937.

———◆———

*"We [will] never be separated nor surrender our remaining rights while alive."*

# Billy Bates and Dick King: Escape from Andersonville

Andersonville, Georgia, 1864

*Fourteen-year-old Billy Bates enlisted in the Ninth Ohio Cavalry in 1862. Dick King joined a Pennsylvania regiment at seventeen. Both boys were captured in battle and thrown together as Confederate prisoners of war. They bounced from prison to prison and wound up at Andersonville, in southwest Georgia. Andersonville was widely known as the worst prison of the Civil War, a place where nearly one in three who passed through its gates died of starvation, disease, or torture.*

Billy Bates was half-asleep during his watch at dawn in Cumberland, Maryland, when his horse snorted restlessly. He looked up, too late. Six Confederate soldiers suddenly sprang from behind rocks, leveled rifles at him, and yelled, "Throw down your guns you infernal Yankee!" Billy got off one shot to alert the others before he was roughly seized and hustled away at gunpoint.

Billy was taken to a prison camp near Wilmington, Delaware. There he joined a group of new prisoners who were told to line up, strip to their underclothes, and throw all their belongings in a pile so Confederate soldiers could have them. Dick King, standing next to Billy, refused. Instead, Dick let his clothes drop at his feet, planted his boot on the pile, and told the commander that no rebel would ever wear his clothes. The commander calmly inspected the pile of garments. He noticed a picture of Dick's mother sewn to a shirt pocket. Looking into the boy's eyes, the commander ripped it from the shirt and ground it into the dust

*Prisoners were forbidden from building shelters at the Andersonville camp. Most lived in holes they scraped in the ground, protecting themselves from the sun and bad weather by making tents of their blankets.*

with his boot. Dick lunged for the commander's throat, and a brawl followed. Dick was knocked unconscious, but when he came to, he found himself in the watery hold of a ship, chained back-to-back with Billy Bates. A lifelong bond formed in that moment. Billy later wrote that "in the presence of Almighty God we pledged that we would be absolutely true to each other; and that we would never be separated nor surrender our remaining rights while alive."

They had no idea how much they would need each other. In the next three months they were transferred to seven different prisons, each bleaker than the one before. A prison chaplain came to visit them the night before their final move. His words were disturbing. "You are going to the worst place in the Confederacy," he said softly, "but you must keep up your courage. Be careful in speech, discreet in action, and constantly plan how to keep up your strength and your hope for deliverance."

The prison at Andersonville, Georgia, sixty miles away, was nothing less than a death camp. When Billy and Dick arrived, it was still being built and contained only twelve hundred men. A year later, thirty-three thousand prisoners were jammed inside its pointed brown stockade fence—three times more than the prison was built to hold. Each inmate struggled to survive on daily rations of a teaspoon of salt, three tablespoons of beans, and a half pint of cornmeal. They drank water from a filthy creek that trickled through the camp and slept in depressions they scraped from the earth with their own hands. Any prisoner who crossed a rail fence twenty-five feet from the prison wall was shot by a guard in a wooden tower called the "pigeon roost." With no clean water or shelter from the weather, disease ravaged the camp. Before the war was over, thirteen thousand soldiers died at Andersonville.

When they arrived, Billy and Dick were searched thoroughly, and everything of value was taken from them—but Billy managed to conceal a pocketknife in the hem of his pants. Though they were among the youngest prisoners, they were leaders from the start. They made a point of greeting each new prisoner in their unit with words of encouragement and friendship. They picked arguments with those who seemed to have given up hope, to try to keep them interested in surviving. They joined a nighttime effort to dig a tunnel under the stockade fence. It failed when one prisoner told a guard. When Billy and Dick refused to name the others, their rations were cut.

Billy and Dick's role in the escape attempt brought them to the attention of the camp's commander, Captain Henry Wirz. Wirz was a hard-drinking Austrian-born doctor who had been given the terrible assignment of overseeing a prison that was too crowded even before

## WORDS FROM ONE WHO SAW ANDERSONVILLE

"My heart aches for those poor wretches, Yankees though they are, and I am afraid God will suffer some terrible retribution to fall upon us for letting such things happen. If the Yankees should ever come to southwest Georgia, and go to Anderson and see the graves there, God have mercy on the land!"
—Eliza Frances Andrews, a Georgia girl who was allowed to look inside the Andersonville prison in 1864

it was finished. He had a violent temper. To teach the boys a lesson Wirz put them in a chain gang. They remained maddeningly cheerful. There was something about Billy, especially, that irritated Wirz. One day Wirz removed Billy from the chain gang and ordered him hung by his thumbs over a gateway in front of the other prisoners. "[My] flesh was cut to the bone by my weight," Billy wrote, ". . . my tongue swelled, my head throbbed almost to bursting."

A fellow prisoner raised a cup of water to Billy's lips but Wirz saw him, pulled out his revolver, and killed the man with five shots. Billy screamed at Wirz from his rope: "You dare not shoot me! I shall see you hang before I die." Wirz put two shots in Billy's leg before Wirz's own men, fearing a prison uprising, dragged him away.

With no guards in sight, a prisoner cut Billy down and carried him to his unit. Billy lay there, near death, until Dick was released from the chain gang and nursed Billy back to health, sharing his own meager food. During a tour of the camp, a few days later Wirz spotted Billy. "I thought I had killed you," he called. Once again Billy dared to talk back and Wirz shot him in the left side. As Wirz's men rushed in to calm him down, the captain demanded that Billy declare an oath of allegiance to the Confederacy. "I'll die in prison first," Billy answered. "I'll bring you under my thumb yet," sneered Wirz, as his men once again led him away.

With nothing to lose, Billy and Dick decided to dig their own tunnel but tell no one. It was a distance of fifty-nine feet from the holes where they slept to the stockade fence. They began late on a moonless night, working with Billy's pocketknife and two small scraps of iron. They carried dirt back out of the hole in their shirts. For months they scraped at the dirt until finally they hit the bottom of the stockade fence and dug under it. Then they came back inside and thought about what to do next. They decided that the right thing to do was to tell those they trusted most and give them a chance to escape, too.

On a warm spring night in 1864, Billy and Dick started down the tunnel alone, Billy first. The others would follow, but they all agreed Billy and Dick, who had dug the tunnel, should have the best chance to escape. Billy and Dick made it out of the camp; then for three weeks they hid by day and traveled by night, living on wild plants and berries. They shook the bloodhounds that were tracking them by hiding in a hollow log in a swamp. A slave family hid them in a cabin for a few days. A month after their escape they reached Union lines near Bridgeport, Alabama.

A few weeks later, they were sent by train to Washington to tell their story to President Lincoln. Lincoln was shocked by their skeletonlike appearance. Billy, now sixteen, weighed

## BASE-BALL

Some Civil War prisoners were allowed a little pleasure. John Delhaney, a teenage Confederate soldier who was captured at the battle of Gettysburg and sent to Fort Henry, wrote, "The prisoners nearly every day are engaged in a game they call 'baseball' . . . I don't understand the game, as there is a great deal of running and little apparent gain, but those who play it get very excited over it."

a little less than sixty pounds. Dick, nineteen, weighed sixty-four. As they began to tell the story, they broke down sobbing. President Lincoln put one hand on Billy's head and the other on Dick's shoulder. "We are all friends here," he said, "and I want you as friends of mine to tell me all you can about Andersonville." When their story ended, Lincoln sprang to his feet and exclaimed, "My God, when will this accursed thing end?"

### WHAT HAPPENED TO BILLY BATES AND DICK KING?

They were sent home by train and reunited with their parents—and then, eleven weeks later, Billy reenlisted. Before Billy and Dick parted, they promised to tell the story for the rest of their lives. After graduating from college, Billy traveled around the country, speaking to schoolchildren until he died in 1909. He kept another promise, too. After the war he went to Washington to testify in the trial of Captain Henry Wirz. Wirz was hanged on November 10, 1865, and remains the only American ever executed for war crimes.

*"What a wonderful revolution!"*

# Susie King Taylor:
# At the Heart of the Sea Islands

Coastal islands of Georgia and South Carolina, 1862–1865

*Thousands of African Americans in the South escaped to Union army camps when Yankee soldiers drew near. Carrying all their belongings, they followed the soldiers wherever they went. The Union officers called them "contrabands"—meaning property seized from the enemy. They wondered how to feed them all and where they would sleep. Some Union officers put them to work as laborers, scouts, guides, cooks, laundresses, and teamsters. Hundreds of teachers and nurses came from the North to help them. Along the coast of Georgia and South Carolina, many people who were suddenly both free and homeless turned to a remarkable teenager named Susie King Taylor.*

Growing up in Savannah, Georgia, Susie Taylor knew that reading and writing had to be important, as so many people were trying to keep her from doing them. She was a slender, dark-skinned girl, with a kind face and an eagerness to learn. Each morning she and her brother walked out their master's front door, pretending to be going out to learn a farm trade. Once out of sight, they made a sharp turn and stepped quickly to that most dangerous of places—an ordinary classroom—run by a widowed friend of Susie's grandmother.

"We went every day about nine o'clock with our books wrapped in paper to prevent the police or white people from seeing them," Susie wrote later. "We went in, one at a time, through the gate to the kitchen. She had twenty-five or thirty children whom she taught, assisted by her daughter, Mary Jane. The neighbors would see us going in sometimes, but they supposed we were there learning a trade." When the teacher ran out of new words to teach Susie, a white friend named Katie O'Connor offered to give her lessons "if I promised not to tell her father."

In 1862, the year Susie turned fourteen, the Union army captured Fort Pulaski, near Savannah, and took shaky control of the Georgia coast. Slaves poured from plantations and city homes and crowded onto military boats bound for Union camps on islands off the Georgia coast. Susie's family joined the exodus. On the boat ride over, she fell into conversation with the captain. He asked her if she could read. Proudly, she said yes, and that she could write, too. He gave her a scrap of paper and challenged her to prove it. She wrote down her name and hometown. The officer was astonished. "You seem so different from the other colored people who come from the same place you did," he finally managed to say. "That's because I was reared in the city," she answered.

There was a reason for the captain's questions. The Union needed someone to teach the illiterate children and adults in the camp on St. Simons Island. Could this newly freed girl handle it? Susie was offered the job and accepted, but refused to begin until they provided her books to work with. When they arrived, she took over a small cabin and started teaching the alphabet to forty children during the day and again to countless adults at night. They were all as hungry to learn as she had once been.

Another important group was stationed on St. Simons Island. Union major general David Hunter, desperately needing soldiers to stave off Confederate attacks on the islands, had given Federal uniforms to a few dozen ex-slaves—although the trousers were red instead of Union blue. He let them fight but didn't pay them. They were the first black

## THE EMANCIPATION PROCLAMATION

"On the first day of January, the year of our Lord one thousand eight hundred and sixty-three, all persons held as slaves within any State, or designated part of a State, the people whereof shall then be in rebellion against the United States, shall be then, thenceforth, and forever free."
—President Abraham Lincoln

## A SECOND NAME FOR THE FIRST TIME

In the spring of 1862, near Hilton Head, South Carolina, Union commander Ormsby M. Mitchel told former slaves they could now give themselves surnames—last names. This was new. Freed people thought hard about what they wanted their second names to be. Some kept the surnames of their former owners, but most didn't.

## THE FIFTY-FOURTH MASSACHUSETTS

Most Union officers doubted that black soldiers could, or would, fight as well as whites. Major General William Tecumseh Sherman asked: "Is not a negro as good as a white man to stop a bullet? Yes...but can a negro do our skirmishing and picket duty? Can they improvise bridges, sorties, flank movements, etc. like the white man? I say no."

But black boys and men wanted to prove the answer was yes; they felt the war was about them. On January 1, 1863, they got their chance, when President Lincoln issued the Emancipation Proclamation, declaring that slaves in the rebel states were free and allowing free blacks to join the U.S. Army. Days later, the governor of Massachusetts formed the first unit of free black soldiers, called the Fifty-fourth Massachusetts Regiment.

Free African Americans, including many boys, hiked to Boston to enlist. Sixteen-year-old John Henry Johnson walked from Salem, Massachusetts, where he had been taking care of a wounded Union officer. Joseph Christy, sixteen, walked from Mercersburg, Pennsylvania, with his three older brothers. Joseph Henry Green of Boston made up a phony name to fool his parents, and James W. Green of Sherborn, Massachusetts, lied about his age.

After training in the North, the Fifty-fourth attempted to seize control of Fort Wagner, South Carolina, from Confederate forces. To do so, they had to charge up a sandy hill into overwhelming fire. About half the unit was killed, but with them died the notion that black soldiers would wilt in battle. Wrote one New York reporter: "If this Massachusetts 54th had faltered ... 200,000 troops for whom it was a pioneer would never have been put into the field. But it did not falter. It made Fort Wagner such a name for the colored race as Bunker Hill has been for ninety years to the white Yankees."

soldiers to fight in the Civil War. One was Edward King, a young sergeant from Darien, Georgia. He and Susie met in camp, fell in love, and were soon married. When his unit was transferred to Port Royal Island, South Carolina, Susie went with him. Though she was officially employed as a laundress, she was far too valuable to spend much time cleaning uniforms. "I taught a great many of my comrades ... to read and write when they were off duty," she wrote. "Nearly all were anxious to learn. My husband taught some also." And while they were learning, she became the unit's postmistress, patiently reading letters to the soldiers and helping them write out replies.

Susie would have fought, too, if she had had a chance. "I learned to handle a gun very well while in the regiment," she wrote, "and could shoot straight and often hit the target. I assisted in cleaning the guns and used to fire them off to see if the cartridges were dry, before cleaning and reloading each day. I thought this great fun. I was also able to take a gun apart, and put it together again."

Above all, she became a skilled and creative nurse. Once, when a group of wounded men ran out of food, she disappeared for a while and returned with a batch of turtle eggs and several cans of condensed milk. From these she whipped up a custard that not only fed her patients but gave them a break from the monotony of dip toast and dry meat.

Susie was only a mile away on the day the soldiers of the Fifty-fouth Massachusetts—the first unit of black soldiers in the Civil War—led their bayonet assault on Fort Wagner.

Many survivors were horribly wounded by the time they got back to Susie and the other nurses. Many men lost arms and legs. Susie worked around the clock to care for them. When she finally had a moment to think about it, she was amazed by her own calmness. "It is strange," she wrote, "how we are able to see the most sickening sights, such as men with their limbs blown off and mangled by the deadly shells, without a shudder; and instead of turning away, how we hurry to assist in alleviating their pain, bind up their wounds, and press cool water to their parched lips, with feelings only of sympathy."

*Private Charles H. Arnum, Fifty-fourth Massachusetts Regiment*

## WHAT HAPPENED TO SUSIE KING TAYLOR?

When the war ended, Susie, then seventeen, went back to Savannah with her husband to begin a new life. Just before their baby was born, Edward King died. Susie opened a school for black children—charging families one dollar a month. Susie later remembered the war years as the best of her life. "What a wonderful revolution!" she wrote. "In 1860 the Southern newspapers were full of advertisements for slaves, but now, despite all hindrances, my people are striving to attain the full standard of all other races born free in the sight of God."

### FIRST ARKANSAS COLORED REGIMENT'S MARCHING SONG

*Oh, we're the bully soldiers*
*Of the First Arkansas.*
*We are fighting for the Union,*
*We are fighting for the law.*
*We can hit a Rebel further*
*Than a white man ever saw.*
*As we go marching on.*
*We are done with hoeing cotton,*
*We are done with hoeing corn;*
*We are Colored Yankee soldiers now,*
*As sure as you are born.*
*When the master hears us shouting*
*He will think it's Gabriel's horn.*
*As we go marching on.*

*"It begins to look as if the Yankees can do whatever they please and go wherever they wish—except to heaven."*—Seventeen-year-old Georgian Eliza Frances Andrews

# Carrie Berry: "They Came Burning Atlanta Today"

Atlanta, Georgia, 1864

*By 1864, the North was winning the Civil War. The Confederate army was running out of supplies and men, while thousands of slaves were strengthening the Union army. Most of the fighting was now taking place in the South. Red-bearded Union major general William Tecumseh Sherman set out to end the war by wiping out the South's ability to produce food and weapons.*

*The Union army reached the outskirts of Atlanta, the South's biggest city, in mid-July. Sherman was amazed by how Atlantans had prepared. "The whole [city] is a fort," he wrote. And he was right. Residents had stripped the wood from the walls of their houses and hammered together fences around the city. Behind the walls were trenches filled with exhausted but determined Confederate soldiers. And behind them were ordinary Atlantans waiting for the worst and hoping for the best. Instead of trying to storm the city, Sherman decided to bombard it from a distance with cannon fire and starve the Confederate soldiers by cutting off roads and railroads that delivered their food.*

*Deep in Atlanta was a ten-year-old girl named Carrie Berry. Until that spring she had lived a happy, ordered life in a big house with her parents, her sister Zuie, and a black servant girl named Mary. Aunts and uncles lived all around her. But when the shelling began, the Berrys frantically dug a hole deep in the ground and covered it with wood and tin. They scrambled to their "cellar" whenever they heard the blast of Union cannons outside the walls. Carrie kept a diary throughout the siege of Atlanta.*

July 19. "We can hear the cannons and muskets very plain, but the shells we dread. One has busted under the dining room . . . One passed through the smokehouse and a piece hit the top of the house and fell through but we were at Auntie Markhams's, so none of us were hurt. We stay very close in the cellar when they are shelling."

August 3. "This was my birthday. I was ten years old, but I did not have a cake. Times were too hard so I celebrated with ironing. I hope by my next birthday we can have peace in our land so that I can have a nice dinner."

August 5. "I knit all the morning. In the evening we had to run to Auntie's and get in the cellar. We did not feel safe in our cellar, they fell so thick and fast."

August 15. "Soon after breakfast Zuie and I were standing on the platform between the house and the dining room. [A shell] made a very large hole in the garden and threw the dirt all over the yard. I never was so frightened in my life. Zuie was as pale as a corpse . . . It did not take us long to fly to the cellar. We stayed out till night."

August 21. "Papa says that we will have to move downtown somewhere. Our cellar is not safe."

August 23. "There is a fire in town nearly every day. I get so tired of being housed up all the time. The shells get worse and worse every day. O that something would stop them."

A few days later Carrie got her wish. On August 31, Sherman's army won a decisive battle and the next day Confederate forces abandoned Atlanta. Carrie heard rumors that the oncoming Yankees were going to burn all the houses in the city, and all the residents would have to evacuate. Union troops began to pour into Atlanta. (Carrie called them Federals in her diary.)

September 2. "We all woke up this morning without sleeping much last night. The Confederates had four engines and a long train of boxcars filled with ammunition and set it on fire last night which caused a great explosion which kept us all awake. Everyone has been trying to [gather up] all they could before the Federals come in the morning. They have been running with sacks of meal, salt and tobacco. They did act ridiculous breaking open stores and robbing them. About twelve o'clock there were a few Federals came in. [We] were all frightened. We were afraid they were going to treat us badly. It was not long before the infantry came in. They were orderly and behaved very well."

> ### ADVANTAGES
>
> The South had bold and brilliant officers, but the North had advantages in materials. The factories of Massachusetts alone produced more manufactured goods than all the Confederate states combined. Northerners had another advantage, too: education. Slaves were not allowed to read, and only one of every three Southern white children was enrolled in school, compared to three of four in the North.

September 4. "Another long and lonesome Sunday . . . We have been looking at the [Yankee] soldiers all day. They have come in by the thousands. They were playing bands and they seem to be rejoiced. It has not seemed like Sunday."

But on September 8, their worst fears were confirmed: Sherman had indeed decided to burn Atlanta. Confederate officers ordered all residents to leave the city. One by one Carrie's friends and relatives departed, but her father, a wealthy businessman, made up his mind to stay even if it meant cooperating with the Yankees. While the rest of the family was packing, Maxwell Rufus Berry went downtown and offered to work for the Union army if it would guarantee his family's safety in Atlanta. He came back home cheerfully announcing they could stay. Early in November, Union soldiers began to enter homes and businesses, first taking anything of value, and then setting piles of furniture ablaze. When flames found the gunpowder that many Atlantans had stored in their homes, explosions rocked the city. Balls of fire arced through the sky, and flying cinders filled the air. One Union soldier called it "the grandest destruction I have ever seen." Carrie was terrified.

November 8. "We lost our last hog this morning early. Soldiers took him out of the pen. Me and Buddie went around to hunt for him and everywhere that we inquired they would say that they saw two soldiers driving off to kill him. We will have to live on bread."

November 12. "I could not go to sleep for fear that they would set our house on fire."

November 14. "They came burning Atlanta today. We all dread it because they say that they will burn the last house before they stop."

November 15. "This has been a dreadful day. Things have been burning all around us. We dread tonight because we do not know what moment they will set our house on fire."

November 16. "Oh, what a night we had. They came burning down the storehouse and about night it looked like the whole town was on fire. We all set up all night. If we had not [stayed up all night] our house would have been burnt up for the fire was very near and the soldiers were going around setting houses on fire where they were not watched. They behaved very badly. They all left town about one o'clock this evening and we were glad when they left for nobody knows what we have suffered since they came in."

With Atlanta in ashes, most of the Union soldiers marched off toward Savannah. Carrie's family had been one of about fifty families to remain in Atlanta. Her house had been spared, but now it stood as an island in a sea of cinders.

*Other cities besides Atlanta were devastated by Union troops. These boys rest in the ruins of Charleston, South Carolina.*

## THE BURNT COUNTRY

After burning Atlanta, General Sherman sent Union soldiers marching eastward in two parallel columns forty miles apart and told them to destroy everything in their path. They did, including major cities, until they reached the Atlantic Ocean. "War is hell," Sherman reminded his troops. Seventeen-year-old Eliza Frances Andrews passed over a stretch of central Georgia just after Sherman's army had left. Here is how she described it in her diary: "There was hardly a fence left standing all the way from Sparta to Gordon. The fields were trampled down and the road was lined with carcasses of horses, hogs and cattle that the invaders, unable either to consume or to carry away with them, had wantonly shot down to starve out the people and prevent them from making their crops. The stench in some places was unbearable; every few hundred yards we had to hold our noses or stop them with cologne."

## WHAT HAPPENED TO CARRIE BERRY?

After the Union soldiers left, her father was arrested for staying in Atlanta with the Yankees, but was soon released. In the new year of 1865, Carrie's mind returned to school, church, and a new sister. She remained in Atlanta throughout her life, married an ex–Confederate soldier, and became the mother of two sons and a daughter.

*Vinnie Ream poses with her bust of Abraham Lincoln.*

*"She seems in fact to think of nothing but her art, having that unbounded enthusiasm in it and love for it that leaves no room for trivialities."*
—A reporter from the *St. Louis Evening News*

# Vinnie Ream: "I . . . Begged Mr. Lincoln Not to Allow Me to Disturb Him"

Washington, D.C., 1865

Vinnie Ream grew up in a log cabin on the Wisconsin frontier, where her father worked as a surveyor. Most of her childhood friends were Winnebago Indians. She was a small, smart, energetic girl, with thick ringlets of black hair.

When Vinnie was ten her father bought her a guitar from a medicine man who came through southern Wisconsin in a covered wagon. The guitar came with a book of songs, and the salesman promised to stay around and teach each new customer how to play. He disappeared the next night, but it really didn't matter. Vinnie learned all the songs within three weeks and taught them to the other five guitar purchasers—all adults. She gave them guitar lessons in her cabin every night and formed them into a band called Little Vin's Musicians. They performed at hoedowns and barn raisings all through her part of Wisconsin. After the family moved to Missouri, she also mastered the harp, banjo, and harpsichord.

The Ream family moved to Washington, D.C., in 1861, when Vinnie was fourteen. It was the first year of the Civil War, and Washington was a city in chaos. As they rode by carriage from the train station to their boardinghouse, they passed makeshift hospitals whose open windows carried the cries of sick and dying soldiers. The streets were congested with army wagons and cannons on wheels. Pigs, chickens, and ducks foraged for garbage in the streets. In the midst of this clamor, Vinnnie spotted a man a head taller than everyone around him, his great height accentuated by a tall stovepipe hat. It was President Abraham Lincoln, making his way calmly through a crowded street as guards scrambled to protect him. Vinnie was amazed that the president of the United States would walk around in public, especially when so many Washingtonians favored the Confederacy. Wasn't he worried about being killed?

Vinnie kept busy. She got a job as a clerk in the post office, replacing a worker who had gone off to war, and also volunteered in hospitals. In her free time, she liked to go sightseeing around Washington. She found herself powerfully drawn to the city's statues. She inspected the many marble busts inside the Capitol building and admired the statues of officers on horseback that had been placed within circles where Washington's major streets came together. She spent hours running her fingers over the smooth surfaces. Somehow, sculptors had been able to turn slabs of cold stone into forms and figures that seemed to breathe and cry. She wanted to learn how to do it herself.

As usual, she found a way. Vinnie met people easily and could, as her father put it, "charm the pearl out of an oyster." One afternoon U.S. congressman James Rollins of Missouri—whom she had met when she lived in that state—escorted her to the studio of Clark Mills, the most famous sculptor in Washington. When Mills learned that Vinnie wanted to try sculpting, he tossed Vinnie a lump of clay (she missed it) and told her to make a model of anything she wished. She wrote, "I felt at once that I, too, could model it … In a few hours I produced a medallion of an Indian chief's head." Mills was so impressed that he offered to take her on at once as a student and assistant.

Vinnie learned so rapidly with Mills that she was soon earning money as an artist, fashioning clay likenesses of people who came into the studio, including several congressmen. But she had a special dream. Ever since the day she had seen Abraham Lincoln walking in the street, Vinnie had longed to mold his features in clay. She felt a deep bond of sympathy with the president. Like him, she had grown up in a log cabin. The Civil War was tearing her apart, too. Her brother had run away to fight for the Confederacy, while the rest of her family supported the Union. President Lincoln became her obsession. Whenever she saw him ride by in his carriage, she stared hard at his face and then rushed

## FEEDING TIME AT THE WHITE HOUSE

At times, the Lincoln White House reminded visitors of a zoo. Abraham and Mary Lincoln's sons Tad and Willie loved animals, and so did their parents. The family had a turkey, rabbits, kittens, a goat, and a dog named Jip. They had their own ponies, which they rode on the White House lawn. "I am in favor of animal rights as well as human rights," Abraham Lincoln said. "It is the way of a whole human being."

back to her studio to try to develop a clay likeness. It always came out wrong. She wanted a chance to fashion President Lincoln in clay as he sat still.

In the fall of 1864, Vinnie made her move. She convinced Congressman Rollins to ask the president to allow her to mold his likeness as he worked at his desk. She said to tell him she would be "quiet as a mouse." It was a good time to ask. Abraham and Mary Lincoln were still trying to recover from the sudden death of their eleven-year-old son, Willie, from typhoid fever in February 1862. The prospect of having a young person around seemed to brighten President Lincoln. He was intrigued by the story of the poor frontier girl who had become Clark Mills's student. To Vinnie's astonishment, the president agreed. Just before Christmas, seventeen-year-old Vinnie sent her tools and a large tub of clay to the White House. A few days later she put on her best dress and made the first of many half-hour-long visits over a period of five months. She described in her diary what it was like to be near him:

"I sat in my corner and begged Mr. Lincoln not to allow me to disturb him. He seemed to find a sort of companionship in being with me, although we talked but little . . . I made him think of Willie and he often said so and as often wept. I remember him especially in two attitudes. The first was with his great form slouched down into a chair at his desk, his head bowed upon his chest, deeply thoughtful. I think [at these times] he was with his generals on the battlefields . . . The second was at the window watching for Willie, for he had always watched the boy playing every afternoon at that window. Sometimes great tears rolled down his cheeks.

"[He seemed] a man of unfathomable sorrow . . . He never told a funny story and he rarely smiled. He had been painted and modeled before, but when he learned that I was poor, he granted me the sittings for no other purpose than that I was a poor girl. Had I been the greatest sculptor in the world, I am sure that he would have refused at that time."

On the afternoon of April 14, 1865, Vinnie worked her usual half hour at the White House. She was almost finished with her clay molding, and Lincoln told her he liked her work. It was the last time she would see him. That night he was shot as he sat watching a play at a downtown theater. He died the next morning.

Not long afterward, Congress appropriated ten thousand dollars for a sculptor to produce a life-size marble statue of the late president, to be placed in the Rotunda of the Capitol. Nearly every prominent sculptor in the United States competed for the award. Besides the great honor, ten thousand dollars was a small fortune in 1865. Vinnie wrote a letter to Congress, pointing out that she had had considerable, recent experience in shaping Lincoln's features. And though she was young, Vinnie had very powerful friends: Congressman Rollins and Senator Edmund Ross of Kansas, who both boarded at her house, supported her. They arranged for other congressmen to see Vinnie's molding of Lincoln, which wasn't quite finished but showed her strong talent.

On January 28, 1866, Congress awarded Vinnie the contract. At the age of eighteen, she had become the first female ever to receive a contract from the people of the United States to make a statue. She had even beaten out her teacher, the famous Clark Mills. Soon thousands wanted to know, "Who is Vinnie Ream?" Some sculptors were jealous. A newspaper columnist wrote that she had flirted her way to the prize. Vinnie tried to keep a level head, decorating her studio with flowers and working each day in a dust-covered smock, an oversized apron, and old shoes with rubber toes. She kept her door open and allowed anyone in who wanted to watch her work.

It took Vinnie nearly five years to complete the statue. At one point she traveled to Italy to pick out the marble with which she would work. The statue was finally unveiled in the Capitol Rotunda on January 7, 1871. A Washington newspaper reporter described how the senators and representatives reacted:

"The veil was raised slowly, disclosing first the base, bearing the simple words ABRAHAM LINCOLN; then the well-remembered form; and finally . . . the head of the patriot martyr. There was a momentary hush, and then an involuntary, warm and universal demonstration of applause gave the verdict of the distinguished and critical gathering."

## WHAT HAPPENED TO VINNIE REAM?

She worked as a sculptor until the age of thirty-one and then married a wealthy naval officer named Richard Hoxie, who didn't want her to work. Reluctantly, she gave in. They continued to live in Washington and had one son. In 1906, suffering from a kidney disease, Vinnie finally convinced her husband that her work meant too much for her to give it up forever. He built her a studio and a chair that could be raised and lowered to help her as she carved. She worked as long as she could. She died in 1914 and is buried in Arlington National Cemetery. Vinnie Ream's statue of Lincoln is still on display in the Rotunda of the Capitol in Washington, D.C.

# PART SIX

# Elbow Room: The West

———◆———

Early in the nineteenth century, many American schoolchildren learned a song that began: "Daniel Boone was ill at ease when he saw the smoke in the forest trees. There'll be no game in the country soon. 'Elbow room!' cried Daniel Boone." It was a popular song because so many settlers dreamed of having more space. Steadily, thousands of them hiked westward over the Appalachian Mountains and paddled and poled their way down broad river valleys. They cleared fields, built cabins, and carved the wilderness into new states. Daniel Boone led his own family across the Mississippi River in 1799. At first they lived on Spanish soil that then became French territory. But in July of 1803, President Thomas Jefferson bought all of France's land in North America for four cents an acre, instantly doubling the size of the United States. Now the United States owned all the land between the Mississippi River and the Rocky Mountains. Most of it was as unknown to whites as the surface of the moon.

Settlers kept on pushing until they were out of elbow room. "There is no more frontier," declared the U.S. census of 1890, and it was true. By then, cattle trails stretched up from Mexico to the railroads like veins in a weathered hand, and steel rails cut gleaming ribbons in the prairie grass from ocean to ocean. There were three times as many people living west of the Mississippi River as there had been in the whole country just eighty years before.

For some, life changed almost totally. The great Sioux chief Sitting Bull grew up in the 1840s hunting buffalo on horseback and learning to be a warrior. By the 1880s, many of his loved ones were dead, his people were confined to reservations, his children attended white-run schools, and the buffalo were all but gone.

Herds of Buffalo and Elk on the Upper Missouri River. *In 1833–1834, Karl Bodmer, a young Swiss artist, traveled twenty-five hundred miles along the Missouri River, painting and drawing western landscapes and native people.*

In January 2000, the U.S. government honored Sacagawea's contribution to the exploration of the West by minting this one-dollar coin.

*"Had the canoe been lost, I should have valued my life but little."*—William Clark

# Sacagawea: "She Inspired Us All"

North Dakota to the Pacific Ocean, 1804–1806

*Between 1804 and 1806, Meriwether Lewis and William Clark led twenty-eight white men and one black man (Clark's slave, York) across the continent and back again. They traveled more than eight thousand miles. History remembers them as the discoverers of the West. But the West was hardly empty when they arrived. When they reached the Great Plains, there were more than thirty tribes living there. Lewis and Clark couldn't have reached the Pacific without the help of native people, especially one remarkable fifteen-year-old Shoshone girl.*

## WHAT LEWIS AND CLARK WERE SUPPOSED TO DO

In 1803, Congress gave President Jefferson $2,500 for a Corps of Discovery to explore and map the new lands of the Louisiana Purchase. Jefferson chose his secretary Meriwether Lewis to lead the expedition, and Lewis picked his ex–army buddy William Clark as co-commander. Jefferson told them to "explore the Missouri River . . . and communicate with the water of the Pacific Ocean." In other words, to see if it was possible to reach the Pacific Ocean from St. Louis on a single river. Jefferson also told them to gather samples of soil and rocks, describe the weather, name the birds and creatures, collect plants, map the land, and see how tough the legendary grizzly bears really were (very tough, it turned out). Finally they were to convince the Indians they met that their real leader was their "Great Father" in Washington, D.C.—Jefferson himself.

Sacagawea's childhood ended when she was ten, on a day when her Shoshone tribe was attacked in a Rocky Mountain meadow by a Hidatsa raiding party. It was no contest: The enemy had guns and her people didn't. She was captured and taken to a Hidatsa lodge, where she lived as a slave with a few other captives. One morning, she and two other girls were pushed toward a big-bellied, hard-drinking white man named Toussaint Charbonneau. She was told that he had won her in a card game and that she now belonged to him.

In the winter of 1804, she rode with Charbonneau to a small fort that had been built by a group of white explorers where the Missouri and Knife Rivers came together. These men had been paddling west for months and had pulled their boats out to spend the winter at the fort until the Missouri's frozen water ran free again. Charbonneau had heard that they were looking for a guide to lead them west to the Rocky Mountains, someone who could speak the languages of the western tribes. Word was they were paying well.

Charbonneau led Sacagawea and another young woman to Fort Mandan, as Lewis and Clark's settlement was called, and announced that he was available to guide them west. Motioning to the women, he said simply that his "two squaws" were Snake Indians.

Lewis and Clark were especially drawn to Sacagawea. Though she was only fifteen and pregnant, here was a girl who could speak both Shoshone and Hidatsa. She had grown up among mountain tribes who might be able to provide them with horses and who could guide them farther west. She had so much to offer that it was worth taking a baby along. Lewis and Clark hired Charbonneau and told him they wanted to take Sacagawea but not the second girl.

Sacagawea and Charbonneau moved to Fort Mandan to help prepare for the trip. In February, Sacagawea began to have unusually violent pains during the birth of her baby. She seemed near death. Meriwether Lewis, the group's doctor, tried everything he knew to help, but nothing worked. Desperate not to lose his guide, he agreed to try a Shoshone custom even though it made no sense to him. Lewis took a rock and ground a rattlesnake's tail into small pieces and then dissolved them in water. Sacagawea gulped down the mixture

*Lewis and Clark's Corps of Discovery took twenty-eight months to go eight thousand miles. By the time they returned, they were able to give America a much clearer picture of itself.*

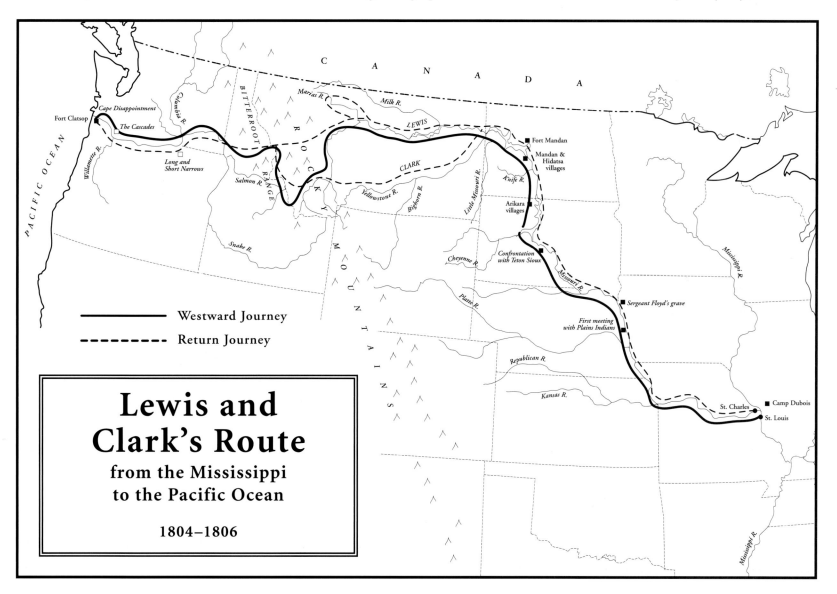

**Lewis and Clark's Route**
from the Mississippi
to the Pacific Ocean

1804–1806

——— Westward Journey

- - - - - Return Journey

eagerly. Ten minutes later she gave birth to a loud, sturdy son. Her boy was named Jean-Baptiste Charbonneau, but everybody called him Pomp.

In April, the men lowered their canoes back into the fast-flowing Missouri, now swollen with melted snow. Sacagawea rode proudly in the largest boat with Pomp strapped to a cradleboard on her back.

From the beginning, Sacagawea proved much more than an ordinary guide. She could tell whether a single moccasin track in the dust came from a friendly tribe like the Shoshones or one that might attack them. When the men were unable to kill game, she used a long pointed stick to scrape up buried roots—licorice, wild artichokes, and something called white apples. She found the places where mice had stored food for the winter. Sometimes she dug enough food to feed the entire exhausted group.

One day a sudden gust of wind nearly tipped over their biggest boat. Charbonneau had been steering and had turned the sail the wrong way. Waves swept over the deck, washing all loose objects into the river. Moving swiftly, Sacagawea plunged into the current and swam after the expedition's maps, journals, instruments, and medicine, rescuing most of them as Clark watched helplessly from shore. That night he wrote, "Had the [canoe] been lost, I should have valued my life but little . . . The Indian woman to whom I ascribe equal fortitude and resolution with any person on board at the time of the accident caught and preserved most of the light articles which were washed overboard."

The explorers were nearly starving by the time they reached the Rocky Mountains, but Sacagawea was overjoyed to be near her home once again. In a mountain meadow, she caught sight of her childhood friend Jumping Fish, who had earned her name by the way she had jumped through a stream to escape the Hidatsa on the day Sacagawea had been captured.

Jumping Fish led the explorers to the Shoshone camp. Soon whites and Shoshones were seated in a circle inside a tent of willows, passing a pipe and trying to communicate with one another. Suddenly Sacagawea, who was translating, stopped speaking. She leaped up, ran across the tent, threw her arms around the chief, and flung a blanket over his head, sobbing. It was her brother Cameahwait. He told her that their parents were dead and only two brothers were still alive.

The Shoshones gave Lewis and Clark horses to cross the mountains, and some members of the tribe went along with them, including Sacagawea and Pomp. When they reached the Pacific, the explorers spent a cold, rainy winter in a fort they built. When the explorers heard that a whale had washed ashore and formed a small group to go see it, Sacagawea insisted that she be allowed to go. It seemed to surprise the others, partly because she had no rights as a slave, but mainly because she had never before taken such a stand. "She observed that she had traveled a long way with us to see the great waters," Lewis wrote, "and that now that the monstrous fish was also to be seen, she thought it very hard she could not be permitted." They let her go.

On the return journey east, Sacagawea found ways to communicate even with Indians from tribes whose languages she had never heard.

On August 17, 1806, Sacagawea, Charbonneau, and Pomp parted with Lewis and Clark and went back to live among the Mandan. Clark found parting with them very difficult. He offered to take Pomp with him to St. Louis and raise him as his son. Sacagawea diplomatically answered, "Maybe next summer," but kept Pomp. Clark paid Charbonneau $500.33 for his "services" on the trip, but not a penny went to Sacagawea. Clark later wrote to Charbonneau, "Your woman who accompanied you that long dangerous and fatiguing

*There are more statues of Sacagawea today than of any female in U.S. history, although no one knows what she really looked like. This early-nineteenth-century magazine illustration shows one artist's vision of her.*

## THE EXCEPTION

The other explorers called Sacagawea "Janey." She was the Lewis and Clark expedition's only Indian, its only female, its only teenager, one of only two slaves—the other being York. And she was the only member of the party who didn't get paid.

route to the Pacific Ocean and back deserved a greater reward for her attention and services on that route than we had in our power to give her."

## WHAT HAPPENED TO SACAGAWEA?

Very little is known of her life after she left Lewis and Clark. She separated from Charbonneau at some point. One missionary wrote that Sacagawea died as a very old woman in 1884, but a more detailed account in the journal of a trader said she died December 20, 1812. The trader wrote: "This Evening the Wife of Charbonneau, a Snake Squaw, died of putrid fever . . . She was best woman in the fort, aged about 25 and she left a fine infant girl." Clark also wrote that by 1828 Sacagawea was dead. Pomp became a successful guide for Western travelers.

*Enrique Esparza in his seventies, still farming near San Antonio and still haunted by boyhood memories of the Alamo*

*"I will never forget the face or the figure of Santa Anna."*

# Enrique Esparza: Inside the Alamo

San Antonio, Texas, February 23–March 6, 1836

*For three centuries the area that is now Texas was ruled by Spain, whose priests had built missions and tried to convert the Indians to Catholicism. In 1821, Mexico finally overthrew Spain and formed a republic like the United States. But soon a tiny, tough general named Antonio López de Santa Anna seized control of the country, canceled the constitution, and declared himself dictator.*

*In these same years people from the United States began to settle in Texas. The Anglos, or English-speaking settlers, were frontier people who wanted the freedom to do what they pleased and all the land they could get, especially land that grew cotton easily. At first they arrived with Mexico's permission, but soon it became clear that most white settlers didn't want to speak Spanish or become Catholics, and they didn't see themselves as Mexicans. Thousands arrived each month, soon greatly outnumbering Mexicans in the area.*

*In 1830, Santa Anna ruled that no more Americans could settle in Texas. Still Americans kept pouring in. In February of 1836, about four thousand Mexican soldiers led by Santa Anna marched into San Antonio to confront fewer than two hundred settlers who were holed up in an old Spanish mission called the Alamo. Enrique Esparza was a San Antonio boy of Mexican descent who was with his family in the Alamo during the legendary battle. Many years later Enrique told his story of the fight to a San Antonio newspaper reporter.*

On a warm February afternoon in 1836, eight-year-old Enrique Esparza looked up from the game he and his friends were playing and saw waves of blue-uniformed troops pouring into his town of San Antonio. First came a horseman carrying a black flag. Behind were horses pulling carts, each containing a polished black iron cannon. Enrique scrambled from the dirt and dashed home to tell his parents—the soldiers are here. Enrique's father, knowing that a battle was coming, had made an arrangement to move the family out of San Antonio, but now it was too late. They were trapped.

A few minutes later, Enrique and his father, mother, sister, and three brothers squeezed through a small window of the Alamo, crawled on their bellies over a cannon, and dropped to the dirt floor. The window closed quickly behind them. They looked around the tall, dimly lit, arched room filled with men, mostly Anglos but some Mexicans as well. A few women and children were in a small chapel off to one side. Men nervously cleaned their rifles and squinted through cracks in the adobe. Enrique could hear the footsteps of guards patrolling the rooftop.

Enrique might have wondered who were the heroes and who were the villains. His beloved uncle Francisco was outside the walls, a soldier in Santa Anna's Mexican army, determined to rout the settlers inside the Alamo. But his father was on the side of the Americans, willing to give his life so that the settlers could govern their affairs. This is how Enrique remembered his next days:

"The scene was one of such horror that it could never be forgotten by anyone who witnessed it . . . We had not been in there long when a messenger came from Santa Anna calling on us to surrender. The reply was a shot from one of [our] cannons . . . Soon after, I heard Santa Anna's cannon reply. My heart quaked when the shot tore through the timbers.

"If I had been given a weapon I would have fought. But weapons and ammunition were scarce and only used by those who knew how. But I saw some there no older than I

## COMANCHES—THE GREAT RIDERS

One reason Santa Anna allowed white settlers into Texas was to help Mexicans kill the great horse Indians—the Comanches, Apaches, and Wichitas—who terrorized the plains. Comanches first reached Spanish settlements in New Mexico in 1705. After raiding corrals and capturing great herds of horses, they soon became brilliant riders. Mounted on swift ponies, Comanche warriors struck swiftly with lances and arrows. They perfected the trick of dodging gunshots by clinging to the side of a galloping horse, and could even shoot from a sidesaddle position. Though greatly outnumbered, the Comanche kept the Spanish from expanding into North America and blocked the French from moving into the Southwest. They were finally stopped by an invention—Samuel Colt's revolving pistol. The six-shooter, a hand weapon that could be fired from horseback, gave one Texas Ranger or U.S. soldier the power of six men.

*In the final siege of the Alamo, Santa Anna's troops flung ladders against the mission's walls and climbed straight into American gunfire.*

who had them and fought as bravely as the adults. This was towards the end when many of the grown persons within had been slain by the foes. It was then that some of the children joined in the defense . . . We must have been within the Alamo for ten or twelve days. They were long and full of horror."

After days of heavy fighting, Santa Anna offered the colonists a three-day truce. During that time anyone who wanted to could leave the Alamo without being fired upon. Inside, Colonel William Travis, leader of the Americans, asked if anyone wanted to leave. Enrique's parents made the decision for the whole family.

"My father replied, 'No. I will stay and die fighting.' My mother then said, 'I will stay by your side and with our children die too. They will soon kill us. We will not linger in pain.' So we stayed."

When the three days were up, the Mexican army waited for nightfall and then struck again with full fury. Enrique woke up screaming from a deep sleep.

"Shots crashed through the doors and windows. Then men rushed in on us. They swarmed among us and over us. Our men had fought long and well but their ammunition was very low and their strength was spent. They struck us down with their escopetas [muskets] . . . And so my father died fighting. He struck down one of his foes as he fell in the heap of the slain.

"By my side was an American boy. He was about my own age but larger. As they reached us he rose to his feet. He had been sleeping . . . As they rushed upon him he stood calmly and across his shoulders [he] drew the blanket on which he had slept. He was unarmed. They slew him where he stood and his corpse fell over me. My father's body was lying near the cannon he had tended. My mother was kneeling beside it with my baby sister. My mother clasped her babe to her breast and closed her eyes . . . She expected they would kill her and her babe and me and my brothers. I thought so too. I grew faint and sick.

"They took us to another part of the building and got all of the women and children who had not been killed into a corner and kept firing on the men who defended the Alamo . . . After all of the men had been slain, we were held until daylight, when we were marched off to a house and placed under guard."

Santa Anna sent for them a few hours later. Again Enrique thought that now they would be killed. They entered a house and saw the dictator himself seated at a table. He was a small man with jet-black hair combed straight back and hard eyes. On the table was a stack of silver dollars and a pile of blankets. They stood before him.

"My mother was called before the dictator. When she appeared, my baby sister pressed closely to her bosom. My brother was clinging to her skirt, but I stood to one side and behind her. I watched every move and listened to every word spoken."

## DAVY CROCKETT

Children who grew up in the United States in the early 1950s learned that the Alamo was the place where Davy Crockett, "king of the wild frontier," died swinging his rifle, Old Betsy, at a horde of Mexicans who swarmed over the walls of the gallant old mission. According to Walt Disney's TV series, Crockett was the last settler to die. Like many stories about David Crockett, it was partly true. He was indeed a brave frontiersman who led a group of Tennesseans west to help the colony of Texas and to find land for himself. He fought valiantly at the Alamo but probably didn't go down swinging Old Betsy. Witnesses say he and five others surrendered to Mexican soldiers and were executed later at Santa Anna's orders. Davy Crockett's personal motto was "Be sure you're right and then go ahead." But like Davy Crockett, the Mexican soldiers who died at the Alamo also believed they were fighting for something that was right—to keep people from taking land they thought was theirs. The illustration above, from Davy Crockett's own *Almanak*, shows Crockett hurrying to Texas.

After questioning her about other settlers who might still be alive, "Santa Anna released my mother. He told her she was free to go where she liked. He gave her a blanket and two silver dollars. After that we gathered what belongings we could and went to our cousin's place on North Flores Street... My mother wept for many days and nights. I frequently went to the main plaza and watched the soldiers of Santa Anna and saw him many times before they marched away toward Houston where he was defeated. He had a hard and cruel look and his countenance was a very sinister one. It has haunted me ever since I last saw it."

## What Happened to Enrique Esparza?

He remained in San Antonio, where he married, had a family, and managed a small farm with his son Victor. Even as an old man, he got up before dawn and spent his days tilling his land behind a team of horses. He was described by a newspaper reporter as "firm-stepped, clear-minded and clear-eyed." And seventy years after it happened, his voice still broke when he talked about his father's death in the Alamo: "I will never forget the face or the figure of Santa Anna."

———————◆◆◆◆◆———————

*"Oh, how did we stand it?"*

# Mary Goble: Walking to Zion

The West, 1856

*In the years after gold was discovered in California in 1848, it seemed as if the whole weight of the country shifted west. Wagon wheels dug deep grooves in trails that went over the Rocky Mountains all the way to the Pacific. In 1862, the Homestead Act promised 160 free acres of land to anyone who would work it for five years. Tens of thousands left Europe and headed to the American West, where they made houses out of the earth itself and tried to survive. Thousands of former slaves, called "exodusters," left the South and sought their future in the prairie states. One group went west as an entire people. Like the Pilgrims before them, they called themselves Saints, but most people called them something else: Mormons. Between 1847 and 1869, more than seventy thousand Mormon pioneers crossed the Great Plains, struggled over the Wasatch Mountains, and skidded their belongings down into the Great Salt Lake valley in what is now called Utah. They called it Zion. Driven by faith, they walked a thousand miles at two miles per hour, hiking beside covered wagons or pushing two-wheeled handcarts. Older children carried their smaller brothers and sisters on their backs. And like the Pilgrims before them, many, including thirteen-year-old Mary Goble, buried their parents on the trail to Zion.*

It all happened so fast. Mary Goble was growing up in Sussex, England, when her parents went to a meeting one night and joined the Mormon Church. Soon she, too, was baptized. The next spring they sold everything they owned and hurried off to Liverpool. Before she knew it, Mary was on a steamship with nine hundred other new Mormons bound for America. "I well remember how we watched old England fade from sight," Mary wrote. "We sang 'Farewell Our Native Land, Farewell.' "

She watched from the rail as a giant shark trailed after the ship for days, disappearing only after a passenger who had died on the ship was buried at sea. Near Newfoundland they almost slammed into an iceberg hidden in the fog. After six weeks at sea, they reached Boston, gathered their belongings, and dashed to the train station. There wasn't an hour to lose. It was nearly July and they still had to get all the way to Iowa City to meet their wagon company. Everyone said that if they started across the Great Plains too late, cold weather in the West would overtake them and they might freeze to death.

In Iowa City, they bought a wagon and a team of oxen. But before they could depart, the sky suddenly darkened and the heavens opened. Violent winds tore apart their shelter, and sheets of rain drenched them all. Mary's infant sister, Fanny, already weakened with measles, was soaked through and through. "The day we started our journey," wrote Mary, "we visited her grave. We felt very bad to leave our little sister there."

On August 1, they finally started to move. "Our ox teams were unbroken and we did not know a thing about driving oxen . . . We travelled fifteen to twenty-five miles a day. We stopped one day in the week to wash. On Sunday we would hold our prayer meetings and rest."

September 1 found them still in western Iowa. Nights were cold now and fear of Indians made them keep their camp dark at night. When they came to the Platte River in Nebraska, some hikers were already weak and ill. Mary watched one group try to

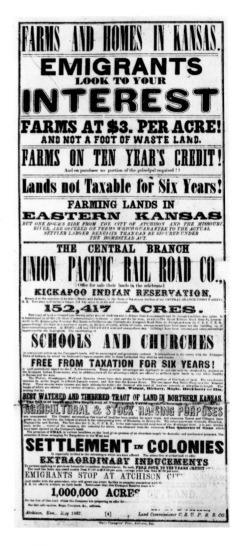

*Ads like this one in 1867 encouraged settlers to emigrate west. Some of the land offered here by the Union Pacific Railroad was part of the Kickapoo Indian Reservation.*

Some Mormon families loaded their belongings on two-wheeled handcarts and pulled them all the way to Salt Lake. Others, like Mary Goble's family and this one, went in ox-drawn covered wagons.

## WHY MORMONS WENT TO SALT LAKE

In 1820, fourteen-year-old Joseph Smith had visions of "two personages whose brightness and glory defy all description." He said an angel then led him to a set of golden tablets, with religious messages written in an ancient language. He translated them into *The Book of Mormon*. In 1830, he started a new religion, which he called Church of Jesus Christ of Latter-day Saints. At first there were only six followers. Soon there were thousands.

Opposition formed. Some resented the church's rapid growth and feared that their own church members might become Mormons. Others objected to the accepted Mormon practice of polygamy—husbands having more than one wife. Anti-Mormon mobs formed and Mormons fought them with their own armed men. Smith moved his followers to Ohio and Missouri, and finally to Nauvoo, Illinois, where they quickly built a city that grew even bigger than Chicago. Joseph Smith even campaigned for president.

But in 1844, Smith and his brother were jailed and then shot to death by a mob. Brigham Young, Smith's successor, sent men west to find a safer home for Mormons. They chose the Great Salt Lake valley, then outside the United States and known only to mountain men and Ute Indians.

drag their belongings through the icy current. "There were great lumps of ice floating down the river . . . The next morning there were fourteen dead. We went back to camp and went to prayers."

They prayed harder and walked on. On September 23, Mary took the last walk she would ever take with her mother. Later that day Mary's mother gave birth to a baby girl. They named her Edith and saw her as a sign of hope, but the labor left Mary's mother too exhausted to walk. From then on she rode in the wagon.

By October, they were out of water and were drinking melted snow. Each hiker was allowed only a quarter pound of a thin gruel called skilly each day. When Mary heard of a spring of fresh water a short distance away, she and a friend trudged off through the snow to try to fill up a vessel for Mary's mother. They came upon an old man who had fallen in the snow and couldn't get up. Mary started back alone to get help but was soon lost. "I began to think of the Indians and . . . I became confused. I waded around in the snow up to my knees . . . When I did not return to camp, the men started out after me. It was eleven o'clock before they found me . . . They carried me to camp and rubbed me with snow. They put my feet in a bucket of water. The pain was terrible. The frost came out of my legs and feet but not out of my toes."

The oxen labored to drag the wagons through deep snow. One day Mary's baby sister, Edith, died of starvation, and a few days later her brother James was gone, too. The cattle looked like walking skeletons. The Gobles abandoned their wagon and joined teams with another family in Wyoming. They were all stumbling through the snow when a horseman galloped into camp with good news: Food and teams of fresh horses from Salt Lake City would arrive the next day. "There was rejoicing that night. We sang songs, some danced, and some cried."

The white-topped covered wagon was a kitchen, living room, and bedroom all in one.

## A FOUR-LEGGED LIFELINE

Children on the trail to Zion—as they called Salt Lake—grew to love and need the animals they walked beside. A cow could be a lifeline. "Our cow was a Jersey and had a long tail," wrote thirteen-year-old Margaret McNeil. "When it was necessary to cross a river, I would wind the end of the cow's tail around my hand and swim across with her . . . Had it not been for her milk we would have starved . . . Every morning I would rise early and get breakfast for the family and milk my cow so that I could hurry and drive her on ahead of the company. Then I would let her eat in all the grassy places until the company had passed on ahead, when I would hurry and catch up with them . . . It was important to see that she was well fed."

## MEETING WESTERN WILDLIFE

Young Mormon travelers met new animals in interesting ways. One barefooted girl wandered off the trail and felt something soft beneath her feet. "I was standing on a bed of snakes, large ones and small ones . . . All I could think of to do was pray, and in some way I jumped out of them." Ohio-born Rachel Wooley spent the night of her twelfth birthday peeking out of her wagon at a pack of wolves. "Some of them would put their feet right on the wagon tongue and sniff in," she wrote.

They arrived in Salt Lake City at night on December 11, 1856. Six months before, Mary had been part of a big English family. Now everything had changed. "Three out of the four that were living were frozen," she wrote. "And my mother was dead in the wagon."

Mary had problems of her own. She was badly frostbitten. Early the next morning Mormon president Brigham Young came to inspect the survivors, accompanied by a doctor. He took one look at Mary's feet and burst into tears. The doctor prepared to amputate, but Young stopped him. "President Young said no, just cut off the toes and I promise you, you will never have to take them off any farther." Months after the operation, Mary's legs were still bent from the frost, but her father came up with an idea to straighten them: " 'I will nail a shelf on the wall,' he said, 'and while I am away to work you try to reach it.' I tried all day and for several days until at last I could reach it. Then he would put the shelf a little higher and in three months my legs were straight and then I had to learn to walk again . . . [When I did] the doctor said that surely was a miracle."

## WHAT HAPPENED TO MARY GOBLE?

She and her husband, Richard Pay, ran a ranch in Nephi, Utah. She learned Native American languages and was known for her ability to get along well with the Pagwat and Ute Indians who lived nearby. She was the mother of ten sons and three daughters and died at the age of seventy in 1913.

<hr/>

*"When the Pony Express dashed past, it seemed almost like the wind racing over the prairie."*—Mary Ann Stucki, a Mormon girl who saw the riders during her journey to Salt Lake in 1860

# William Cody: Racing the Wind

California to the Mississippi River, 1860

*If you wanted to deliver a business letter or newspaper across the West in 1860, the fastest way was to send it by Pony Express. That's how people in Salt Lake City learned that Abraham Lincoln had been elected president, and that's how San Franciscans found out that the Civil War had begun.*

*Though some historians doubt the authenticity of this advertisement, there is little doubt that the company was after young, light daredevil riders.*

The Pony Express was a two-thousand-mile-long relay race against time. Investors spaced 190 stations about ten miles apart between Sacramento, California, and the Mississippi River. Each station had two or three fast horses ready to go. Every morning a rider took off from Sacramento with a leather pouch full of letters written on the thinnest paper available and galloped east as fast as he could to the first station, Folsom.

*A Pony Express rider gets set to leap from one horse onto another.*

## YOUNG, LIGHT DAREDEVILS

It cost five dollars, paid in advance, to send a letter on the Pony Express. The goal was to advance the mail 250 miles per day. Only business letters were allowed. Riders were hired for strength, stamina, and lightness. Their average age was eighteen. They made about $120 a month, a good wage then, and got bonuses for especially quick rides. The riders who brought news of one Civil War battle to Sacramento a day before schedule divided a bonus of $300.

There he leaped off the horse, gulped down water, grabbed his mail pouch, jumped onto a fresh mount, and thundered off. The switch took two minutes. The same thing happened with a westbound rider starting from St. Joseph, Missouri. Riders rode about eight switches before they rested. They took pride in never slowing down for anything—storms, Indians, thieves, or even fatigue.

They were lightning fast. News of Lincoln's election traveled from St. Joseph to Denver—a distance of 665 miles—in two days and twenty-one hours. The text of Lincoln's inaugural address traveled two thousand miles in seven days and seventeen hours. Many of the riders were teenagers, because they were light and adventuresome. Young J. H. Keetley rode the first eastern leg, starting each morning from St. Joseph, Missouri. People got up early and lined the streets just to catch a glimpse of him as he tore out of town. Keetley later wrote, "[We] bounded out of the office door and down the hill at full speed . . . It was then that all St. Joe, great and small, were on the sidewalks to see the pony go by . . . We always rode out of town with silver mounted trappings decorating both [rider] and horse and regular uniforms with plated horn, pistol, scabbard and belt and gay flower-worked leggings and plated jingling spurs resembling, for all the world, a fantastic circus rider."

The most famous rider of all was William F. Cody, later known as Buffalo Bill. He was a boy who grew up in the saddle. After his father died, eleven-year-old Bill found a job delivering messages by mule for a Kansas freight company. He was fourteen when he heard that the Pony Express had started up. He thought the job had been invented for him. At first the hiring agent at his local station said he was too young, but finally gave in and let Bill take a test run. Bill won his job by blistering the course between Red Buttes and Three Crossings in nearly record time.

He quit after two months but then missed the excitement and tried to get a job at a station farther west. According to Bill, this is how his job interview went: "My boy, you are too young for a Pony Express rider," the hiring agent said. "I rode two months last year on Bill Trotter's division," Bill replied coolly. "I filled the bill then and I think I'm even better now." The agent's eyes widened in recognition. "What! Are you the boy that was riding there, and was called the youngest rider on the road? . . . I've heard of you."

And so Bill Cody was off again, wringing adventure from every mile. Once, when the rider expected at Three Crossings station didn't show up (he had been shot dead in a saloon the night before), Bill grabbed the man's mail sack and took off in

*Eighteen-year-old Richard "Ras" Egan rode a seventy-five-mile route between Salt Lake City and Rush Valley.*

his place. He rode 322 miles by himself from station to station without mishap and arrived on time, even though he spent part of his ride bent flat back in the saddle dodging robbers' bullets. According to Bill Cody (who was known to stretch a story), that was the day he set the all-time Pony Express endurance record.

The Pony Express lasted only eighteen fabulous months. It lost a race to electricity, which could push messages along a telegraph wire even faster than Bill Cody could urge a half-breed California mustang along a dusty trail.

## WHAT HAPPENED TO BILL CODY?

He served as a Union scout in the Civil War, then became, among other things, a wrangler, hotel owner, gold-panner, rancher, and meat hunter for the Union Pacific Railroad. In one year alone, he boasted of killing 4,280 buffalo. In 1883, he started Buffalo Bill's Wild West Show, which toured America, and in which he, of course, starred. He died in 1917.

## GOLD MOUNTAIN MALES

Nearly twelve thousand Chinese went to Gold Mountain in 1852. Only seven were women or girls. Fifty years later only 5 percent of all Chinese in the United States were females. According to Chinese custom and religion, women were expected to stay within the walls of their villages and tend to their families. Also, it was very expensive for two to go, and families thought that if a wife stayed at home, the husband would be more likely to return to China. Many of the Chinese teenagers and men who left were married, and their wives knew they might never see them again. One song warned:

*If you have a daughter, don't marry her to a Gold Mountain man . . .*
*The spider will spin webs on top of the bedposts,*
*While dust fully covers one side of the bed.*

*"If you will, you can."*—Ng Poon Chew's grandmother's parting words to him when he left China for the United States

# Ng Poon Chew and Lee Chew: Gold Mountain Boys

Pearl River Delta, China, and San Francisco, California, 1850s–1880s

*In 1848, nuggets of gold were discovered in several California rivers, triggering a worldwide gold rush. A few Chinese merchants living in California got lucky, and in the winter of 1850–1851, they journeyed back to their villages carrying fortunes of between $3,000 and $4,000 each. Overnight, thousands of young Chinese men and teenage boys borrowed the money for the trip and crowded aboard small ships bound for Gam Saan, or "Gold Mountain," as California was called. Many who set out to be miners ended up with very different jobs. Ng Poon Chew and Lee Chew were two of China's Gold Mountain boys.*

One day thirteen-year-old Ng Poon Chew looked up to see his long-lost uncle coming up the road from the Tam River. Overjoyed, Ng followed him inside the family house and watched him reach into the folds of his blue traveling blouse and pull out eight heavy sacks. He dropped them one by one on the table and smiled. Each was filled with 100 Mexican silver dollars. From that moment on, Ng could think of nothing but reaching Gam Saan.

Such scenes were taking place throughout Kwangtung Province, on the coast of south China. Nearby, sixteen-year-old Lee Chew quickly lost all interest in farming when he saw all the things a neighbor who had returned from Gold Mountain could buy: "He took ground as large as four city blocks and made a paradise of it. He put a large stone wall around and let some streams through and built a palace and a summer house . . . The man had gone away from our village a poor boy. Now he returned with unlimited wealth. It filled my mind with the idea that I, too, would like to go to the country of the wizards and gain some of their wealth."

Parents couldn't hold the boys. Some parents mortgaged a field or sold a pig to secure a loan from a ticket seller in Hong Kong. Their children promised to send money soon to pay off the loan and then bid tearful good-byes. Ng Poon Chew set off with his cousin in 1880. Each boy attached a bedroll containing a package of herbal medicines to a bamboo

*Chinese boys and men bound for Gold Mountain aboard the steamship* America

pole, hoisted the pole across his shoulders, then headed for the river. They had their heads shaved, except for a single long braid in back, and wore loose blue jackets and broad, umbrella-shaped hats that shaded them from the sun. They boarded a slow-moving boat called a junk, which pulled them down the Tam River into the mouth of the Pearl River and across the bay to Hong Kong.

Lee Chew sailed with five friends. He had a hundred dollars from his father tucked into his blouse. His grandfather had told him that Americans were "wizards" and "barbarians," and he was worried that maybe his grandfather was right. Things were different from the

## DIFFERENT DIETS

The habits of Chinese railroad workers were very different from those of the whites who worked with them. At the end of a workday, exhausted men from both groups put their tools down and went to dinner. But first, each Chinese worker filled his tub with hot water from a giant boiler the cook had ready. He sponged himself and changed clothes. Then he sat down to his evening rice. It was flavored with oysters, abalone, cuttlefish, mushrooms, and bamboo shoots brought from China. Chinese workers drank hot tea several times a day. Whites ate beef, beans, bread, butter, and potatoes, and they drank water that was not boiled free of impurities. Some thought that the Chinese workers were able to work longer because they had a healthier diet.

*Candidates for California's Workingmen's Party campaigned on anti-Chinese sentiment.*

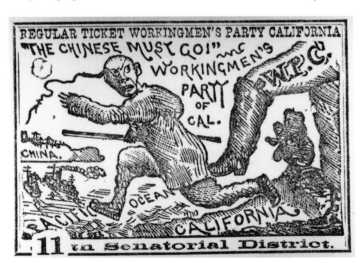

start. He couldn't sleep on the ship: "All my life I had been used to sleeping on a board bed with a wooden pillow, and I found the steamer's bunk very uncomfortable because it was too soft. I was afraid of the stews [we ate], for the thought of what they might be made of by the wicked wizards of the ship made me ill. Of the great powers of these people I saw many signs. The engines that moved the ship were wonderful monsters, strong enough to lift mountains."

Two months later, they arrived in San Francisco. They went through customs, were examined for diseases and frisked for opium, and then tromped down the ship's ramp into the clamor of San Francisco's waterfront. At first Chinese immigrants were welcomed to America, but as more and more arrived, attitudes had hardened. Many whites feared that the Chinese, who were tough and disciplined workers, would take away their jobs. Furthermore, most Chinese kept to themselves, cooked their own food, worshiped in their own way, and usually did not speak English.

Some whites wouldn't tolerate these differences. Gangs of boys and young men often waited for the half-starved Chinese newcomers at the bottom of the ramp and greeted them with a shower of stones, potatoes, and mud. The Chinese made their way to agents of "Six Companies"—groups of Chinese businessmen—who separated them by their home villages and hustled them off to the city's Chinese quarter. Sometimes the gangs ran alongside, screaming curses and pulling them out of the wagons by their braids. "Often," wrote one who watched such scenes, "they reach [Chinatown] covered with wounds and bruises and blood." Most recovered quickly. "A few days living in the Chinese quarter," wrote Lee Chew, "made me happy again."

Many Chinese boys got their first jobs as houseboys in the homes of whites. Ng was hired by a rancher who couldn't pronounce his name. For two dollars a week he worked from dawn till nightfall gardening, cleaning, watching children, cooking, and serving meals. The worst times were when he had to go to the store and was beaten by gangs and forced to surrender the groceries. Lee Chew earned $3.50 per week working for a family of four. "I didn't know how to do anything, and I did not understand what the lady said to me, but she would take my hands and show me how to cook, wash, iron, sweep, dust, make beds, wash dishes, clean windows, paint and brass, polish the knives and forks."

In the 1860s, thousands of teenage boys and young men went from China to California to build the western portion of the first transcontinental railroad. Two companies were racing to see which could build the most miles of track. Workers for the Union Pacific Company began in Omaha, Nebraska, and headed west. Workers for the Central Pacific began in Sacramento and moved east. The Union Pacific crew, consisting mostly of Irish immigrants, got off to a great start, racing over the flat prairies. But in 1865, after two years of trying, the Central Pacific had managed fewer than fifty miles of track. Few workers in California seemed interested in the backbreaking labor of blasting a railroad bed through the rugged Sierra Nevada mountains.

Frustrated, the Central Pacific hired fifty Chinese workers in 1865. This was embarrassing because one of the company's main investors, Leland Stanford, had been elected governor of California partly by vowing to prevent more Chinese from entering the United States. At first whites refused to work with the Chinese. But the Chinese proved well organized, hardworking, and quick to learn. After hearing one complaint too many, Charles Crocker, superintendent of the Central Pacific, faced down a group of whites. "If you can't get along with [the Chinese]," he said, "we'll let you go and hire nobody but them."

*Young Chinese workers prepare to move by handcart to another section of the Central Pacific Railroad.*

As teams chipped and blasted through the Sierra Nevada, the railroad company sent ships to China to get more workers. Groups of uneducated young Chinese farmers of the Sinning and Sinhwui districts clustered around marketplace notices advertising jobs for a long-term project in the Gold Mountain. Seven thousand Chinese workers sailed off to San Francisco in little more than a year.

They were taken to the mountains, organized into camps, and put to work for one dollar a day. Their mightiest challenge came when the tracks reached Cape Horn Pass. There, a sheer cliff rose fourteen hundred feet straight up from the deep green American River. The job, somehow, was to blast a flat ledge out of the cliff face near the top. It had to be wide enough to make a bed for railroad tracks. Some accounts say that the problem was solved when a Chinese interpreter told a crew boss how they had built roads along steep cliff faces in the Yangtze valley. Days later, loads of reeds were brought up from San Francisco, and by campfire the Chinese stayed up weaving waist-high wicker baskets and attaching them to ropes. Symbols were printed on the baskets to repel evil spirits.

The next day teams of three climbed to the top of the cliff, carrying the baskets. Ropes were attached to each corner of the basket and then lashed to a central cable. Then one Chinese worker got in. Only the bravest, smallest, and lightest—and probably often the youngest—were chosen to be "basket men." Once seated, they were lowered over the cliff ledge on long ropes. Trying not to look down, they swayed in the wind like spiders on long strands along the cliff faces, sometimes bumping into one another. When they reached the level of the railroad bed to be blasted, they grabbed a twig or branch to steady the basket, chipped a hole into the cliff with a small ax, inserted gunpowder into the hole, and lit a fuse. When the fuse caught, the worker in the basket waved frantically for his partners above to pull him up, crying out for them to hurry. Some didn't wait and shinnied up the ropes before the rock exploded in a shower of stone. Some didn't make it. All summer and fall the boys and men worked the face of the cliff. It took three hundred basket men and boys ten days to blast a single mile of railroad bed at Cape Horn Pass.

When the transcontinental railroad was finished in 1869, most Chinese workers were left on their own without a job or future. Though some twelve hundred Chinese workers had died, they received little recognition for having conquered the Sierra and done the hardest work of the project. Some tried to find work with other railroad companies, while others returned to San Francisco. Railroad work had not prepared them to be houseboys like Ng Poon Chew or Lee Chew, so they looked for work in factories. Some decided it was enough to have wrestled both the Sierra Nevada and Gold Mountain. They tucked their savings into their traveling blouses and went home.

### WHAT HAPPENED TO NG POON CHEW AND LEE CHEW?

Ng Poon Chew survived many hard times, including the deliberate burning of his school, before becoming the first Chinese Presbyterian minister on the Pacific Coast. Lee Chew saved his houseboy's wages and opened a laundry business for railroad workers. Then he moved to New York City, where he bought his own laundry shop in Chinatown.

*"I never had a boyhood."*

# Teddy Blue Abbott: Cowpuncher

*Texas to Nebraska, 1871–1878*

*Between the end of the Civil War and the 1890s, cowpunchers pushed millions of balky cows, bulls, longhorn steers, and horses from Texas north to the new railroads. There the animals were jammed into boxcars and sent to slaughterhouses to feed the masses in eastern cities. Many cowboys were former Confederate soldiers still hungry for action. Their lives were so hard that two out of three never went on the trail again after their first time. But boys throughout the country yearned to become cowboys, and some had their dreams come true. One was Teddy Abbott, a frail ten-year-old boy born in England and brought to Nebraska in 1871 by his parents. Soon after arriving, his dad went to Texas and bought a herd of cattle. Teddy got to go with the cowpunchers who drove them north to his father's ranch.*

*One afternoon in 1876, sixteen-year-old Teddy Abbott (above) staggered drunk out of a saloon and paid a photographer to take his picture. His mother hated it. Three years later he bought new clothes, slicked down his hair, and tried to make up with a new photo (below).*

"I was the poorest, sickliest kid you ever saw, all eyes, no flesh on me whatever," Teddy Abbott wrote. "If I hadn't have been a cowpuncher I never would have growed up. The doctor told my mother to 'keep him in the open air.' She kept me there, all right, or fate did. All my life."

Even at the age of ten, Teddy had troubles with his father. Mr. Abbott was a distant man, absorbed in his already mounting business losses. As they drove the cattle north along the broken, treeless trail, he had little to say to Teddy except to give him orders and bawl him out for one mistake or another. When they came to the first dangerous crossing, at the Red River, Mr. Abbott decided it was time to make a "man" out of Teddy.

"[My father] said he was to tie me to my horse to cross the Red River, so if the horse drowned I'd be sure to drown too. I kicked like a steer, as I could swim, and the rest of the men talked him out of it."

When they got back to Nebraska, Teddy's father ordered him to take care of the cattle. Since Mr. Abbott knew little about livestock, Teddy had to learn on his own. That was fine with him.

"In the summer [the cattle] were turned out on the range and I was out there with them, living in camp ten miles from home and cooking my own grub like a man. That was

## THE GREAT BUFFALO SLAUGHTER

As the range filled up with white settlers and their cattle, buffalo nearly disappeared. When Lewis and Clark explored the West, from 1804 to 1806, there were about sixty million buffalo. The animals gave Plains Indians food, shelter, clothing, beds, blankets, fuel, strings for bows, glue, thread, saddle coverings, even boats. But just fifty years later two-thirds of the buffalo were gone. After the railroads came, the land stank of rotting buffalo meat. Passengers shot them from train windows. President Teddy Roosevelt once spoke of a friend who rode all the way across Montana and "was never out of sight of a dead buffalo, and never in sight of a live one." By 1883, only a few buffalo survived in parks. Below are an estimated 40,000 hides purchased for a Dodge city firm in 1874.

how I got to be so friendly with Texas cowpunchers and tried to be just like them . . . One of the Texas fellows gave me my first six-shooter when I was about thirteen. The cylinder was burnt out, and he said, 'Promise me you'll never load it' . . . but one day I had it home, and my older brother Frank got hold of it, and he loaded it though I told him not to. It pretty near blew his hand off . . . My father found out and took it outside and smashed it with an ax. As soon as I could I got another one."

Though he was young, Teddy developed a reputation for understanding the Nebraska range and being good with cattle. Each summer the cowpunchers came up from Texas, driving cattle to the B&M railroad in Lincoln. Teddy started a business, charging local ranchers $1.50 per animal to take care of their cattle and helping the Texans get their cattle to the trains. These long drives made him even tougher:

"There never was enough sleep. Our day wouldn't end until about nine o'clock, when we grazed the herd onto the bed ground. After that [we] had to stand two hours of night guard . . . Sometimes we would rub tobacco juice in our eyes to keep awake. It was like rubbing them with fire . . . The cook yelled 'roll out' at half past three. I would get maybe five hours' sleep when the weather was nice. If it wasn't so nice you'd be lucky to sleep an hour. But the wagon rolled on in the morning just the same."

When Teddy was fifteen, three Texans hired him to help deliver a herd of five hundred cows to a Nebraska rancher. On that job he got his first look at every cowpuncher's nightmare—a stampede:

"That night it come up an awful storm. It took all four of us to hold the cattle and we didn't hold them, and when morning come there was one man missing. We went back to look for him, and we found him among the prairie dog holes, beside his horse. The horse's ribs was scraped bare of hide, and all the rest of horse and man was mashed into the ground as flat as a pancake. The only thing you could recognize was the handle of his six-shooter . . . I'm afraid his horse stepped into one of them holes and they both went down before the stampede . . . After that, orders were given to sing when you were running with a stampede so the others would know where you were."

Teddy began to spend his nights in the saloons of Lincoln, Nebraska. His pockets were stuffed with the silver dollars he had earned with his own hard work. He tried to impress men at the bars by buying them round after round of whiskey, and they felt no guilt about

*On the trail*

soaking up a boy's pay. One day when he was sixteen, Teddy staggered out of a saloon and hired a photographer to take his picture. It shows a boy with a sagging face, half-closed eyes, and a cigar jammed in his mouth.

A preacher went to warn Mr. Abbott that Teddy was on the wrong path. "My old man went up in the air . . . But what could he expect? He'd kept me out there with the cattle, living with all those men, and all they'd talk about was bucking horses and shooting scrapes and women. I never had but three winters at school, and they was only parts of winters. I was a man from the time I was twelve years old—doing a man's work, living with men, having men's ideas."

At the end of his seventeenth summer, Teddy came home from his camp on the range, his pockets jingling with silver dollars. He was very proud of himself. His father didn't even look up. He told Teddy, "You can take old Morgan and Kit and Charlie and plow the west ridge tomorrow." That was it. Instead, Teddy took off. He stopped in town and bought a bed, a tent, three horses, and a gun. Then he rode all the way to Austin, Texas, and hired on with a trail outfit to help drive seven thousand wild horses back north.

It took nearly a year to get back to Nebraska. After a lot of thought, Teddy decided to visit his family. He wanted to show his mother that he had amounted to something. First he stopped in town and bought some new clothes and had another picture taken for her, to wipe away the memory of the old one. He loved the way it turned out. "I had a new white Stetson hat that I paid ten dollars for and new pants that cost twelve dollars, and a good shirt and fancy boots. They had colored tops, red, white and blue, with a half-moon and star on them. Lord, I was proud of those clothes! They were the kind of clothes top hands wore, and I thought I was dressed right for the first time in my life."

But the visit went sour from the start: "When I got there and my sister saw me she said, 'Take your pants out of your boots and put your coat on. You look like an outlaw.' " It didn't take Teddy long to head back for the trail.

## WHAT HAPPENED TO TEDDY ABBOTT?

He became a well-known Montana rancher, songwriter, and western storyteller. When Teddy was an old man, a writer described him like this: "Today he is seventy-eight years old, tough as whipcord, diamond-clear as to memory and boiling with energy. He can ride me into the ground any day."

*"I tried praying to Jesus for candy and oranges."*

# Chuka: "I Did Not Want My Shirt Taken from My Back"

Arizona, 1899

*By 1877, there were forty whites for every Indian in the West. Up until 1890, whites and Indians struggled to control the same land, with Indians steadily losing ground. In battle after battle, U.S. army units, filled with Civil War veterans, gunned down Indian men, women, and children. Indians were herded onto government-controlled "agencies" and then given reservations on the poorest land.*

*Scholars and government officials debated what to do about the "Indian problem." Some, like Civil War hero William Tecumseh Sherman, thought it best that they be put to death. A group of white church leaders and government officials who called themselves Friends of the Indian had a different idea. Starting in 1883, they set up nearly two hundred Indian schools around the nation. Children as young as five were taken from their families and sent off to learn the ways of whites. One was a stout, curious Hopi Indian boy whose people lived in the high desert near the Grand Canyon. His name was Chuka, which means "Mud." As an adult, he wrote about what going to an Indian school had been like.*

"I grew up believing that whites are wicked, deceitful people. It seemed that most of them were soldiers, government agents or missionaries, and that quite a few were Two-Hearts. The old people said that the whites were tough, possessed dangerous weapons, and were better protected than we were from evil spirits and poison arrows."

When Chuka was small, a school run by white missionaries was opened at the foot of a mesa in New Oraibi, where he lived. One September morning he watched as his older sister became the first in his family to go down the hill to the school. He was shocked when she returned:

"The teacher cut her hair, burned all her clothes, and gave her a new outfit and a new name, Nellie. She stopped going after a few weeks, and tried to keep out of sight of the whites who might force her to return. About a year later she was captured by the school principal [who] compelled her to return to school. The teacher had forgotten her old name and called

her Gladys. Although my brother was two years older than I, he managed to keep out of school until about a year after I started, but he had to be careful not to be seen by whites. When finally he did enter the day school at New Oraibi, they cut his hair, burned his clothes and named him Ira."

When Chuka was nine, it was his turn. He made up his mind to go to school on his own terms: "I did not want a policeman to come for me and I did not want my shirt taken from my back and burned. So one morning in September I left it off, wrapped myself in my Navajo blanket, the one my grandfather had given me, and went down the mesa barefoot and bareheaded.

"I reached the school late and entered a room where boys had bathed in tubs of dirty water. Laying aside my blanket, I stepped into a tub and began scrubbing myself. Suddenly a white woman entered the room, threw up her hands and exclaimed, 'On my life!' I jumped out of the tub, grabbed my blanket and started back up the mesa at full speed . . . Boys were sent to catch me and take me back. They told me that the woman was not angry and that 'On my life!' meant that she was surprised. They returned with me to the building, where the same woman met me with kind words that I could not understand . . . She cut my hair, measured me for a good fitting suit, called me Max, and told me through an interpreter to leave my blanket and go out to play with the other boys."

## HOPI GAMES

Most of Chuka's time was spent in play until he went to school. "We shot arrows at targets, played old Hopi checkers, and pushed feather-edged sticks into corncobs and threw them at rolling hoops of cornhusks. We wrestled, ran races, played tag, kickball, stick throwing and shinny. We spun tops with whips and made string figures on our fingers. Another game I liked was making Hopi firecrackers. I mixed burro and horse dung, burned a lump of it into a red glow, placed the coal on a flat rock, and hit it with a cow horn dipped in urine. It went 'bang' like a gun."

The lessons Chuka learned in school seemed strange: "The first thing I learned in school was 'nail,' a hard word to remember. Every day when we entered the classroom a nail lay on the desk. The teacher would take it up and say, 'What is this?' Finally I answered 'nail' ahead of the other boys and was called 'bright' . . . I learned little at school the first year except 'bright boy,' 'smart boy,' 'yes' and 'no,' 'nail,' and 'candy.' "

When Chuka was eleven, he switched to a boarding school a two days' burro ride away from home. His mother and father rode to school with him and dropped him off. When they mounted up to return home, his father gave him some parting advice: Don't run away, he said, because "we would not know where to find you and the coyotes might eat you." And then they were gone. A teacher cut his summer hair again and gave him new clothes. When he did not answer to the name Max, they called him Don. He gave up and tried to think of himself as Don. His confidence faded. He had been a big, tough boy at home, but now he lost fights. The food tasted terrible— hash, prunes, and tea. The matron told him to pray to Jesus each night, so he cupped his hands and prayed for oranges and candy but none came down from the sky. Sometimes in the evenings he and a friend climbed a high hill and looked out over the land. On the clearest days he could faintly see his mesa. Especially at these times, he longed with all his heart to go home.

*The same Navajo boy, now called Thomas Torlino, a short time after enrolling at the Indian school at Carlisle, Pennsylvania, in 1886*

## A Boy Who Grew Old Too Early

Crow Foot was born in 1876, on the eve of the last major Indian victory over whites, the battle of the Little Big Horn. He was the son of Sitting Bull, the greatest of Sioux chiefs. Crow Foot spent his youth fleeing with his family from U.S. soldiers who wanted to capture his father for his role at Little Big Horn. He deeply admired his father.

"Crow Foot was not like the rest of the boys," wrote one who met him. "He grew old too early. He did not get out and mingle with the boys and play their games. He was more with the old men . . . [They were] training him for the chieftainship." When food ran low, Sitting Bull reluctantly surrendered. But instead of giving his rifle to army troops, he handed it to Crow Foot, saying, "This boy wants to know how he will make a living."

Crow Foot went to a white boarding school at the Standing Rock reservation, but he had little use for white ways. In 1890, Sitting Bull prepared to travel to the Pine Ridge reservation to find out more about the Ghost Dance, a new religion that he hoped could revive the old Indian ways. The Indian agent at Standing Rock ordered forty policemen to stop him. Heavily armed, they burst into the family's home at dawn. Crow Foot, then fourteen, urged his father to resist. Minutes later, both father and son were shot dead.

In June, his father came for him and he returned home. Riding through the desert on the burro, he thought about what he had learned in his two years of white education: "I had learned many English words and could recite part of the Ten Commandments. I knew how to sleep on a bed, pray to Jesus, comb my hair, eat with a knife and fork, and use a toilet. I had learned that the world is round instead of flat, that it is indecent to go naked in the presence of girls . . . I had also learned that a person thinks with his head instead of his heart."

He went home for the summer and helped his father hoe weeds and tend sheep. As the third school year approached, Chuka's grandfather worried that Chuka was losing his Hopi ways. The old man reminded him to spit four times if he had bad dreams while at school. That would drive evil influences from his head. One morning in September, Chuka was preparing to set off for school when armed police appeared and surrounded his village.

"Their intention was capturing the children of Hostile families and taking them to school by force. They herded us all together at the east edge of the mesa. Although I had planned to go later, they put me with the others. The people were excited, the children and the mothers were crying, and the men wanted to fight. I was not much afraid because I had learned a little about education . . . The next morning we took a bath, had our hair clipped, put on new clothes and were schoolboys again."

## WHAT HAPPENED TO CHUKA?

Throughout his life he struggled to live in two worlds. He took the name Don Talayesva for whites but kept his Indian name and belief in Hopi customs. He was such a good student of English that he was able to co-write his autobiography. He lived to be an old man and stayed in his village of New Oraibi. When his uncle died, Chuka became a tribal official. He married and had four children. To his great sorrow, each of them died as a baby.

*A classroom at the Riverside Indian School at Anadarko, Oklahoma, in 1901*

# PART SEVEN

# Shifting Gears in a New Century

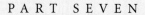

American cities sizzled with energy in the first years of the twentieth century. Overnight, dirt roads became rowdy neighborhood streets filled with farm families, immigrants, and African Americans from the South who poured into cities. In 1908, a young Brooklyn teacher described her third-grade class in a letter to her mother: "There are twenty-eight students. Six speak English, and the rest speak eight other languages, of which I know a few words of only three. We use sign language and get along as best we can."

New inventions changed the way nearly everyone lived. Between 1875 and 1925, Americans were introduced to electric lights, movies, radios, telephones, bicycles, airplanes, subway trains, typewriters, washers, dryers, irons, refrigerators, cars, and tractors. Engineers used new ways of making steel to send buildings up into the clouds and stretch bridges across even the widest rivers. They built one steamship that was four blocks long. It was called the *Titanic*.

By 1880, nearly 20 percent of all workers were fifteen or younger. "The most beautiful sight we see is a child at labor," said the founder of the Coca-Cola Company. Families came to depend on the incomes of children, who worked long hours and struggled to stay awake as increasingly powerful machines ground on. "We don't have many accidents," one mill owner told a government investigator. "Once in a while a hand gets mashed, or a foot, but it doesn't amount to anything."

The children fought back. Young millworkers, stitchers, miners, and newsboys—even golf caddies—joined and led strikes for higher pay, shorter hours, and safer conditions. It may be that young Americans never worked or played harder, or suffered more, than in the tough, raucous years of the early twentieth century.

*Boys working the night shift at Indiana Glassworks in 1908*

*"One hundred Forty-fourth Street between Brook and Willis Avenues was all America to us."*—Jimmy Savo, born in 1895 in the Bronx

# Gene Schermerhorn: A New City Every Day

New York City, 1848–1922

*The New York City neighborhood that Gene Schermerhorn moved into as a boy in 1848 seemed like another planet when he revisited it at the end of the century.*

When young Gene Schermerhorn moved to Twenty-third Street in New York City in 1848, his favorite game was to try to lasso the pigs from the farm next door as they ran squealing between the apple trees that lined muddy Sixth Avenue. In the evenings he flew kites and played baseball in front of his house with his father and uncle. But before long a new law was passed that forbade kite-flying in the street. City officials explained that it was important to keep string from getting tangled up on the new poles and wires. Then Gene's street was paved, and after that his family had to move so his house could make way for a brick building with plate-glass windows.

The changes were almost too fast to keep up with. The cattle barn across the street turned into an apartment building. Horse-drawn carriages gave way to railroad tracks on Fourth Avenue. Then, in 1883, a new bridge over the East River connected Manhattan and Brooklyn. To prove that it was safe, circus master P. T. Barnum led a herd of elephants across the Brooklyn Bridge. The same year, electric streetlights pushed back the darkness on Pearl Street in lower Manhattan, allowing children to stay out and play longer.

Games changed to fit new spaces. Back on Twenty-third Street, there had been enough room for Gene and his friends to play "how many miles," a game in which marbles were shot across a great ring of smooth dirt in his road. But in his new neighborhood, there was only space to shoot through "a little spot of bare earth about two feet by four."

Some young New Yorkers took advantage of the changes. An unfinished bridge could be a perfect winter sledding hill. Young people swung on wrecking balls after the construction workers went home and wrenched open fire hydrants to cool off the block in summer. Apartment windows became launching pads for matchstick airplanes and water balloons. Anything could be a baseball field; comedian George Burns remembered his: "A

In 1909 Lewis Hine photographed this game of baseball in a city alley.

manhole cover was home plate, a fire hydrant was first base, second base was a lamppost and Mr. Gitletz, who used to bring a kitchen chair down to watch us play, was third base."

Younger children began to ask for store-bought toys instead of the toys family members made for them. In its 1874 catalog, R. H. Macy's department store advertised dolls made in thirteen different countries. One jump-rope rhyme, probably made up by a disappointed girl whose family couldn't afford to buy a doll, went:

*I won't go to Macy's any more, more, more*
*There's a big fat policeman at the door, door, door*
*He'll grab you by the collar and make you pay a dollar.*
*I won't go to Macy's any more, more, more.*

With no pools or lakes, children plunged into fast-moving, increasingly filthy rivers. Willie Sutton, who became a famous jewel thief, remembered that as a boy, "We swam through the raw, untreated garbage [of New York's East River] . . . We dove off the cargo barges . . . Before I was out of my early teens I was swimming [from Brooklyn] to Manhattan and back with such ease that I was able to rescue friends of mine who couldn't make it."

> ### TRAFFIC WARS
>
> Some children waged war against cars by controlling traffic lights with mirrors that reflected the sun's rays. "You could focus the reflection on to the red . . . or green," wrote Julius Sokolsky of the Bronx. "We'd keep them there for five minutes, and see the drivers get all frustrated."

In 1887, when Gene Schermerhorn was forty-five, he took a walk through his old neighborhood. He could barely recognize it. "It seems hard to believe that Twenty-third Street could have changed so much," he wrote when he got home. "The rural scenes, the open spaces have vanished; and the small and quiet residences, many of them built entirely of wood, have given place to huge piles of brick and stone, and to iron and plate-glass fronts of the stores which now line the street." Worst of all, workers had filled in Beekman's Pond, his old swimming hole, to make Madison Avenue.

Even bigger changes lay ahead. In 1902, developers finished one of the world's tallest buildings on the block where Gene grew up. It was a twenty-two-

*One of New York's first skyscrapers, completed in 1902, was the Flatiron Building, rising twenty-two stories from former pastureland at Fifth Avenue and Twenty-third Street. It's still there.*

story skyscraper called the Flatiron Building, shaped like a giant slice of pie. In the years that followed, street after street was paved for use by automobiles. The results were tragic. In 1922, the year Gene Schermerhorn died, 477 New York children were killed by cars. That summer, fifteen hundred angry young New Yorkers marched up Fifth Avenue to rally for safer streets. But nothing could stop the automobile. Parked cars soon lined the city streets. New roads sliced through meadows and fields. One young New Yorker named Michael Gold later wrote of his neighborhood: "We defended our playground through force of arms but the Schiff Parkway was an opponent we could not defeat."

## WHAT HAPPENED TO GENE SCHERMERHORN?

He became an important fire department official in New York City. He remained a walker and a lover of New York's streets, neighborhoods, and history throughout his life. Though he had no children of his own, he wrote letters about the city of his youth to his young nephew Phil so that the boy would have an idea of what New York had once been like. Gene Schermerhorn died at the age of eighty.

*"I am the new feller hand."*

# Rose Cohen: First Day in a Sweatshop

Russia and New York City, 1892

*Rose Cohen grew up in a tiny Russian village where Jewish life was brutally controlled by the army of the czar. Jews were forced to live within a barren region that stretched from the Baltic Sea to the Black Sea. Rose's father fled to America, bribing troops at the border to let him pass. Rose heard nothing more from him until the day in 1892 when she received a package covered with mysterious stamps. Inside were two steamship tickets to America—one for Rose, then twelve, and one for her aunt, a few years older. Her father sent for Rose first because he had taught her to sew. She could help him make enough money in New York to send for the others. Rose's father met her ship in New York City and then led her to their new home—a grimy tenement on the Lower East Side. Like many immigrants before and after them, father and daughter vowed that they would work hard so that next year at that time the family would all be together. Rose Cohen wrote of her first two days in a New York sweatshop.*

*European immigrants like Rose Cohen bundled all their belongings onto ships like this one bound for America.*

## A CLOCK THAT CALLS

"Often I get there soon after six o'clock so as to be in good time, though the factory does not open till seven. I have heard that there is a sort of clock that calls you at the very time you want to get up, but I can't believe that because I don't see how the clock would know."

—Sadie Frowne, sixteen, a sweatshop worker born in Poland

"About the same time that the bitter cold came, father told me one night that he had found work for me in a shop where he knew the presser. I lay awake long that night. I was eager to begin life on my own responsibility but was also afraid. We rose earlier than usual that morning for father had to take me to the shop and not be late for his own work. I wrapped my thimble and scissors, with a piece of bread for breakfast, in a bit of newspaper, carefully stuck two needles into the lapel of my coat and we started.

"The shop was on Pelem Street, a shop district one block long and just wide enough for two ordinary sized wagons to pass each other . . . Father said, 'good-bye' over his shoulder and went away quickly. I watched him until he turned onto Monroe Street.

"I found a door, and pushed it open and went in. A tall, dark, beardless man stood folding coats at a table . . . 'Yes,' he said crossly. 'What do you want?'

"I said, 'I am the new feller hand.' He looked at me from head to foot. My face felt so burning hot I could scarcely see. 'It is more likely,' he said, 'that you can pull bastings than fell sleeve

*A sweatshop on New York City's Lower East Side*

lining.' Then turning from me he shouted over the noise of the machine: 'Presser, is this the girl?' The presser put down the iron and looked at me. 'I suppose so,' he said. 'I only know the father.'

"The cross man said, 'Let's see what you can do.' He kicked a chair, threw a coat upon it and said, 'Make room for the new feller hand.' One girl tittered, two men glanced at me over their shoulders and pushed their chairs apart a little . . . All at once the thought came, 'If I don't [sew] this coat quickly and well he will send me away at once.' I picked up the coat, threaded my needle and began hastily, repeating the lesson father impressed upon me: 'Be careful not to twist the sleeve lining, take small false stitches.' "

The man inspected the sleeve and then silently tossed Rose two other coats to sew. She reached her apartment well after dark. She went back out the next day before the light of dawn. Everyone was already at their stations. The boss bawled her out for being late. This is not an office, he told her. She bent down low and began to work.

"From this hour a hard life began for me. [The boss] refused to employ me except by the week. He paid me three dollars and for this he hurried me from early until late . . . He was never satisfied. By looks and manner he made me feel that I was not doing enough. Late at night when the people would stand up and begin to fold their work away . . . he would come over with still another coat. 'I need it first thing in the morning,' he would give as an excuse. I understood that he was taking advantage of me because I was a child. And now that it was dark in the shop except for the low single gas jet over my table and the one over his at the other end of the room, and there was no one to see, more tears fell on the sleeve lining than there were stitches in it.

"[When I got home] my father explained, 'It pays him better to employ you by the week. Don't you see if you did piece work [and got paid for each coat] he would have to pay you as much as he pays a woman piece worker? But this way he gets almost as much work out of you for half the amount a woman is paid.'

"I myself did not want to leave the shop for fear of losing a day or even more perhaps in finding other work. To lose half a dollar meant that it would take so much longer before mother and the children would come . . . Often as the hour for going home drew near I would make believe they were home waiting. On leaving the shop I would hasten along through the street keeping my eyes on the ground so as to shut out everything but what I wanted to see. I pictured myself walking into the house. There was a delicious warm smell of cooked food. Mother greeted me near the door and the children gathered about me shouting and trying to pull me down. Mother scolded them saying, 'Let her take her coat

## SWEATSHOPS

Clothing workers filled factories called sweatshops on New York's Lower East Side. Workers made dresses and shirts and coats in an assembly line, the way cars are made. A worker finished one part and then passed the garment on to the next worker. A boss stood behind, nagging. Most workers smoked, so a thick blue haze hung over the shop. A peddler brought in beer and whiskey from time to time. Some Jewish women sang songs in Yiddish as they worked, but always, always they bent over their garments.

off, see how cold her hands are!' I used to keep this up until I turned the key in the door and opened it and stood facing the dark, cold silent room."

## WHAT HAPPENED TO ROSE COHEN?

She kept working in shops and helped make enough money to send for the rest of her family. She became a union leader and organizer. She refused to marry a man her father had picked for her and later married Joseph Cohen. When their daughter Evelyn was born, Rose stopped working in sweatshops. She took writing classes and followed her passion, writing. She wrote five short articles and a book about her life. All were praised. She died in 1925.

———◆◆◆———

*"Mom, I'm not going back tomorrow to work."*

# Joseph Miliauskas: Breaker Boy

Scranton, Pennsylvania, 1900

*Joseph Miliauskas's family emigrated from Lithuania in 1900. They settled near Scranton, Pennsylvania, so his father could mine coal. Joseph, not yet ten, begged his parents to let him work, too. Finally they gave in and let him begin as a "breaker boy." Early each morning he picked up his lunch bucket and proudly walked to the tallest building in the colliery—or coal factory. He sat down on a wooden board in a row behind several other boys. At 7 A.M. a belt clicked on and a river of coal chunks began to tumble down toward them. A rising cloud of coal dust soon blackened their skin and clothes. It was far too noisy to talk. There wasn't even time to straighten their backs, and many breaker boys ended up with curved spines. Joseph later recalled that he earned seventy cents a day for his labor.*

"There were five slate pickers on our chute. The last one was the cleaner. He got one cent more than the boys in front of him. It was up to us to watch and pick the slate [rock that couldn't be burned] out. We had to throw it to the side and let the clean coal go down.

"The boss was behind us with a broom and if he caught you slipping up and letting some slate come down, boy, you'd get it in the back with a broom. Oh, he'd sock you. If you were the first one, and if you don't throw [out] much slate, he'd come back up of you and let you have it . . . Sometimes when the boss wasn't looking we let more of it go through. Usually he was there though watching you and he'd slam you with the broom.

"[My] second day [on the job] my fingers were all cut up and bleeding. I asked the boss if I could go home and he hit me with the broom and said, 'Stay there.' Twelve o'clock came and the whistle blew. I took my dinner pail out and went home. I come home and said to my mother, 'Mom, I'm not going back tomorrow to work anymore. My fingers are all bloody.' 'Oh, yes you are,' she said. 'We didn't tell you to get this job. You got it on your own. You started it; you're going to stay with it.' So I stayed home that afternoon and then went back. [After] you're there two or three weeks, your fingers get hardened up. No more blood. You get used to it."

## "I COULD NOT DO THAT WORK AND LIVE"

In 1905, a writer named John Spargo tried to do a breaker boy's work in a Pennsylvania mine. He lasted only half an hour. He wrote, "I tried to pick out the pieces of slate from the hurrying stream of coal, often missing them; my hands were bruised and cut in a few minutes; I was covered from head to foot with coal dust and for many hours afterwards I was spitting out some of the small particles of [coal] I had swallowed. I could not do that work and live."

The breaker boys looked for chances to get back at the bosses who beat them. Sometimes they fired pieces of coal at a boss who turned his back. When they really got mad, they jammed the machinery with pieces of board or rock, bringing the whole factory to a standstill. But getting caught meant big trouble at home, since no one got paid when the machines were down. For Joseph, the best part about being a breaker boy was lunch:

"[We] worked from seven to noon, then a half hour to eat, then back to work till 5:30. [When the noon whistle blew for lunch] we ate our sandwiches in no time, then started playing tag. We knew every hole in that breaker, and we'd hide and go through in complete darkness. We'd go over the machinery and around it. You get to know it because everything stops during lunch hour. We got to know it like a bunch of rats."

When he turned twelve, Joseph became a "nipper" in the underground mines. All he had to do was sit on a bench outside the door and open it when he heard a train or a mule coming with a coal car from another part of the mine, and then close it again. At last he was free of noise, dust, and bosses. He fed crumbs of bread to the rats that kept him

*Young mule drivers at work. Mules lived in stables deep in the mines, where the boys fed them, combed them, cleaned up after them, and treated them as pets.*

company and made friends with the mules that hauled coal cars along the underground railroad tracks. It was warm and peaceful deep inside the earth. But Joseph soon found out how important it was to stay alert.

"Once I got up a little late and missed the cage that took us down the shaft to work . . . I got there late, but thank God, there were no empty cars and nothing had come through [my door]. I was all wet with perspiration. I stretched out on my bench, put my lamp along side of me, and fell asleep. First thing I knew I heard a bang and I jumped up. The bib to my overalls was on fire [from the lamp] and there was my door on top of a loaded car . . . A short time later [the boss] came through. I told him the whole story of how I got up late. All he said was, 'Well, Joe, be a little more careful.' "

## WHAT HAPPENED TO JOSEPH MILIAUSKAS?

Unlike most of his friends, Joseph left the mines after being a nipper. He went to school and became a Roman Catholic priest in a Pennsylvania coal town. He lived into his seventies.

### MULE DRIVERS

Nippers usually went on to become mule drivers when they were about thirteen. Mule drivers sat on the front bumper of a coal car and commanded the mule with words and a whip to pull the car along the underground railroad tracks. Sometimes a mule would obey only one particular boy. Most boys loved their mules. Often a driver gave up part of his lunch to his mule, and he would even break off plugs of tobacco and jam half into his mule's mouth. The mule drivers' favorite song began:

*My sweetheart's the mule in the mines*
*I drive her without reins or lines*
*On the bumper I sit*
*I chew and I spit*
*All over my sweetheart's behind.*

———✦✦✦———

*"We are not just fighting for ourselves, but for decent conditions for workers everywhere."*

# Jennie Curtis: Strike Leader

Pullman, Illinois, 1893–1894

*George Pullman invented a luxurious sleeping car for railroad passengers.*
*His company took off in 1865, when a Pullman car was attached to the funeral train*
*carrying Abraham Lincoln's body. After that, Americans dreamed of riding in style.*
*Pullman built an entire town near Chicago for the workers who manufactured his cars.*
*He seemed to take care of their every need. But when the company's fortunes sagged,*
*life for a Pullman worker became brutally hard. One fearless teenage girl sparked*
*a demand for justice in one of America's most famous strikes.*

*Inside a Pullman Palace Car. For a few dollars more, one could cross the prairie in style, sleeping on a pull-down bed and eating good meals served on white linen tablecloths.*

Jennie Curtis started life in a squalid Chicago tenement with her parents and little sister. Her father, Alexander Curtis, could barely make enough as a peddler in Chicago's downtown streets to keep them alive. And then one evening he came home red-faced and talking fast. A dream had come true! He had a new job with the Pullman Palace Car Company, the one that made fancy railroad cars. They were moving to Pullman Village, the new town Mr. Pullman had built just for his workers. Now they would live in a two-story house with a private entrance and a backyard. There would be hot and cold running water and gas for cooking. Every day someone would come to pick up the garbage!

Pullman Village was amazing. There were theaters, a library, and a hotel—all just for the Curtises and their neighbors. They chose the biggest and most expensive of the three kinds of houses offered, even though the rent ate up nearly half of Mr. Curtis's paycheck and meant he had to work nearly all the time he was awake. Jennie's mother made the children's clothes to save money and they planted a vegetable garden.

Jennie liked Pullman well enough, but she knew it wasn't a paradise. The company controlled everything. It set the prices everyone had to pay for food, rent, and heat. Living in Pullman was more expensive than in Chicago, and there were company spies everywhere. Mr. Pullman kept calling the residents his "children."

Jennie went to work for Pullman when she was thirteen. At first she worked in the room where they sewed fancy carpets and draperies for the sleeping cars. The work was boring. She hated the long hours, but the pay was good—$2.25 a day. She kept telling herself that she was making good wages for a girl.

But in 1893, the American economy collapsed and orders for luxury railroad cars dropped. Pullman slashed everyone's wages again and again, but his rent and prices for heat and food stayed high. Children walked barefooted through his wide streets, and the big houses turned cold when renters couldn't afford heat. Jennie's wages were cut twice in a single week. Soon she was making only eighty cents a day. When she complained, she was transferred to the repair shop, where it was even harder to make good money.

One of the seamstresses was assigned to supervise the others. The woman seemed to change overnight with her new authority. Jennie wrote: "She had sewed and lived among us for years . . . You would think she would have compassion on us . . . [but] she seemed to delight in showing her power in hurting the girls in every possible way . . . She was getting $2.25 a day and she did not care how much we girls made, whether we made enough to live on or not, just so long as she could figure how to save a few dollars for the Company."

Jennie organized a petition to have the supervisor removed. After fifteen of eighteen girls and women signed it, Jennie took it to the superintendent. He ignored it, but he began to look at Jennie Curtis as a troublemaker.

Then Jennie's world collapsed. Her father died after a long illness. Alexander Curtis had worked for Pullman for thirteen years. The company reacted by informing Jennie that her dad still owed them sixty dollars for rent and it was up to her to pay it. They would be taking money from her weekly paycheck until the debt was paid. At first she tried to keep up the payments, just so her family could stay in their house, but it got to be too much. Trips to the bank grew ugly. Jennie wrote: "When I could not possibly give them anything, I would receive slurs and insults from the clerks in the back, because Mr. Pullman would not give me enough in return for my hard labor to pay the rent for one of his houses and live."

Jennie's co-workers depended on her more and more as times got worse at Pullman. They recognized her as a leader. She kept her cool under fire even when she was angry. Though she was young, she always seemed to find the words to express what they all felt. Many Pullman workers were signing up for the American Railway Union (ARU), led by a brilliant organizer named Eugene V. Debs. The Pullman company hated the ARU, which threatened its control. At first Jennie wasn't convinced they needed a union

## PULLMAN PALACE CARS

Suppose you need to travel from Omaha to Sacramento in 1875. You could pay forty dollars and sit on a hard bench for most of a week. You could pay seventy-five dollars for a little more room, but you would still be eating stringy buffalo steak for dinner. Or—for just four more dollars a night—you could ride in a Pullman Palace Car. Now, when dinnertime comes, your waiter unfolds an embroidered white tablecloth and serves you fresh trout with lemon and melted butter. After dessert he lights the reading lamp and you settle in with a good book while people gather round the organ and sing. You hum along until you become drowsy, and then fold your seat down into a soft bed and pull your curtain around you. You douse the light and watch the moon gleam on the rails until prairie dreams overtake you.

at Pullman. She thought the company might still listen to reason. In May of 1894, she and four other leaders went to see the company superintendent, Thomas Wickes, in his paneled office. They demanded the company either restore their full pay or cut rents in Pullman Village. Wickes barely looked up from his desk. Three of the five workers were fired after the meeting. Jennie was allowed to keep her job, perhaps because she still owed the company money.

The very next day Jennie signed her American Railway Union card and was quickly elected president of the Girls' Union, Local 269. Only eighteen, she now spoke for thousands of women at Pullman. Jennie and other union leaders went to Chicago in June to urge the ARU to support the Pullman workers in a strike against the company. Thin and tired, Jennie stood up in a downtown union hall and addressed 450 ARU delegates. The room fell silent as she explained that some of the women in her sewing room were starving. Tough men wept as she told the story of her father's death and the unpaid debt. When she finished, one of the ARU delegates leaped up and urged a strike. A roar of approval filled the hall. But Debs urged caution. The ARU, he pointed out, was only one year old and still fragile. A loss might further weaken them, and he wasn't convinced they could win against the wealthy railroad managers. Then Jennie rose again to face the delegates. "We ask you to come along with us," she pleaded, "because we are not just fighting for ourselves, but for decent conditions for workers everywhere."

At Debs's urging, the Pullman workers tried twice again to negotiate with the company. It was no use. So they stopped work, and fifty thousand railroad workers throughout the nation joined them. Engineers refused to drive trains carrying Pullman cars. All traffic on the twenty-four railroad lines going out of Chicago stopped. With no cars moving, Pullman's business ground to a standstill. George Pullman himself asked the mayor of Chicago and the governor of Illinois to send police to force the workers back to work. Both refused.

But President Grover Cleveland felt differently. Declaring that the U.S. mail had to keep moving, he sent thousands of federal troops to Illinois. Riots broke out. Thirty strikers were killed and hundreds injured. A federal judge declared all strike activity illegal. Union leaders were arrested, and Eugene Debs was imprisoned. The Pullman strike collapsed in August and the factory reopened, minus one thousand union members who had been fired for taking part in the strike.

## WHAT HAPPENED TO JENNIE CURTIS?

All record of her life after the strike seems to have disappeared. She was probably fired because she was a well-known union member and strike leader. Maybe she changed her name so she could get another railroad job somewhere else. In 1994, there was a gathering in Chicago to honor the one hundredth anniversary of the Pullman strike. Historians scrambled to find any record of the girl whose words had jolted the ARU convention back to life and sparked the strike. All efforts failed. One wrote in tribute, "Perhaps if we try hard enough, we can feel her spirit on this centennial."

*Six hundred freight cars burn on the Panhandle Railroad, July 6, 1894, as striking railroad workers battle federal troops.*

*"Mr. Pulitzer, the people seem to be against us."*

# Kid Blink and the Newsies: Bringing Down Goliaths

New York City, 1899

*William Randolph Hearst and Joseph Pulitzer were two of the richest and most powerful men in America in 1899. Each owned a giant newspaper in New York City, and both competed to grab readers with sensational headlines and extra editions. They depended on a large network of city children and teenagers to get papers to readers. When the two millionaires tried to gouge the "newsies" for a few pennies more, it was nearly their downfall.*

Newsies hollered out the day's headlines from busy street corners and subway entrances, from positions outside the revolving doors of office buildings, and from sidewalks near the lunch counters where secretaries and businesspeople grabbed quick meals. Some newsies stayed on the streets all day long, avoiding school, while others raced to their positions as soon as school was finished. They made their profits by buying papers from the newspaper company and then selling them to readers for a little more, pocketing the difference. They kept about a nickel for every ten papers they sold. If they didn't sell a paper, they had to take the loss. It was a tough deal, but a straight deal: At least a newsie knew what to expect.

The trouble started when Hearst and Pulitzer decided to make up for slow sales by raising the price that newsies had to pay for their papers. They didn't figure boys could do anything about it. They were very wrong. In July of 1899, three hundred newsies gathered in City Hall Park and formed their own union.

*Newsies competed for customers fiercely at each corner and subway entrance, but they banded together as a union when they had to.*

They elected officers and made up committees. They announced that they would refuse to deliver Hearst's *New York Journal* or Pulitzer's *New York World* until their buying price went back to normal. "We're here for our rights and we will die defendin' 'em," explained ten-year-old Boots McAleenan to reporters.

The strike lasted two weeks. The newsies demonstrated at the places where delivery carts usually gave them their bundles of papers. They put signs up on nearby lampposts that read HELP THE NEWSBOYS and OUR CAUSE IS JUST. Their tactics were not gentle: Sometimes hundreds of boys surrounded the carts and threatened the drivers, who quickly tossed the papers over the side and fled. Mobs of boys threw rocks at the men Hearst and Pulitzer hired to replace them. Soon nobody would even pick up the papers for fear of being confronted by angry boys. Police were caught in the middle—the public supported the newsies, but the companies and replacement workers demanded protection. And boys could almost always outrun the police.

*Girls, too, sold papers throughout New England and in major cities to the south.*

The newsboys' strike spread throughout New Jersey, Connecticut, and Massachusetts. As newspaper sales dropped, Pulitzer and Hearst began to lose big money. Advertisers demanded lower rates because of the strike. But other New York newspapers cheerfully made heroes of the newsies. Pulitzer's assistant sent him a worried message: "The people seem to be against us; they are encouraging the boys and tipping them . . . and refraining from buying the papers for fear of having them snatched from their hands."

One summer night the newsies organized a mass rally in lower Manhattan and five thousand boys showed up. A great cheer arose when a leader named Kid Blink vaulted up onto the speakers' platform. He raised his hands for silence and scratched his head as if something were puzzling him. "I'm trying to figure it out," he said, "how ten cents on a hundred papers can mean more to a millionaire than it does to newsboys, and I can't see it." The newsies vowed to continue the strike until they brought Pulitzer and Hearst to their knees.

When sales dropped by two-thirds, Hearst and Pulitzer gave up. They offered a deal that kept the prices the same but let the newsies return unsold papers and get their money back. In the end it meant more money than before. The newsies took it, disbanded their union, and went back to selling papers.

# John Thayer: Becoming a Man
# Aboard the *Titanic*

The Atlantic Ocean, 1,000 miles due east of Boston, April 14–15, 1912

*In April of 1912, seventeen-year-old John Thayer took a trip to Europe with his parents. It was spring break of his last high school year and the number one topic of conversation was his future. His father had it all mapped out for him. The next year John would start at Princeton University, then on to London, Vienna, Paris, and Berlin for an apprenticeship in commercial banking. After that he would manage a bank in the United States. All that was fine with John. He was too excited to think about it now. As he stepped aboard the luxury liner* Titanic *to return home, he was eager to explore the biggest ship in the world.*

John thought the *Titanic* was astounding. It was really a floating city, four blocks long. You could work out in the gymnasium, take steam baths, or lounge around the pool. There were shops everywhere; even the barber shop sold flags from around the world. As a first-class passenger, John could go anywhere and talk to anyone he wanted to, even the ship's owner.

On the evening of Sunday, April 14, after a dinner conversation with a judge's son named Milton Long, John stepped out onto the deck for some fresh air. He later wrote: "There was no moon and I have never seen the stars shine brighter—they sparkled like cut diamonds . . . It was the kind of night that made one glad to be alive." Yawning, he went down to his stateroom, said good night to his parents, and slipped on his pajamas. He was about to climb into bed when he felt the ship sway very slightly. He wrote, "If I had had a brimful glass of water in my hand not a drop would have been spilled."

The engines stopped and then started up again, and he heard voices outside his door. He put on his overcoat and went to the deck to see what was happening. There were chunks of ice scattered about. A crew member told him they had struck an iceberg. The deck seemed to be tilting a little to the right. A few minutes later, John passed the ship's

## BOYS AND MEN

Who was a boy and who was a man? The White Star Line charged anyone fourteen or older an adult fare. But there was no official age for adults when the ship was sinking, and getting a seat on a lifeboat meant the best chance to survive. What happened to teenage boys depended on which officer managed the lifeboat they wanted to enter, whether their families fought for them, how old they looked, and when they tried to enter. At the beginning, even a few dogs were allowed into lifeboats, some of which took off only half-filled. But as time ran out, it got harder and harder to get a place. Thirteen-year-old Jack Ryerson was climbing into boat number four when an officer called out to his parents, "That boy can't go!" Jack's father shouted back, "Of course he can go—that boy is only thirteen." They let him pass, and he survived.

Elsewhere on the ship, a boy in his midteens was discovered hiding in lifeboat number fourteen. An officer named Lowe drew his pistol and ordered him out. The boy wouldn't budge. Lowe switched tactics, telling him to "be a man" and let a woman or younger child into his spot. Finally the officers seized the boy and lifted him from the lifeboat. There is no record of his name or what happened to him.

Some young passengers, like the children of the Sage family, who traveled third class, refused to be separated from their parents. When the oldest daughter, Stella, saw that her mother wasn't following her into the lifeboat, she got out. None of the little children would enter either. All died in the tragedy.

designer, Thomas Andrews, in a corridor. Shaken, Andrews told John he didn't think the ship could float for more than an hour. John's heart began to race. He got dressed, woke his parents, and rushed back to the deck with them to put on life vests and wait for a lifeboat. Milton Long appeared and asked if he could join them.

There was room in the lifeboats for only about half the passengers and crew, so choices had to be made. "Women and children first," people were yelling. John didn't even ask whether he qualified. He could see that much younger boys than he were being kept from the boats. John knew that on this, maybe the last night of his life, he was considered a man.

At 12:45 A.M. John hugged his mother good-bye, watched her step into a lifeboat, and hurried to the deck on the other side of the boat with his father and Milton. The roar of the steam was deafening. Sailors sent rockets arcing high into the sky to try to attract passing ships. The ship's orchestra was still playing in the background. People were screaming. A surging crowd separated John and Milton from John's father.

As one side of the ship continued to list, John and Milton climbed to the upper deck and looked down onto the scene. They

*John Thayer and twenty-seven others clung to this lifeboat after the* Titanic *went down.*

had few choices, and none of them was good. They thought about trying to fight their way aboard one of the last two lifeboats, but it looked like those boats would be crushed under the ship anyway. John wanted to slide down a rope, leap into the water, and swim for a lifeboat, but Milton convinced him to wait to jump until the water was close to the deck. The two climbed onto the deck railing as the water drew nearer. "So many thoughts passed so quickly through my mind! I thought of all the good times I had had, and of all the future pleasures I would never enjoy; of my Father and Mother; of my Sisters and Brother . . . It seemed so unnecessary, but we still had a chance, if only we could keep away from the crowd and the suction of the sinking ship."

When the water reached them, John and Milton shook hands and wished each other luck. Milton jumped first, and then John sat on the rail, placed his feet outward, gulped as much air as he could, and leaped. He and the *Titanic* went down at about the same time. "The shock of the water took the breath out of my lungs. Down and down I went, spinning in all directions." John stayed under for at least a minute and then struggled to the surface, popping up just in time to see the great ship split in two. Then the suction dragged him under again. Swimming with all his might, he broke the surface with his hand and grabbed onto an object. It was an overturned lifeboat. Soon twenty-seven other passengers were clinging to it as well.

They hung on in the freezing sea for five hours, singing hymns and trying to keep talking, until they were rescued by sailors from the ocean liner *Carpathia*. John was able to climb the rope ladder by himself. At the top of the ladder, the first face he saw was that of his mother. Hours later, they realized John's father had not survived.

*John Thayer* (right) *and his surviving family after the disaster*

## WHAT HAPPENED TO MILTON LONG AND JOHN THAYER?

John Thayer became a successful banker, a husband, and the father of six children. He was haunted by memories of the *Titanic* until he took his own life at the age of fifty-one. Milton Long's body was found in the Atlantic shortly after the *Titanic* went down.

*"He broke two of my fingers taking my banner away."*

# Edna Purtell: Suffragist

Hartford, Connecticut, and Washington, D.C., 1918

*By her midteens, Edna Purtell was already a well-known leader in Connecticut. At sixteen, she was elected secretary of her local tobacco stripper's union and became president of a women's organization that supported Irish independence from Britain. In 1917, after the Connecticut legislature voted down suffrage—the right of women to vote—Edna went to work for the National Women's Party. Many party members had seen the inside of a cell, and their militance fit Edna's combative style just fine. In the summer of 1918, she got an unexpected chance to go to a suffragist rally in Washington, D.C. Still in her teens, she became the youngest suffragist to be jailed and go on a hunger strike. More than sixty years later, she remembered it well.*

*Suffragists parade through the streets of New York City in 1912.*

Women in some parts of the country were able to vote long before the U.S. Congress got around to passing a constitutional amendment. In the 1860s, when Wyoming was a territory rather than a state, there were six times as many men as women living there. Still, suffragist leaders invited both candidates for the territorial legislature to teas and got them to promise to support the women's vote if elected. They also made candidates promise to help give women the vote once Wyoming became a state. Colonel William H. Bright, a Democrat, won the election, and he kept his word. So in 1869, the Wyoming Territorial Legislature became the first to grant women the right to vote, and Louisa Ann Swain became the first woman to vote in a public election in U.S. history. Eighteen years later, when Wyoming applied for statehood, some U.S. Congressmen objected to Wyoming's tradition of allowing women to vote. Wyoming's male political leaders telegraphed this response: "We may stay out of the Union a hundred years, but we will come in with our women." And they did.

"One day I was in Brown Thompson's Department store when Mrs. Hepburn [the mother of the famous actress Katharine Hepburn] came along. I knew her because I used to help [suffragists] give out posters. Mrs. Hepburn said, 'Could you go to Washington, to be arrested and demonstrate?' I said, 'I've got a week's vacation coming but I can't afford to go.' She said, 'I can't go because I'm pregnant, but will you go if I pay your way?' I said, 'Certainly I will!' She said, 'You know, you may be jailed. Some of the women are not sure they're going to come out of it all right. Are you sure that you want to go?' I said, 'yes,' and I did. There were an awful lot of [other] working women who would have loved to have gone, but they couldn't afford it."

Edna took the train to Washington. On August 6, she and hundreds of other suffragists hoisted long, streaming banners and began to march toward Lafayette Park, shouting slogans as they advanced. They were angry that Democrats in the U.S. Senate had gone on summer recess without voting on a proposed amendment to the U.S. Constitution that would give women the right to vote. At the park, they demanded that President Woodrow Wilson come out of the White House to speak with them. But whenever one of the women tried to speak, she was grabbed by the police and forced into a patrol wagon. Outraged, a few women scaled a statue of Lafayette and shouted their defiance from the top to all who could hear. Edna was one of them:

"I was so young that I could climb the statue and call out, 'Lafayette, we are here!' The police wouldn't arrest you until you began to speak. Those were their orders. I was arrested four times for climbing the statue. Some of the police would throw us in the wagon, others would help us in. They would take us down to the jail, then they'd let us go. The older women couldn't go back to Lafayette Park, but I went back. I carried the American flag, and sometimes another banner that said, 'I come from Connecticut, the Cradle of Liberty.' It was purple, white and gold [suffragist colors].

"The last time I was arrested a young policeman came over [and said] they had orders to take those banners away from us. I said to him, 'Oh, I can't give you this banner. This banner is my banner of liberty' . . . [Then] a great big cop came along and told him, 'Take [her banner] away.' The young cop said to him, 'You take it away.' [The other cop] bent back my fingers, and he broke two of them taking it away . . . We were taken to the Washington District workhouse. Many of the women were desperately ill. We couldn't even drink the water in that place."

The Washington District workhouse was set in a swamp. Years before, it had been declared "unfit for human habitation" and had been closed down. Shortly after they entered, the women voted to go on a hunger strike. That meant they would live only on the reddish brown drinking water that trickled through rusted pipes. One prisoner after another became ill. U.S. senators who visited were shocked by the conditions and demanded their release. President Wilson received a flood of telegrams from outraged citizens, and, after five days, the women were freed. Edna's broken fingers were still untreated when she stepped outside. The women immediately applied for a permit to hold a second rally in Lafayette Park. This time, police made no attempt to stop them.

*Edna Purtell* (fourth from right with her face at the foot of the bed) *and other suffragists arrested in the Lafayette Monument rally try to sleep in the abandoned District workhouse in Washington, D.C.*

Edna's arrest and imprisonment made the Hartford newspapers. When she returned to her job in the filing department of the Travelers Insurance Company, her admiring co-workers greeted her with a large sign reading VOTES FOR WOMEN. The company president wasn't pleased.

"When I came back, Batterson [the president] called me down [to his office]. He said, 'You know, Miss Purtell, you're liked very well here, but we don't want you to be talking about suffrage . . .' I said to him, 'Mr. Batterson, during work hours I'll take care of my job. But once I get in that elevator, what I talk about is my business, not yours. And on our coffee break, that's our coffee break, and I'll talk about anything I want.'"

## WHAT HAPPENED TO EDNA PURTELL?

The Nineteenth Amendment to the U.S. Constitution was adopted by Congress in 1920, and Edna proudly voted in the presidential election of that year. She became well known for her commitment to human rights and many urged her to run for mayor, but she didn't. She joined the Connecticut Labor Department in 1933 and crusaded against the tobacco industry and for laws banning child labor. She died at the age of eighty-six.

*"I'd rather be in prison in Detroit than to be free in the South."*

# Charles Denby: Bound North

Lowndes County, Alabama, to Detroit, Michigan, 1924

*A million African Americans left the South for northern cities between 1915 and 1930 in what has been called the Great Migration. A second, even bigger wave started in the 1940s, when the invention of a mechanical cotton picker put southern field hands out of work. At the beginning of the twentieth century, African Americans were the most rural of Americans. By the end they were the most urban. Seventeen-year-old Charles Denby joined the migration when he left his Alabama plantation for Detroit in 1924.*

Charles Denby, a tall, ambitious boy who shaved his head clean, was bound for Detroit. The main reason was simple: "We heard that you could make twenty-five or thirty dollars a week in a factory," he later wrote. "After a few years I'd have several thousand dollars." He planned to send money home to his parents, so they could "build a home like the white people had."

There were other reasons, too. Except for his family and friends, Charles wasn't leaving much behind in Alabama. He lived in a shack that looked out on forty acres of worn land where his father grew cotton. The whites he knew were cruel to him and his family. There was no future in sharecropping. His one-room school was "so full of cracks that a child could raise a plank in the floor and slip away without the teacher knowing." The only subjects offered were reading and arithmetic; their teacher had only a sixth-grade education; Charles's fifteen-year-old brother, Buddy, was still in third grade.

Charles was ten when some of the older boys on the plantation went off to Detroit and Cleveland and Chicago to work in factories during World War I. Good jobs were available to young black males at that time mainly because the whites who normally had them were fighting in Europe. Southern blacks, long used to hard work, suddenly looked so good to northern factory owners that they sent railroad cars south to haul them up north.

Many soon came back home to visit with money in their pockets and stories of better treatment. Charles listened keenly. "All the things we heard was like reading in the Bible," he wrote, "milk and honey and pearly gates."

Early in 1924, when Charles turned seventeen, a friend gave him the address of a Detroit boardinghouse and urged him to get a job in an automobile factory. Charles bought a ticket in Montgomery, Alabama, and boarded the "Negro car." It was packed so tightly that people slept standing up. Just ahead were the roomier cars for whites.

They pulled away and darkness soon came. Charles hoped it would be light when they reached the Mason-Dixon Line, so he could finally see it. The Mason-Dixon Line was an imaginary border between the North and the South. Once it had separated the slave states from the free states, and now it separated states that had systems of racial segregation laws from those that didn't. Like many southern blacks, Charles assumed the line was real. "I thought it would look like a row of trees with some kind of white mark like the mark in the middle of the highway," he wrote. Just as the sun was rising, the train reached Covington, Kentucky, on the southern side of the Ohio River.

## FATHERS AND SONS

In 1917, an African-American preacher from Mississippi thought about the differences between his father and his son: "My father was born and brought up as a slave. He never knew anything else until after I was born. He was taught his place and was content to keep it. But when he brought me up he let some of the old customs slip by . . . and in bringing up my own son, I have let some more of the old customs slip by. He has been through the eighth grade; he reads easily. For a year I have been keeping him from going to Chicago; but he tells me this is his last crop; that in the fall he's going. He says, 'When a young white man talks rough to me, I can't talk rough to him. You can stand that; I can't. I have some education, and inside I have the feelings of a white man. I'm going.'"

Charles looked in vain for the line, until someone told him the bridge ahead over the Ohio was the Mason-Dixon Line.

Once they had crossed, Charles boldly decided to see if his life had really changed. Back on the plantation, Charles had been careful to address every white man as "sir." A slip could get you shot. But now they were north. Charles stepped out of the Negro car and edged into the next car, filled with whites. Heart pounding, he sat down in an empty seat beside a white man. The man was reading a paper and didn't look up for over an hour. "When he finished half, he pushed it to me and asked if I wanted to read. He wanted to know where I was going and said, 'Detroit is a nice place.' This was the most relaxing time I had."

*Boys dress up in their finest for Easter Sunday in their new neighborhood on Chicago's South Side.*

When Charles reached Detroit, he realized he had locked the address of the boardinghouse in his trunk, and the trunk room wouldn't be open until the next day. So he and a friend spent the whole night walking through the city, knocking on doors, trying to find someone who knew the name written on the paper. House by house, the reality of the North set in: "One white woman said that our friends couldn't possibly live on her block because no colored lived on her end of thirtieth. We walked off her porch wondering why. We didn't want to believe in discrimination up North but it kept going around in our heads."

The next day Charles rented a room and quickly found a factory job. His task was to shake out oil pans that fit under the motor of a car. He hated it: "Take a mold, knock it out, set it back. Over and over for nine, ten, eleven and twelve hours a day. The foreman would say, 'Do it. If you can't do it there are plenty of men outside who will.'" Charles got paid five cents a pan and found out that his pay was quickly eaten up by the ten dollars a week he had to pay for room and board. Soon he quit thinking about buying his parents a house.

After being laid off several times, Charles ran out of money and headed back to Alabama. For a while it seemed good to be back. But then, shortly after arriving home, he went to the plantation store to help his mother buy groceries. The owner asked him a question and, not thinking, Charles answered "Yes" rather than "Yes, sir." The man stormed out from behind the counter and confronted Charles. "Don't think just because you've been up north you can forget you were raised here," he yelled. Charles mumbled an apology and walked out into the sunlight with his mother. He felt sick, but it had taught him a lesson. "I told my mother that I'd rather be in prison in Detroit than to be free in the South," he wrote.

## WHAT HAPPENED TO CHARLES DENBY?

He married, became a father, and moved back to Detroit. There he was an auto worker, union leader, and newspaper columnist. He died in 1983 at the age of seventy-six.

---

### BETTER SCHOOLS

The chance for children to get a good education drew parents to northern cities. In 1910, fewer than half of all black children under the age of ten attended school in Alabama, Mississippi, Georgia, and Louisiana. By contrast, in 1920 the Chicago Board of Education told students of all races, "Your job today is to go to school." Wendell Phillips High School, on Chicago's South Side, attracted so many southerners that it soon became the largest high school in the city. But it wasn't a paradise. Students born in the city often made fun of the newcomers, and whites controlled clubs and sports teams. Racial fights broke out. Some northern cities refused to allow black students to mix with whites. In 1927, Indianapolis concentrated all the city's black high school students and teachers into one building, Crispus Attucks High. On the day the school opened, hundreds of hooded Ku Klux Klansmen paraded through the streets of downtown Indianapolis.

*"Be a good boy and cry."*—Jackie Cooper's grandmother

# Jackie Cooper: "Lights, Action, Cry!"

Hollywood, California, 1930

*On April 23, 1896, a few people in a New York City music hall saw the first exhibition of motion pictures in the United States. Ten years later, small, shabby theaters called nickelodeons had sprung up all over the country to gobble the nickels of working children. The boys and girls sat in the dark, biting off chunks of gooey candy, as adventure stories passed before their eyes. By 1911, 16 percent of all schoolchildren in New York City saw at least one movie a day. Hollywood talent scouts combed the country for children who could act. One was a quick-thinking boy with a mop of blond hair named Jackie Cooper. His big break came in 1930, when, at the age of eight, he beat out three hundred other children for the lead role in a movie called Skippy. The fun ended when it was time for him to cry.*

"My first crying scene came at the end of a long, hard day. [The director] told everyone on the set to be quiet. My grandmother said, 'Be a good boy and cry.' They waited. I tried. No tears . . .

"The director screamed, and he hollered. He shouted that it had been a mistake to have hired me and he called me a 'lousy ham actor.' He told his assistant to start getting the standby kid ready to replace me . . . It made me angry rather than unhappy. Angry kids don't cry . . . I hit things and slammed things and maybe even broke things but not one tear was shed.

"As I waited, I saw a new figure on the set, another kid dressed exactly as I was dressed, in the Skippy costume. They always have two of everything on a set, and they had quickly put it on one of the other kids . . . The idea that they would give my part to another boy was enough to make me very sad very quickly.

"I came apart at the tear ducts. I really cried . . . They rushed me into the scene, and I did it, and then they gave me an ice cream cone, and [the director] said I was a fine actor, and my grandmother said I was a good boy."

---

### AT LAST, MONEY OF THEIR OWN

"Never before have such numbers of young boys earned money independently of the family life, and felt free to spend it as they choose."
—Jane Addams, 1909

---

Jackie Cooper got bigger and bigger parts. As a ten-year-old he was earning more than the president of the United States. But later he felt he had paid a price:

"I had no friends. I did not receive a good education. I grew up with pressure and responsibility from the time I was seven or eight. The pressure to get the scene right, to learn the words, to act this way or that way, to smile or cry or look scared for the cameraman, to do a nice interview . . . Why should an eight-year-old kid have that kind of pressure?"

And adults controlled the money. In 1921, a seven-year-old actor named Jackie Coogan (a different boy from Jackie Cooper) got the title role in a film called

*Jackie Cooper* (left) *and Jackie Coogan star together.*

*The Kid* and soon was earning nearly $10,000 per week. When he turned twenty-one, he tried to claim some of the $4 million he had earned as a boy. Lawyers told him he had no right to it. He sued to win his salary, but the courts always ruled that money he had earned when he was a minor belonged to his parents. He won in the end, and other child actors with him. The California State Legislature passed the Child Actors Bill, which said that at least half of a child actor's earnings had to be set aside in a fund that could be claimed when the actor turned eighteen.

## WHAT HAPPENED TO JACKIE COOPER?

He went on to become a well-known actor and a director of the long-running television series *M*A*S*H.*

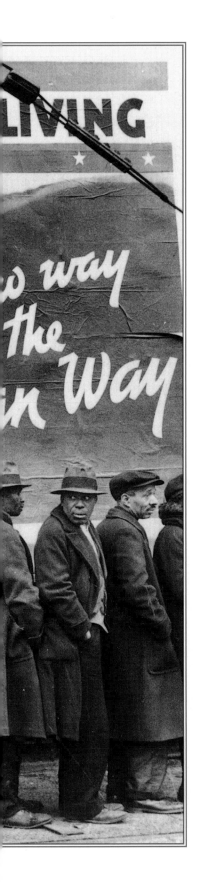

# PART EIGHT

# Hard Times: Wars, Depression, and Dust

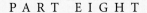

At first, World War I seemed to be a European family feud that the United States could stay out of. On one side were the Central Powers: Germany, Bulgaria, Austria-Hungary, and the Ottoman Empire. On the other were the Allies, including Britain, France, Russia, Japan, and Italy. For three years, the United States shipped food and materials overseas, mainly to the Allies, but didn't send troops. But in April 1917, German submarines began to sink U.S. supply ships, prompting President Woodrow Wilson to declare war. "The world must be made safe for democracy," he said. Confidently, he proclaimed the Great War the "war to end all wars."

Though the fighting took place in Europe, the war changed life in the United States. Families worked harder and ate less to supply Allied troops in Europe. Some Americans turned against European immigrants, accusing them of having stronger loyalties to their former homelands than to their new nation. Neighbors spied on one another, and laws were passed to punish those who didn't support the war.

Even the weather turned grim. A decade after World War I ended, it stopped raining in parts of the Great Plains for nearly ten years. Gusts of wind picked up soil from the Great Plains and carried some of it all the way to the Atlantic Ocean. Farm families went west to look for a future and instead found armed guards at the California state line. The stock market collapsed, and America's economy went into a freefall, leaving many jobless and without food. Thousands of young Americans, with nothing to hold them, drifted around the country.

And far from ending all wars, World War I produced a desperate rage in Europe that ignited into a second, even bigger, war. A popular song of the 1930s was a plea that went "Hard times, hard times, come again no more." Indeed, very few Americans who lived between the beginning of World War I and the end of World War II escaped hard times.

*Margaret Bourke-White's photograph of a bread line in Louisville, Kentucky, 1937*

*"I hung at the back of the crowd, watching with distaste as the grownups made fools of themselves."*

# Margaret Davidson: War on the Home Front

Hamburg, Iowa, 1914–1918

*Eight-year-old Margaret Davidson lived in a small Iowa town during the final year of World War I. The war caused trouble in her town that was even more upsetting than the fighting overseas. The problem seemed to revolve around the word* patriotism. *To some, it meant supporting American soldiers and making sacrifices for the Allied cause. But to others, the word meant making life miserable for the German-Americans in Hamburg. Margaret later wrote about the forces that tore apart Hamburg, Iowa, during the Great War.*

When America entered the war in 1917, the citizens of Hamburg, Iowa, exploded with patriotic activity. Red Cross chapters rolled miles of bandages, knit khaki sweaters and socks, and made flannel nightgowns. "As the draft board began calling up and sending off our young men . . . we students learned all four verses of the 'Star

Spangled Banner' and sang them every morning along with 'The Marseillaise' (which had one verse in English) and 'God Save the King.' We sang patriotic songs reaching all the way back to the Civil War—and also 'Tipperary' and 'Keep the Home Fires Burning' and 'Over There.' Surely no group of kids ever knew so many patriotic songs as we."

Like Americans everywhere, the Davidsons went without food and coal so that they could be sent overseas. They learned to cook without sugar or flour. They even followed the government's advice and "Fletcherized" their food, chewing each bite thirty to forty times before swallowing. Supposedly, Fletcherizing let them

*German soldiers were drawn as beasts in many World War I posters.*

*Boys at a Cooperstown, New York, school knit blankets for World War I soldiers.*

eat less, save more for the troops, and still squeeze the full nutritional value out of each bite. Margaret thought it was crazy, but she remembered the soldiers and dutifully chewed away.

The Davidsons sat through endless speeches at Liberty Bond rallies to raise money for the war. Margaret followed battle reports in the newspaper and felt heartsick when she read that a soldier from Hamburg had died, especially if she knew his brother or sister. But she was troubled even more by a conflict brewing right in Hamburg.

One large group of men was trying to use the overseas war against Germany to turn townspeople against their neighbors of German ancestry. Some of the men were out-laws who had settled in Hamburg because it was conveniently close to both the Nebraska and Missouri borders if Iowa authorities came after them. They made speech-es declaring that no German-American could be trusted and accused anyone who dis-agreed with them of being unpatriotic. Unfortunately, that included Margaret's father, who published the town newspaper.

## "HYPHENATED AMERICANS"

World War I made things much harder for millions of European immigrants in the United States, especially those who came from enemy lands. Former president Theodore Roosevelt led the attack on what he called "hyphenated Ameri-cans," mainly German-American and Austrian-American residents. "They play the part of traitors," Roosevelt declared. "Once it was true that this country could not endure half American and half slave. Today it is true that it cannot endure half American and half for-eign. The hyphen is incompatible with patriotism."

To Margaret's dismay, anti-German fever spread rapidly. Early in 1917, a mob attacked Hamburg's German Lutheran church, smashing the windows and smearing the sanctuary with yellow paint to symbolize cowardice. "Only a few people were shocked or indignant at this incident," Margaret wrote with alarm. German dolls—her favorites—were pulled from store windows. German classes were banned in the high school, where students heard horror stories of German atrocities in Belgium and France. Younger children were taught to hate the kaiser.

Soon the town was deeply divided. Many remembered that German immigrants had founded and built Hamburg the century before, naming it after a German city. Margaret didn't see why their descendents still living in town couldn't be both patriotic Americans *and* citizens proud of their German heritage. One fall day in 1917, she took a small stand of her own against intolerance:

"When I went home for lunch, I heard that some super-patriot had the bright idea that all the German books in the town should be burned in a public bonfire. My sister Letha was away at college. She had studied German four years in high school and owned a half-dozen or so German books. I hid them where my mother couldn't find them. I had a strong feeling that these books belonged to Letha and that it was for her alone to decide what to do with them. The bonfire blazed in a vacant lot across from the post office. A large crowd waved flags, yelled and danced as they threw more books into the fire. I hung at the back of the crowd, watching with distaste as the grownups made fools of themselves."

On November 7, 1918, word reached Hamburg that an armistice had been signed and the war was over. Jubilant people poured out of their houses to share the

## A National Draft

After declaring war, President Wilson called for a million men to volunteer, but six weeks later only seventy-three thousand had signed up. So, in May of 1917, Congress passed the Selective Service Act, allowing the armed forces to draft young men into the military whether they wanted to serve or not. It was the first time in U.S. history that young men were drafted into a national army. Blacks were drafted, but only about one-tenth of those who served were allowed to fight. Most performed food and maintenance work.

Senators debated the proper draft age. Said Senator Nelson of Minnesota, "Make the age limit eighteen. If you want good soldiers, take the young men." Senator Lodge of Massachusetts countered, "A boy of eighteen is still in the growing stage." The age was first set at twenty-one but quickly lowered to eighteen as more troops were needed. Most reported to their draft boards, but many others did not—risking a year in jail. The government encour-

aged neighbors to report so-called slackers and tried to shame them into induction with poems like this one, which took the stern voice of a father:

*I'd rather you had died at birth or not been born*
*    at all*
*Than know that I had raised a son who cannot*
*    hear the call*
*To save the world from sin, my son, God gave his*
*    only Son*
*He's asking for MY boy today, and may His will*
*    be done.*

Another poet gave a different view:

*I love my flag, I do, I do, which floats upon the*
*    breeze*
*I also love my arms and legs, and neck and nose*
*    and knees*
*One little shell might spoil them all and give*
*    them such a twist*
*They would be of no use to me; I guess I won't*
*    enlist.*

news with their neighbors. "Someone played 'America' on the steam whistle at the light plant. And yet, some people weren't quite sure it was true. They were right—it wasn't."

It was a false alarm, but soon definite news arrived that the war in Europe would cease at 11 A.M. on November 11. Europe may have been at peace, but Hamburg wasn't.

"I didn't hear about it until I got to school, where we were told that school would be dismissed at 11 A.M. We were crazy with excitement. The teachers lined us up ten abreast and prepared us to march down the school house hill singing 'Columbia the Gem of the Ocean.' Then I was looking for a wild and wonderful day with my Dad who always took me with him to exciting events. Suddenly, from nowhere, he appeared and snatched me roughly from my line and pulled me over to the edge of the street. He said, 'I want you to go right home and don't go out of our yard again today no matter what happens.' " Then he disappeared.

It turned out that Margaret's father was trying to protect a store owner who refused to close his store at eleven o'clock. The man insisted upon waiting until noon. Some of the "super-patriots," as Margaret called them, were so angry that they had already smeared his store with yellow paint and were looking around for a rope to lynch him. Margaret's father was one of only four men in town trying to save the storekeeper's life.

The standoff lasted the whole day, paralyzing the center of town and ruining Hamburg's victory celebration. After dark, Margaret's father came home, explaining that the men had finally gotten tired and gone home to bed. That suited Margaret just fine. She was tired too—tired of living in a divided, angry town. "By midnight the streets were nearly clear," Margaret wrote. "Peace descended on Hamburg. The War was over."

## WHAT HAPPENED TO MARGARET DAVIDSON?

She went to college and, like her mother, became a librarian. During a long career she worked in three Iowa public libraries. Margaret died in 1984.

---

> ### "WHY DID GOD SEND THE EPIDEMIC?'
>
> One spring day in 1918, Margaret Davidson found herself at the funeral of three of her classmates—all from the same family. A week later, four from another family died. The Spanish influenza had struck Hamburg. Children made up a rhyme for it: "I had a little bird, its name was Enza. I opened up the window, and in-flew-Enza." It was a mystifying plague that raced through the world, killing twenty million people in less than a year. The flu swept through the army camps of World War I, killing soldiers so fast that doctors stacked up their bodies like wood. Doctors couldn't see the flu virus in their microscopes and wondered why everyone was dying. Some thought it was a German plot. With no vaccine, people stayed home, wore masks, and tried to breathe only through their noses. Nothing worked. Schools, theaters, church services, and other public gatherings were stopped in most U.S. cities. The crisis ended when the disease vanished just as mystifyingly as it had appeared.

*Throughout the 1930s, winds swept the powdery soil of the Great Plains into towering "black blizzards." Kansas farmers joked that they could see Texas and Oklahoma whizzing past their windows.*

*"It was coming too fast to be a thunderstorm."*

# Harley Holladay: Black Sunday

Near Dodge City, Kansas, 1935

*Years after it ended, World War I darkened the skies of Kansas, Oklahoma, New Mexico, Colorado, and Texas. Farmers had answered the call to "win the war with wheat" by plowing under native grasses and planting wheat to feed the soldiers. The strategy led to an environmental disaster. A drought began in 1931 that lasted for nearly ten years. Windstorms swept up the soil that had once been held together by deep-rooted grasses and whipped it into black, towering clouds. The Great Plains simply blew away. Noon seemed like midnight when the dust flew. The worst storm of all hit on April 14, 1935, producing a terrifying cloud seven thousand feet high. That noon, thirteen-year-old Harley Holladay had just gone outside to enjoy a rare day of fresh air on his family's Kansas farm.*

"It was such a nice clear Sunday. We had hung the laundry out on the line that morning, and mother had washed the upholstered chairs and set them out to dry. I walked up to our horse pond and had picked up a stone to skip across the water. While I was throwing I happened to look up and noticed this long gray line on the horizon. It looked like a thunderhead, but it was too long and flat and it was rolling toward me way too fast. I sprinted to the house to tell my parents that the dust was coming but they wouldn't believe it until they went outside and looked for themselves. Then we started hauling in clothes as fast as we could, just snatching them in armloads and running. The cloud caught me outside with a load of clothes. I couldn't see anything at all. It was black as night. I got down on my hands and knees and tried to crawl toward the house. I finally felt the porch, and reached up and opened the screen door and crawled inside.

"For a long time it was total blackness inside, except for one thing. When I looked out the window I could see our radio antenna outlined in static electricity. There were little balls of fire all over it caused by dirt particles rubbing together. It was spooky. Finally the sun began to shine as a faint glow of orange light coming in through the windows. As it got lighter, I could see baskets and brush sailing past us. It felt like we were flying through space."

When the storm was over they stepped outside. Dust was heaped in the yard like sand dunes in a desert. Cattle and farm equipment were buried. Jackrabbits loped through the dunes. As always, Harley and his family cleared their throats and dug out.

"I guess we had gotten used to it, because it had been that way for a long

## CALIFORNIA BOUND

During World War I, the government had set a very high price for wheat, and many farmers made more money than ever. They used their profits to buy more and more land to plant more and more wheat. But after the war ended, the price of wheat declined, a situation made worse when it stopped raining in 1931. With no crops to sell, many families couldn't keep up their bank payments and lost their farms. More than three million people, like the Arkansas family shown here, left the Great Plains in the 1930s and headed for California, looking for a better life. Most Dust Bowl families were met with hostility and scorn.

time. Our windows were taped up and the cracks in our walls were stuffed but nothing kept the dust out. Whenever we ate a meal we had to turn our plates and cups and glasses over until the exact time the meal was served. Even then, you could write your name in dust on your glass by the time the meal was done. Every night before we went to bed we scooped a little water into our noses and blew out the dirt. We put covers over our faces and a sheet over my little sister's crib. Some people slept with masks on.

"You didn't want to get caught out in a storm, either. Some families strung clothesline between the house and the barn so that they could always find their way back to the house. We always made sure we had food and water with us when we left the house. When the dust started flying and I was away from the home I tried to find a fenceline to follow. My father used my brother and I as guides when he was plowing with the tractor in the fields. I'd stand at one end of the field with a kerosene light and my brother would shine a light at the other end. My dad would try to drive straight between us. The dust came so fast that it would cover up the tractor's tracks."

At the end of a workday their clothes were caked, their hair was matted, and their skin was streaked with dust. They bathed in a tub on the porch before they entered the house, but nothing kept the dust out. No matter what they did, the rain stayed away, the soil blew away, and very little grew. In 1935, the government established the Soil Conservation Service. The aim was to encourage Dust Bowl farmers to plant grass, rotate their crops, plow the land into strips that caught rainwater, and plant rows of trees to break up the wind. It helped, but true relief didn't come until rain finally came—five years later. By then, Harley Holladay was a soldier in Italy.

"I was in World War II when the rain came back to Kansas, but I was still thinking a lot about the farm. One night in Italy I had the most wonderful dream. I was back on the farm in Kansas and we were having a rainshower at last. It was a big, loud thunderstorm, with buckets of rain just soaking the ground. I was so happy. And then someone was shaking me awake and there were tracer bullets and anti-aircraft fire all around. We were under attack. But in my dream the thunder of gunfire was a great blessing. That's how much rain meant to a Dust Bowl boy."

### WHAT HAPPENED TO HARLEY HOLLADAY?

After World War II, he farmed his family's land for twenty years. Then he became a husband, a father, a potter, a brickmaker, a research scientist, a schoolteacher, a tour guide, and an actor, and he drilled a few oil wells along the way. "I was one of those guys who never settled down," he says.

———◆✕◆———

*Peggy Eaton, age fifteen*

*"You'll be back for supper!"*—Peggy Eaton's father

# Peggy Eaton: Ridin' the Rails

Wyoming, Idaho, and Washington, 1938

*During the Great Depression of the 1930s, nearly one-third of all working-age Americans were out of work. Many teenagers left home to hitchhike and ride freight trains around the country. Their reasons varied: Some schools were closed and there was little work to be found. Some, like sixteen-year-old Clarence Lee, were told by their parents, "Go fend for yourself. I can't afford to have you around any longer." Fifteen-year-old Peggy Eaton left her home on a Wyoming ranch in the summer of 1938, after an argument with her father.*

"The real problem was there was just no money. I was going into my junior year in high school and I wanted decent clothes to wear when school started . . . I was taking care of sheep for my brothers, and milking cows for my dad, but it just didn't look like I was going to make any money. I was mad a lot that summer.

"One night the cow I was milking whopped me in the eye with her dirty tail. I got up and whopped her right back with my stool and cussed her out. My dad heard me. He came over, boxed me up one side of the face and down the other. He said, 'Don't you ever let me hear you talk like that again!' I said, 'I'll leave home!' He said, 'You'll be back for supper!'

"A couple of weeks later my friend Irene asked me if I wanted to go with her to see her folks in Issaquah, Washington. She said I could make lots of money out there picking fruit. I didn't tell my folks. I just rolled up a few pieces of clothing and tied it with rope and slung it over my shoulder. Irene stuffed her things in a suitcase made of tin. We took off hitchhiking on July 12.

"The first day we got rides all the way to Cokeville, Wyoming, near the state line with Idaho. We were walking down the highway when we came to a railroad yard. There were two out-of-work bums cooking their dinner in an old gallon bucket over a campfire. They asked if we were hungry and of course we said yes. They served us a nice vegetable stew and coffee out of tin cans. They said their names were Joe and Slim. They were going to Washington, too, and they said we'd do better riding the rails than trying to hitchhike.

"Soon a train stopped to water up and we all four climbed into an empty freight car. Slim and Joe showed us a lot of things about riding. They warned me not to swing my legs out the open door because they could get caught on a railroad switch and pulled right out. When night came and the cold came in, they showed us how to roll up in the paper that lined the walls of the boxcar.

"Two days later we jumped off at Nampa, Idaho. Slim and Joe went off to beg for food, and Irene and I walked over to a grassy area where dozens of hobos were living. Everyone had their eyes on this one boxcar door, the only open door on a train that was about to leave for La Grande, Oregon. Every hobo in that yard wanted to get inside that car. The bulls [railroad police] were patrolling the area with rifles and lanterns. Everyone was a little nervous because the day before one of them had shot a bum off the top of a boxcar in the La Grande freight yard.

"When the engine started up a wave of bums rose up like one person and rushed for that open door. I was the first one there. Someone behind me picked me up by the nape of the

neck and the seat of the pants and pitched me into the car. Irene was right behind me. It was dark inside, and scary. We were the only girls. We crawled into a corner and Irene put her tin suitcase in front of us. Slim and Joe made it on board and slept in front of us, too, that night.

"When we got near the La Grande freight yard the train sped up instead of slowing down. It looked like a trap, especially since it was the same place where the bull had shot the man the day before. We went for the door and jumped out while the train was going at least thirty-five or forty miles an hour. I tumbled head over heels when I hit the ground.

"We couldn't catch a freight out of La Grande because the bulls were too thick so we split from Slim and Joe and went back out on the highway and caught a ride in a gasoline truck. The old road took us over what was called 'Cabbage Hill' between La Grande and Pendleton. We reached the top of the hill right at sundown. There were hundreds of little farms, in all different colors spread out before us. I had never seen anything so magnificent in my life.

"We hitched into Pasco, Washington, found a room for a dollar and then walked down to the tracks the next morning. The only available boxcar was full so we climbed up onto the top of the train and rode up on the catwalk, where railroad workers can walk across the top of the train. When the train first got going we were scared to death and clung tight to the edge, but soon we were sitting up and looking around at the desert. Suddenly we saw a man coming toward us on the catwalks, jumping from car to car. When he reached us he sat down to visit. He was a bull all right, but sort of a friendly bull. He didn't know how to roll a cigarette so we rolled it for him. He told us we'd have to get off in Yakima, because after that there were low tunnels through the Cascade Mountains and he didn't want to see us get decapitated.

"So we got off at Yakima. When we finally made it to Irene's home in Issaquah she came down with the mumps. We started back east as soon she got well. We never did pick fruit or make any money.

"Going back east people were less generous. In Nampa, Idaho, we got arrested for vagrancy, fingerprinted and thrown into a dirty jail cell. The next morning the judge fined us ten dollars apiece, but instead of making us pay he wrote us out a voucher for a free breakfast and a personal note that said, 'Eat your breakfast and get out of town.' That was fine with us.

"We went on to Soda Springs, Idaho, where there was a rodeo. A couple of cowboys who had pitched their tent in the city park shared a pot of beans with us. They let us use their tent to sleep in and got us into the rodeo free the next day. Before long Irene fell for one of them and that split us up. She went on to the next rodeo and I started back home alone.

"It took me a few more days to make it back. My mom and dad welcomed me home and my dad never said another word about me leaving. I had traveled over three thousand miles, experienced a few bad incidents and many acts of kindness. I had seen hundreds of people, even whole families, bumming rides to try to find work during those hard times. And I had proved to my dad that I would not be back for supper."

A teenage hobo climbs aboard another freight car after four years on the road.

## WHAT HAPPENED TO PEGGY EATON?

She continues to live a life of adventure. She has run day care centers, worked as a grocery wholesaler and in a children's hospital, and served as a missionary in Trinidad. Once she rode a steam engine from Anchorage, Alaska, to Whittier, California. At the age of seventy-five she climbed a mountain and drove 4,212 miles in her van. "My whole life has been interesting," she says.

### HUMAN FREIGHT

"Men and boys swarm on every freight in such numbers that the railroad police would be helpless to keep them off . . . From September 1, 1931, to April 30, 1932, the Southern Pacific Railroad, with 9,130 miles of track, recorded 416,915 trespassers ejected."
—*Monthly Labor Review*, 1933

*Calvin Graham in his navy uniform*
*at age twelve*

# Calvin Graham: Too Young to Be a Hero?

Houston, Texas, and the Solomon Islands, 1942

*On December 7, 1941, Japanese warplanes dropped bombs on U.S. ships in Pearl Harbor, Hawaii, killing 2,403 Americans and destroying much of the U.S. Pacific Fleet of warships. The next day President Franklin D. Roosevelt declared war on Japan, and the United States entered World War II. Calvin Graham of Houston, Texas, was one of many thousands who enlisted in the U.S. Navy. The unusual thing about him was that he was only twelve years old. Military historians call him the youngest U.S. soldier of the twentieth century.*

The U.S. Navy looked good to Calvin Graham in the spring of 1942. His life was hard. His father had died five years before, when he was seven and his brother, Frank, ten. Their mother married a man who drank heavily and forced the boys out of the house. On their own, the boys shined shoes after school, earning just enough to rent a single room in a shabby hotel. Their only furnishings were a bed, a mirror, a washstand, and a water pitcher.

Until America declared war against Japan, Calvin couldn't even imagine a future for himself. He was in sixth grade but rapidly slipping behind his classmates. But then, at the age of fourteen, Frank forged some papers and faked his way into the navy, even though the law said you had to be seventeen to enlist. After Frank left, Calvin drifted from one flophouse to another, but at last he had a plan. If Frank could enlist, so could he. Calvin decided to wait until the end of the school year to make his move. That way, if his plan didn't work, he could always go on to seventh grade. Until then, he would try to eat more and get stronger, since he had heard you had to be at least five feet two and 125 pounds for the navy to take you. He found a razor and started shaving to try to get a beard to grow.

In August of 1942, Calvin went to the recruiting station with his friend Cleon Jones, also underage. The recruiting officer wasn't fooled when he looked at Calvin, but he needed sailors, since Japan still controlled much of the Pacific Ocean. "The man told me not to tell him my age," Calvin said, "just to sign my mother's name and tell him I was seventeen."

He took a train to San Diego for boot camp, where a dentist noticed that Calvin's twelve-year molars weren't in yet. He ordered Calvin to take his file to the medical officer to be discharged from the navy. Instead, Calvin waited until the dentist's back was turned and placed his file in a stack with all the others. Five weeks later he was aboard the battleship *South Dakota,* headed for the Solomon Islands in the Pacific, which were controlled by Japanese forces. Soon the crew was trying to survive an all-out assault in the battle of Santa Cruz. Calvin was assigned to a gun crew that shot down seven Japanese planes.

When the battle ended, Calvin and his crewmates formed a line to be congratulated by Lieutenant Sargent Shriver. Shriver stopped when he got to Calvin. "He asked how old I was. I told him 'Thirteen in April, sir.' " Shriver sent him to the captain, who told Calvin that he would have to go home at once. Calvin insisted he had only been kidding, that he was really seventeen. "[The captain told me] it wasn't anything to be ashamed of," Calvin said. "He had already sent three other [underage] boys home that same day." Calvin desperately wanted to stay. He had a home now, food, friends, and a job. He stuck to his story and the captain couldn't prove him wrong. He stayed.

In November, they fought in the battle of Guadalcanal, one of the bloodiest episodes of World War II. The *South Dakota* was hit again and again by enemy fire. One explosion threw Calvin down three decks of stairs. Another shell whistled in and knocked out the ship's electrical power. The *South Dakota* drifted unseen in the dark until a nearby U.S. ship trained a spotlight on it. That made the ship a sudden target: Shell after shell boomed onto Calvin's part of the boat. The room quickly filled up waist-high with reddened seawater. Dead and wounded men were all around. Screams and exploding shells and planes made hearing nearly impossible. Calvin's partner went out for more supplies and never returned. Calvin was hit by a shell fragment, sending a bolt of pain through his head and crushing a part of his mouth. All night long he did what he could to keep his mates alive. Often all he could do was take belts off the dead to tie tourniquets for the living.

After the battle, they sailed back to Brooklyn, New York, for repairs. Calvin was awarded the Purple Heart, the Bronze Star, and several other medals for his bravery, but the ship's captain was still troubled by how young he looked. He ordered Calvin to go home to Texas to get a letter of consent from his mother allowing him to stay in the navy. When Calvin got back with the letter, the captain had been reassigned. The new officer in charge ordered Calvin back to Houston to turn himself in to naval authorities there. "They're the ones who signed you up," he said sternly. "Let them straighten this out."

## A GRADE SCHOOL IN 1943

Students throughout America did everything they could to help the war effort. The yearbook of North School, serving grades 1 through 8 in Portland, Maine, lists the following student activities in 1943:

- Raised $5,315 to buy war stamps and bonds.
- Made bookmarks for injured soldiers.
- Collected flower vases to send to a Veterans' Hospital.
- Pooled pennies to buy yarn.
- Collected 10,017 tin cans to be used by the military.
- Collected 28 pounds' worth of keys to be turned into bullets.
- Formed a first aid class in case of attack.
- Sold 13,350 half-pints of milk to raise money for war bonds.
- Room 103 alone collected 100 pounds of tin foil, 200 keys, and 100 tin tubes.

Lessons were often about war. Children in Room 209 learned games from a book titled *Fun in a Fallout Shelter.* Eighth grader John Romano wrote his spring essay about the importance of chewing gum. "Gum is good for aviators when they go into a power dive," he wrote. "So do not argue with your grocer if he has no gum. The men in the service need it more than you do."

Then Calvin's nightmares really began. He hitch-hiked home and reported. But the navy officials got his story backward. They thought he was seventeen and trying to get *out* of the navy by pretending he was twelve, not the other way around. He was arrested as a deserter and placed in a naval prison in Corpus Christi, Texas. His medals were taken away from him.

He stayed behind bars for three months. No one knew where he was. Finally his sister found him and got a newspaper reporter to write about him. The navy released him but refused to grant him an honorable discharge or veterans' benefits. Two days after his thirteenth birthday, Calvin Graham, the battle-hardened war veteran, rejoined his classmates in seventh grade.

## WHAT HAPPENED TO CALVIN GRAHAM?

He enlisted in the marines when he finally turned seventeen. While on duty he fell from a pier and broke his back and leg, causing him to spend the rest of his life in a wheelchair. The government paid him for that injury but still refused to return his medals or to pay him for the injuries he suffered as a boy on the *South Dakota*. He kept writing to the navy and to his congressional representatives, asking for help. He won his pay and all his medals back except the Purple Heart, awarded for being injured

*During the war years, students throughout America—like these from Butte, Montana—collected mountains of scrap metal, which were quickly transformed into planes, tanks, and ships.*

in battle. That was the one that meant the most to him. In 1988, a TV movie was made about him. Calvin dedicated it to all the boys who faked their age and fought in World War II. "They helped win that war," he said. "The Americans were losing the war . . . we thought that if we got in and did our part, we could turn that thing around. And we did." In 1994—two years after his death—the navy finally gave Calvin's widow his Purple Heart.

*"Daddy held me and told me it was my responsibility to take care of the other kids."*

# Terry Grimmesey: "What Had We Done?"

Poston, Arizona, 1942

*Terry Grimmesey moved from Japan to California in 1938, when she was six years old. Her mother was Japanese and her father American. Terry loved California. She lived in a big white house surrounded by an orange grove. Cousins lived nearby. Her new classmates seemed to like and accept her until December 1941, when Japanese warplanes bombed Pearl Harbor. Suddenly Terry was a "Jap," one of the enemy. Three months later, President Roosevelt signed Execcutive Order 9066, declaring that Americans of Japanese ancestry on the West Coast were to be removed from cities and taken to prison camps in the desert. Terry was bused to a new home, one that was wrapped in barbed wire and patrolled by armed guards.*

*Terry Grimmesey* (left), *her brother, Bob, and her sister Barbara at Poston Camp, in Arizona*

"We didn't talk about the war much at home but I read the paper from cover to cover trying to find out what was going on. And then one day there was a telephone call from my grandmother. When Daddy hung up we gathered in the living room. I could see the panic on the faces of the adults. The Japanese had bombed Pearl Harbor. Daddy worried if the U.S. declared war on Japan, Mother would be sent back to Japan because she was not a U.S. citizen. I became frightened. Right away Mother began to teach me how to wash and iron clothes and clean house so I could take care of the family without her. I was only ten years old but I was the oldest of four.

"I felt I was both Japanese and American. I loved both countries. I didn't look Japanese, but it didn't matter—soon we got a notice saying that in a few days we were to report to the Riverside bus station and be ready to move somewhere else. Just me and mother and the other kids. Daddy *couldn't* go because he was not Japanese. We didn't know if we could ever go back home. I have never seen my mother so upset.

"We packed our belongings in the one suitcase we were allowed and went to the bus station. Daddy held me and told me it was my responsibility to take care of the other kids. Then the bus pulled away and he

A gust of wind whips the desert dust and straightens the American flag at the Manzanar Relocation Center, in California's desolate high-desert country.

was gone. My brother was crying on my lap and I tried to keep him calm. We headed straight out into the desert. After what seemed like days the bus passed through a fence and came to a stop in front of a group of flat buildings. The sun was blinding and the wind was blowing hard. I stepped off the bus into about six inches of dust. There was no shade anywhere. A Japanese gentleman handed me a white sack and directed me to go behind a building and fill it with straw.

"We were led to a long building with a roof made of tar paper. We pushed open a door that had no lock and looked in at our new home. It was one small room with bare walls. Five metal cots had been shoved into the center of the room. A little light slanted in through a tiny window. My mother just slumped down onto one of the cots and we kids started filling our mattresses with straw before the sun went down.

"We woke up the next morning and started our new life. First we walked to a building and waited in line to use the bathroom. Then we waited in another line to use the sink to brush our teeth. Then we went to a building to eat breakfast—powdered stuff, cooked prunes and oatmeal. How I missed the oranges from our orchard! Then we got back in line to wash our clothes by hand in a tub in the bathroom. Then we went to our room to hang them up.

"After that there was nothing to do. I walked out to the barbed wire fence by myself and watched the guards walk back and forth, carrying their rifles. Why did they need guns? What had we done?

"That summer I did a lot of fighting. I couldn't take people staring at me because I didn't look Japanese. At school that had made life easier, but here it counted against me. And I fought anyone who picked on my brother or sisters. But I discovered that if you can beat a boy, he becomes your friend. I played a lot of baseball and made a fishing pole with a stick and string. I caught frogs and snakes and scorpions, mainly. I didn't make friends with girls because I didn't know how. I wasn't into dolls or pretend games.

"The adults who gathered at the washtub gossiped that we'd never get out. News of the war was kept from us, and I expected that we'd be there a long time. But then one day my father came to visit with the news that the U.S. Government had agreed to release Japanese who were married to Americans, and their families. He said we would be out in time for school.

"When we got home, people treated us differently than before. One day two FBI men came to see us. They made me sit down on the sofa between them. They told me that if I ever spoke Japanese again I would be sent back to camp behind the barbed wire. I became so terrified that I never could speak Japanese again. And at school it no longer mattered that I didn't look Japanese—now I was a 'Jap.' The first Valentine's Day after we came back I got many nasty and insulting Valentines. I was so hurt I couldn't look anyone in their eyes.

"But two kind things also took place on that day. After school, a small boy came to me and handed me a box of chocolates. I cried at that gesture of kindness. And a girl named Sybil invited me to her home. They lived in a garage attached to a small house. They had come from the Midwest to work in the orange and lemon groves of California. They invited me to stay for dinner and all we had was corn soup and bread. They were the first poor people I had ever met but they didn't seem poor because they were so rich with love.

"Soon we lost all our money. The U.S. government and the Japanese government took away everything we had. Before Pearl Harbor, Daddy had

---

### AN APOLOGY

"We now know what we should have known then—not only was that evacuation wrong, but Japanese-Americans were and are loyal Americans."
—President Gerald Ford, in a statement that ended the power of Executive Order 9066 in 1976

*Two Japanese-American girls lead their class in the Pledge of Allegiance, just a few weeks before they were forced to leave their homes for an internment camp.*

been the number one executive for Columbia Records in China and Japan. Now he worked packing fruit, trying to make enough money for us to rent a place to live."

## WHAT HAPPENED TO TERRY GRIMMESEY?

She married and became the mother of three boys and three girls. But being in a prison camp as a girl left scars inside. "For years I could not look people in the eye," she says. "It took away my self-worth. It got better when I decided that what happened was not my fault. I decided to try to help others." For twenty-six years she taught math and pre-algebra to junior high students. "Teachers have the chance to teach children not to hate, and to show kindness to one another," she says. "I never spoke to my students about what happened to me, but I could relate to any child who was hurting inside, or who felt like they didn't fit in."

———◆✕◆———

*"It really* was *Stan Musial . . . This was not junior high."*—Joe Nuxhall

# Joe Nuxhall and Anna Meyer: A Wartime Chance to Play Ball

Cincinnati, Ohio, and Kenosha, Wisconsin, 1944

*World War II touched everything—even baseball. When shiploads of major league players went off to war, President Franklin Roosevelt thought about stopping professional baseball until the war ended. But then he decided the game meant too much to too many people to take it away. The games went on, and major league baseball scouts looked in unusual places for players. One Saturday afternoon in 1944, a fifteen-year-old junior high school student named Joe Nuxhall found himself on the pitcher's mound against baseball's toughest lineup, the St. Louis Cardinals.*

"It was the summer between eighth and ninth grade when they found me. My dad and I were playing in the same Sunday league in Hamilton, Ohio, but we were on different teams. One Sunday some scouts came up from Cincinnati to watch my dad play, but our game got started before his so they watched me pitch. I was only fourteen, but I was already 6′3″ and 190 pounds. I didn't have a curveball but I could really throw hard. 'Straight ahead and let 'er fly,' that was my motto.

"The scouts introduced themselves to me after the game and said they wanted to sign me right up. I wouldn't do it, because I wanted to play ninth grade basketball. So I waited until right after basketball season, and in February of 1944 I signed a contract with the Cincinnati Reds. I got a five hundred dollar bonus and $175 a month. I thought I was a millionaire. The deal was that whenever the Reds were in Cincinnati and I didn't have school I'd go down to Cincinnati and put on a uniform and sit on the Reds' bench.

"The players were really nice to me. The first day I walked into the clubhouse, an outfielder named Eric Tipton looked up at me and asked me how old I was. I said 'fifteen.' He said, 'Son, you're big enough to kill a bear with a switch.' When the games started I'd sit in the dugout with them, and we'd talk about what was going on, but I never even dreamed of getting to play.

*Joe Nuxhall, a major leaguer at age fifteen*

"Then this one Saturday afternoon we were playing the St. Louis Cardinals and they were beating us 13–0. The ninth inning came, and I was sitting there thinking, 'Boy, these guys can hit' when all of a sudden our manager, Mr. McKechnie, walked down to my end of the bench and told me I was going in. I was scared to death. The Cardinals were the world champions that year. They had the hardest-hitting lineup in baseball.

"When I walked out there I was so nervous I don't even remember what my catcher said to me. The first batter grounded out, I walked the second and the third popped up. Not bad, I was thinking, and then Stan Musial came up. I just stood there staring at him. It really *was* Stan Musial, the most feared hitter in the league. There was that famous red number six. This was not junior high. I looked at him for a while until I had to throw the ball. Then I did, as hard as I could. He cracked it even harder to right field for a single. If he had hit it higher it would have been a homer. After that I never got anyone else out. I walked five and gave up two hits and threw a wild pitch. They scored five runs. My earned-run average was sixty-something when they took me out.

"None of my friends or family were in the crowd that day because no one expected that I would ever get into a game. But when I got home everyone was excited. My mom had heard it on the radio. All the

*Anna Meyer's first baseball card*

## ALL-AMERICAN GIRLS PROFESSIONAL BASEBALL LEAGUE

At first their game was more like softball than baseball. Women pitched underhanded and played with a larger ball on a smaller field than men in the major leagues. The rules quickly changed when officials and fans saw how well they could play. The league drew many fans even after major leaguers came back from war. Attendance dropped off in 1949 when officials pulled money out of the league and gave control of the teams to local investors. The league disbanded in 1953.

kids in the neighborhood wanted to know how it felt to pitch to Musial. They were happy for me. We didn't know for a while that I had become the youngest person ever to play in a major league baseball game."

*That same year, the war gave another fifteen-year-old a chance to play professional baseball. The All-American Girls Professional Baseball League was started in 1943 by Philip K. Wrigley, a millionaire chewing-gum-company owner who also owned the Chicago Cubs. Wrigley believed that with so many major league stars away, Americans fans would pay to see good female players. He was right. Wrigley sent scouts out around the United States and Canada, holding tryouts in small towns and cities, signing the best players. The youngest player to sign a contract was fifteen-year-old Anna "Pee Wee" Meyer, who played with the Kenosha Comets and Minneapolis Millerettes in 1944.*

"I grew up in an Indiana town with five baseball-playing brothers who threw grounders at me in the barn from the time I was two. After a while they were smashing them at me—in my family, it was run, catch it or get killed. By the time I reached my teens, I was playing with them on a church league team, and doing very well.

"When my dad heard that there was going to be a pro league for women, he wrote a letter to league officials, recommending this anonymous girl he had seen with great talent. He got a letter back telling him to send her to an upcoming tryout in Peru, Illinois, as long as she wasn't working in an important war-related job.

"Everyone around town said, 'She'll never make it,' and my mom thought I was too young to leave home. On the day Dad and I went to the train station she said, 'I hope you don't make it.' She was crying when we left. I was so determined, though. All the way up on the train I pounded a ball in my glove, not really listening to anyone, just thinking about what I had to do. When we arrived, there were so many women trying out that they had to use six diamonds. They made us all wear little dresses, which was terrible when you had to slide because your legs were unprotected.

"It was a two-day tryout. The first day was a disaster. I tried out at shortstop and made a bunch of errors. I had never been away from home before and I was very nervous and just trying too hard. That night my dad and I had a talk in the hotel. He said I had done terribly and I surely wasn't going to make it, and he wondered what I was going to say to everyone when we got home. I just looked at him and said, 'I'm not going back home, Dad.' The second day I just burned up the diamond. I fielded everything and threw like a rocket. By the end photographers were taking my picture, and I knew I had made it. After the workout they offered me a contract, for forty dollars a week, plus expenses. That was five dollars more than my dad made.

"I wept a bit when I sent my dad off home, but not for long. I was too busy. We finished spring training and then went off to Kenosha, Wisconsin. Two great players, Pepper Pare and Faye Dancer, took me under their wings. Pepper was a catcher, and we worked endlessly on throws to second base. 'Look,' she kept saying. 'Prepare yourself for a terrible throw and then you'll be ready for anything. If it's a good throw, that's gravy.' We studied how to position ourselves for certain batters, footwork, anticipation. I learned so much. I lived with a roommate in a family's home, and we traveled from city to city in trains filled with soldiers. The women smoked, drank, and swore. I didn't but I loved them anyway and I loved being around all the soldiers. I learned a lot about life. Midway through the season I got traded to Minneapolis. There were even bigger crowds and I signed even more autographs.

"We made the playoffs and I didn't get home until nearly October. My teachers let me make up lost work at night, and I got quite a reception. I was named my town's 'Athlete of the Year' and rode through town in a float. I had to wear a dress but it wasn't so bad. There I was, a fifteen-year-old girl making my living as a professional athlete. What a time it was! I loved every minute of it."

## WHAT HAPPENED TO JOE NUXHALL AND ANNA MEYER?

Joe spent seven more years in the minor leagues and finally worked his way back up to the Cincinnati Reds, where he became a fine major league pitcher. He pitched fifteen years for the Reds, with a record of 135 wins and 117 losses. At this writing he is the radio voice of the Cincinnati Reds. Joe is married and has a son.

Anna played five more years and then left to go to college and was soon married. To help pay expenses she took a job in a leather factory and was invited to play on the company's softball team. She had told no one about her baseball career. Early in the first game she fielded a grounder at third and fired the ball to home plate. The catcher went down in a heap. "They had to bring in the rescue squad," Anna recalls. She is the mother of two boys, and, like all former players in the All-American Girls Professional Baseball League, a proud member of the Baseball Hall of Fame.

# PART NINE

# Times That Kept a-Changin'

After World War II, the economy roared back to life and many young Americans shared in the wealth. By 1956, the average American teenager had $10.55 a week to spend. That was about the same amount an entire American *family* had to spend after bills were paid at the end of the Great Depression. And spend it they did, on music and clothes, movies and cars. Whole industries sprang up to relieve teens of their spending money. In 1959, teenagers bought ten million record players and countless transistor radios, machines that gave them the freedom to listen to their own music. Most of it was rock 'n' roll, a new music that often separated them from their parents.

Not everyone was invited to this party. Many young blacks were still stuck in poverty, and in the South they were still humiliated by segregation laws. But their times were changing, too. In 1951, a Farmville, Virginia, high school junior named Barbara Johns led her classmates out of their school to protest their overcrowded building, broken-down desks, and inferior supplies. The students stayed out for two weeks, and their strike developed into a lawsuit against the town. Such behavior was shocking, but it was only the beginning. In the years to follow, young people, white and black, powered the Civil Rights movement, sometimes sacrificing their lives to overthrow segregation laws. As Dr. Martin Luther King, Jr., put it, "The blanket of fear was lifted by Negro youth."

Their example inspired other young Americans to step forward in the following years. They challenged America's involvement in the Vietnam War and fought to expand opportunities for women and girls. Young environmentalists insisted on the importance of a safe and beautiful planet.

In 1963, songwriter Bob Dylan wrote "The Times They Are a-Changin'." The song became an anthem of the day, and with good reason. Times changed like lightning in the second half of the twentieth century, and young people had never been more at the center of the action.

*"I paid my fare . . . It's my constitutional right!"*

# Claudette Colvin: The First to Keep Her Seat

Montgomery, Alabama, 1955

*The Civil War may have ended slavery, but it did not end racial prejudice.*
*In the decades after, whites passed hundreds of laws to keep whites and blacks from living,*
*playing, working, and riding buses or trains together, and even from being buried*
*in the same cemeteries. Called Jim Crow laws, after a character in an old song, these rules*
*were often enforced by violence. Jim Crow was strongest in the South, but it swaggered*
*through the North, too. In Indianapolis, for example, nearly all black residents lived in*
*one swampy area on the northwest side of town. There were separate parks for colored*
*residents and a high school just for black students and teachers.*
*One of the first successful challenges to Jim Crow came in Montgomery, Alabama.*
*There, in December 1955, forty-two-year-old Rosa Parks refused to give up her seat*
*to a white passenger on a segregated bus. She was arrested and soon freed on bail.*
*Her stand sparked a boycott of the Montgomery buses that lasted more than a year.*
*But few people know that nine months before, a defiant fifteen-year-old girl*
*did the same thing in the same bus system. And later, this same girl stood up for*
*freedom in a historic lawsuit that ended legal segregation in Montgomery.*

Claudette Colvin got on the Highland Gardens bus in downtown Montgomery at about 4 P.M. on March 2, 1955, and settled in for the long ride home to her neighborhood on the north side. She knew the seating rules well—everyone did. You paid your fare in the front and then walked around to the back door so you wouldn't brush up against white people. There were ten seats in the front for whites and ten in the back for blacks. In the middle were sixteen seats where black riders could sit unless a white rider came on and the driver told you to get up. Then you had to move back. Whites and blacks couldn't sit in the same row.

When Claudette got on, there were no whites on the bus. The riders were mostly students like her, going home. Claudette slid into a seat in the middle section, next to the window. It had been a long day, and she was tired. She was daydreaming as the bus began to fill up with white passengers. A white lady took a seat across the aisle from her. As more and more white people got on and began to stare at her, she realized she was supposed to move. Any other day she might have changed seats, but this time she didn't feel like it. She found herself getting angry. Claudette was a tough-minded, smart girl, already a year ahead of others her age in school. She hated racial segregation and she despised the bus laws in particular. "I knew I had to take a stand sometime," she later recalled. "I just didn't know where or when."

The driver looked through the rearview mirror and ordered Claudette to get up. She didn't speak or move. All conversation stopped. "Hey, get up!" the driver yelled. Claudette remained in her seat. The driver told the crowd that he would not drive on until that girl got up. Now other riders started in. "Why don't you get up?" one said. A black student answered from the back, "She doesn't have to. Only thing she's got to do is stay black and die."

The driver got out and hailed a police officer. A traffic patrolman boarded the bus and stood over Claudette. "Aren't you going to get up?" he demanded. And then she faced him. "No," she said loudly. "I do not have to get up. I paid my fare . . . It's my constitutional right!" Words began to pour out fast. Tears formed. She spoke of her rights under the Constitution and the Bill of Rights. The traffic cop went for help. Two more officers entered the bus and each grabbed one of Claudette's wrists, sending her books flying to the floor. She struggled with all her might, flailing her arms and legs and screaming at them that they had no right to do this to her. They shoved her into a police car, pinned her arms back, and slapped handcuffs on her. They insulted her all the way to city hall.

Hours later, Claudette's father bailed her out, but now she was in big trouble. She was charged with violating the segregation law, disorderly conduct, and even "assaulting" the two policemen who had dragged her off the bus. A few days later a judge threw out the first two charges but made her family pay a fine for the assault charge. She was placed on probation for a year. Claudette was furious. She wanted to fight.

She didn't know it, but a group of black leaders in Montgomery had been searching for someone brave enough to do just what she had done. They wanted to challenge Montgomery's segregation laws in court. Now, suddenly, a schoolgirl had been arrested. They debated: Should they use Claudette Colvin's arrest as the test case? In the end, the leaders, including the new minister in town, Dr. Martin Luther King, Jr., backed away from her. Why? People remember it in different ways. Some thought Claudette's arrest had happened too

## ALBERTA SCHENCK: OUTSPOKEN ALASKAN

The experience of black soldiers in World War II began to change attitudes toward racial segregation. At the beginning of the war, black soldiers in the navy could serve only in the mess halls. But as the war unfolded and more soldiers were needed to replace the dead and injured, the army let soldiers of color fight alongside whites in integrated fighting units for the first time in history.

Their bravery raised a question back home: If people of color were good enough to die for their country, weren't they also good enough to eat, swim, study, ride, and shop anywhere they liked? The question spread all the way to a movie theater in Nome, Alaska. One night in 1943, a seventeen-year-old half-Inupiaq girl named Alberta Schenck sat down with her soldier boyfriend in the "white" section of Nome's downtown movie house. An usher told her, "Get over there with the Eskimos!" Alberta refused, and her boyfriend, who was white, insisted that Alberta was his guest in the section. Police lifted her from her seat and hauled her off to jail. Furious, Alberta wrote a telegram of outrage to Alaska's governor. The words seem to scream: "My father was a soldier in World War I. I have two brothers in the army in this war." Her stand led to the passage of an anti-discrimination act in Alaska in 1945.

*Signs like this one in a Florida bus station greeted generations of blacks throughout the South and in some northern cities.*

suddenly for the community to prepare well. When asked, some of the other black passengers who had been on Claudette's bus said they wouldn't appear as witnesses for Claudette in court because they were frightened of what might happen to them. Some leaders thought a girl who had been dragged kicking and screaming from the bus would be too hard to control in court. As one historian later summed it up: "Blacks weren't ready to give up their reliance on their buses for a teenager's troubles."

Claudette thought she was overlooked because her family was poorer than the black leaders in town. "We weren't in the inner circle," she later said. "The middle-class blacks didn't want us as a role model." And her parents were terrified. "[They] didn't sleep at night," she later recalled. "They expected some response from the white community."

Claudette went back to Booker T. Washington High and tried to get on with her junior year. She joined the National Association for the Advancement of Colored People (NAACP) Youth Council and gave speeches to other students about what had happened to her. Some listened, but not many. She became discouraged. "The kids in school wanted to avoid me because they said, 'She's the girl that was in the bus thing.' Sometimes I felt I did something wrong . . . I lost a lot of friends," she later said.

In December, nine months after Claudette's arrest, Rosa Parks also refused to give up her bus seat to a white passenger. She, too, was arrested and released. Now ready, Montgomery's black leaders rallied around Mrs. Parks and quickly organized a boycott of the city buses. Black elementary and high school students passed out thirty-five thousand flyers, telling people to stay off the buses and use car pools instead.

But the bus boycott alone would not end the segregation laws—it was more than just the buses. A young NAACP lawyer named Fred Gray decided to sue the city in federal court, claiming that the segregation laws were unconstitutional. He combed Montgomery for blacks who would testify in court how they had been mistreated on the buses. It would take real courage, because violence was a serious possibility. Gray decided not to use Rosa Parks in this case, because she was already challenging her own arrest in court. After weeks of searching, Gray could find only four blacks in all of Montgomery willing to stand up to the city in court: three women and Claudette Colvin.

The court hearing took place on the sparkling morning of May 11, 1956. The case was called *Browder v. Gayle*, after Mrs. Aurelia Browder—one of the four litigants—and W. A. Gayle, Montgomery's mayor.

Claudette wore a fine blue dress to the hearing. When she heard her name called, she walked to the witness stand and raised her right hand, her eyes sweeping over the three white judges. The city's lawyer attacked right away, trying to trap Claudette into saying that Dr. King and other leaders had manipulated Montgomery's blacks into boycotting the buses against their will.

"Who are your leaders?" the city's lawyer demanded.

"Just we, ourselves," Claudette answered evenly. "We are just a group of people."

"Don't make speeches," snapped one of the judges, so Claudette answered the next few questions with only one word. She kept that up until the lawyer asked her, "Why did you stop riding on December fifth?" Then her eyes narrowed and steel entered her voice: "Because we were treated wrong, dirty and nasty," she replied.

The hearing lasted five hours. A local reporter later wrote, "If there was a star witness . . . it had to be Claudette Colvin." A month later, the judges issued a shocking decision: Montgomery's segregation laws were unconstitutional. Montgomery's lawyers appealed to the U.S. Supreme Court, but the decison was upheld, leaving Montgomery with no choice but to integrate buses and other facilities.

In court and on the bus, Claudette Colvin's courage as a Montgomery teenager set the stage for the first major victory of the Civil Rights movement. As she later put it, "I was just saying 'enough is enough.' "

## WHAT HAPPENED TO CLAUDETTE COLVIN?

She moved to New York City in 1958, where she now lives. She is a caregiver in a nursing home and is the mother of two sons. "I'm glad I did it," she has said. "My generation was angry."

---

### DON'T RIDE THE BUS TO SCHOOL

"Another Negro woman has been arrested and thrown into jail because she refused to get up out of her seat on the bus and give it to a white person. It is the second time since the Claudette Colvin case that a Negro woman has been arrested for the same thing [seven months after Claudette Colvin, a second teen, Mary Louise Smith, was also arrested for refusing to move to the back of the bus] . . . We are, therefore, asking every Negro to stay off the buses on Monday . . . Don't ride the buses to work, to town, to school . . . You can afford to stay out of school for one day if you have no other way to go except by bus."

—From a flyer written and distributed December 5, 1955, just after Rosa Parks was arrested

### FLESH

Signs of racial discrimination were in toys and games, too. Starting in 1949, Crayola crayon boxes included a color called Flesh, which was pinkish orange. Bowing to the Civil Rights movement, the crayon manufacturer renamed it Peach in 1962.

*"It seemed a kind face, [and then] . . . she spat at me."*

# Elizabeth Eckford:
# Facing a Mob on the First Day of School

Little Rock, Arkansas, September 4, 1957

*Elizabeth Eckford was a fifteen-year-old tenth grader in the fall of 1957. She was one of the Little Rock Nine—the first black students to attend Central High School in Little Rock, Arkansas.*

## BROWN V. BOARD OF EDUCATION

Linda Brown was a third-grade student from Topeka, Kansas. She had to walk five long blocks to her school every day, even though she lived much closer to a segregated school for whites only. Linda's father sued the city government to let her go to the all-white school. The case was combined with several similar cases around the country, and it was argued all the way up to the U.S. Supreme Court, as *Brown v. Board of Education of Topeka, Kansas.* Lawyers from the NAACP represented Linda and the other black students. On May 17, 1954, the Supreme Court ruled 9–0 that segregated schools did not give black students an equal chance for a good education. Some school systems integrated smoothly, but other communities took more than ten years to open their schoolhouse doors to children of all races.

On the morning of September 4, 1957, Elizabeth Eckford got up early and pressed the new black-and-white checkered dress her mother had made her for the first day of school. As she was ironing, her little brother turned on the TV. The reporter was wondering if the nine black students knew that there was a mob waiting for them in front of Little Rock Central High School. Well, at least now *she* did.

Elizabeth sat down and waited for the adults who were supposed to pick her up and take the six girls and three boys to school. Eight o'clock came. Then 8:15. No one showed up. Since her family had no phone, she had no way of knowing that the adults had changed the pickup plans. Finally, Elizabeth grabbed her notebook and started out the front door toward the bus stop. Her mother called her back into the living room. Together they knelt in prayer. And then Elizabeth left.

The bus let her off a block from Central High. She could see hundreds of white people gathered across the street from her school, restrained by a police barricade. When they spotted her, they started toward her but the police held them back. Soldiers surrounded the giant redbrick school. She assumed they were there to help her get inside. As television cameras recorded her every step, she made it to the nearest corner of the school and tried to push through the soldiers to the building. The soldiers refused to let her through. They wouldn't even tell her why.

She tried the main entrance, farther down the block. This time the soldiers moved closer together and crossed their rifles in her face. Then she realized they were there to keep her *out.* With nowhere to go, she stepped back into the street and the mob surged toward her. This time the Little Rock police let them go. Clutching her notebook, she tried to keep moving forward toward the bus stop as she was engulfed by the hateful crowd. Some were screaming,

"Lynch her!" At one point she looked into the eyes of an old woman. "It seemed a kind face," Elizabeth remembered, "[and then] . . . she spat at me."

Elizabeth made it to a bench by a bus stop and sat down. The crowd closed in. And then, mercifully, the bus pulled up and a sympathetic white woman took her by the arm, led her in, and sat down beside her. The doors closed against the angry faces and the bus pulled away.

For the next three weeks the Arkansas National Guard, under orders from Governor Orval Faubus, kept the nine black students out of school. Finally, a judge ordered the governor to remove the guardsmen from Central High. President Dwight Eisenhower sent one thousand federal troops to Little Rock to protect the six girls and three boys. Each day, the students were picked up by U.S. soldiers who stayed with them until they went in through a side door.

The girl in a white dress yelling at Elizabeth Eckford is Hazel Bryan Massery. Like Elizabeth, she was fifteen on that day. The words on her tongue were "Go home, nigger." This photograph made Hazel feel ashamed, and she called Elizabeth five years later to apologize. In 1997, she told a reporter, "I grew up in a segregated society and I thought that was the way it was and that's the way it should be . . . I don't want to pass this on to another generation."

But there were no troops to protect them when they got inside. "Once we got into the school, it was very dark," recalled Melba Pattillo Beals, another of the nine. "It was like a deep dark castle. And my eyesight had to adjust to the fact that there were people all around me . . . There has never been in my life any stark terror or fear akin to that." All year long they were taunted and tripped, ignored and called names. "We'd be showering in the gym and someone would turn your shower into scalding . . . you'd be walking out to the volleyball court and someone would break a bottle and trip you on the bottle. I still have scars on my right knee. After a while I started saying to myself, 'Am I less than human?' 'Why did they do this to me?' "

Their parents were terrified. People threatened to kill Elizabeth Eckford's father at work. But the Little Rock Nine didn't quit school, even though some whites refused to attend classes with them. Every one of them finished the year at Central High. Ernest Green, the group's only senior, became the first black student to receive a diploma there.

## WHAT HAPPENED TO ELIZABETH ECKFORD?

She went to college in Illinois and then returned to Arkansas, where she worked as a substitute teacher in the Little Rock public school system. Like all members of the Little Rock Nine, Elizabeth received the U.S. Congressional Gold Medal in 1997. It is the highest award given to a civilian by the U.S. Congress.

———◆✕◆———

*"Three minutes."*—Anonymous warning

# Carolyn McKinstry: On the Firing Line

Birmingham, Alabama, 1963

*Martin Luther King, Jr., called Birmingham, Alabama, the hardest city in the United States for blacks to live in. The city's police commissioner, Eugene "Bull" Connor, was an outspoken racist who enforced the city's Jim Crow laws with an iron fist. In the spring of 1963, civil rights leaders came up with a plan to integrate Birmingham's downtown stores. Using the Sixteenth Street Baptist Church as a base of operations, they sent groups out to demonstrate in front of the stores. They knew Connor's police would arrest them, but the strategy was to fill up the Birmingham jails so completely that there would be no place else to put additional marchers, who would then be free to picket the stores. The strategy would also call the nation's attention to a town that would arrest so many freedom fighters. But soon all the adults who were willing to go to jail were either behind bars or out on bail and not eager to go back. One night at a church meeting, Dr. King asked for new volunteers to be arrested. Only a handful of adults stood up, but Dr. King noticed that a large group of young people were also on their feet. Some appeared to be third and fourth graders, others teenagers. At first Dr. King told them they were too young, but with few other volunteers available he changed his mind. He decided to train the children in nonviolence and let them take part. On May 2, 3, and 4, 1963, thousands of children poured from the church and from their schools and filled the streets of Birmingham. One was studious, church-going fourteen-year-old Carolyn McKinstry.*

*Fourteen-year-old Carolyn McKinstry (right) with her grandfather and cousin in the summer of 1963.*

"My parents tried to shield me from the embarrassment of the segregation laws. When we'd go to a store downtown my mother would say we didn't need to try on clothes. She'd say, 'This is fine, this'll fit.' She would hold the jeans out in front of my brothers and say, 'Oh yes, this is perfect,' because she knew the stores wouldn't let us try the clothes on. I was fifteen before I rode a city bus. We rode a special bus to school, but any time it wasn't running my parents drove us. They drove themselves to death with six kids because they didn't want us to have bad feelings about ourselves on the city buses.

"It was no use. You couldn't help but know the rules in Birmingham. My dad worked at the Birmingham Country Club. He could wait tables but I couldn't visit him there. My elementary and high schools were all black. I never really even had a conversation with a white person until I went off to college. I knew that our textbooks had been to white schools first because they were full of obscenities that seemed written *to* us. It all seemed so wrong."

Carolyn was so sure that her parents wouldn't let her take part in the civil rights demonstrations, she didn't even ask permission. Besides, the center of action was the one building in town where they always let her go—her church.

"I could always say, 'Mom, I have to work at the church today from ten to two.' There were always excuses to be there: Choir rehearsal. Vacation Bible school. Volunteer candy striping. I was the only one in my family that went, so I heard a lot about what was going on and I knew when the mass meetings and rallies were. My parents didn't know about all that was going on at the church.

"Those meetings were powerful. First there would be this wonderful music. Songs like, 'Ain't Gonna Let Nobody Turn Me Around' or 'Woke Up This Morning with My Mind Stayed on Freedom.' You were feeling good, really motivated. You knew everybody around you. My classmates were beside me. And then Dr. King would speak. He said things in a way that we as children could relate to. He'd say, 'We want the right to sit down in a restaurant and eat a hot dog after we shop . . . We want the right to use the water fountain because all water is water, and it's *God's* water.'

"Then there were classes for the children who were willing to march. It was all about nonviolence. They told us if we were knocked down we should stay down. They told us not to resist the dogs. Just stand there. Don't run from them. Before we went out they passed around big wastebaskets and told us to put in anything that could be seen as a weapon. A fingernail file, even a sharp pencil. We were not to give police any reason to say, 'We knocked that child down because she pointed that fingernail file at me.' "

On the morning of May 2, 1963, Carolyn was one of nearly one thousand children who marched out of the Sixteenth Street Baptist Church and into the streets of Birmingham, carrying signs and chanting for freedom. Police arrested them by the hundreds. Singing, they climbed into the police wagons until the police ran out of wagons. Then they ran out of police cars. Then fire trucks. Six hundred young people were in jail after the first day alone. "I have been inspired and moved today," Dr. King told their families at a rally that evening. "I have never seen anything like it."

Word raced around the country. The next morning, dozens of reporters and photographers flew into the Birmingham airport. A second march started at midmorning. The police were angry and embarrassed. They felt the children had made them look foolish. This time they were determined to keep them away from the downtown business section without making arrests. Carolyn hadn't been arrested the day before, though she had wanted to be. Her parents didn't even know she had marched. As she joined nearly four hundred students from her school and began the second day's march downtown, she was hoping she could be more fully involved. She was with a large group of students from her school when she first saw the police.

"I couldn't believe the firepower they had. They had giant water hoses that took several police just to lift and aim. They yelled through megaphones and told us to disperse. 'Go home.' Then it was, 'You have two minutes . . . You have one minute.' And they counted to ten."

Police hoisted the heavy fire hoses into place and turned the water on. The blast of water slammed into the fleeing students, sending them sprawling onto the sidewalk. Some held on to one another and tried to sing. The police waded forward, increasing the pressure. The children tumbled backward and smashed into buildings. Carolyn was running for the church when the water reached her.

"It felt like the side of my face was being slapped really hard. It hurt so bad I tried to hold on to a building so it wouldn't push me down the sidewalk, and it just flattened me against the building. It seemed like it was on me forever. When they finally turned it off I scooted

*A police-directed "water cannon"*
*finds Carolyn McKinstry (left) and two*
*schoolmates with no place to hide.*

around the side of the building and felt for my sweater. They had blasted a hole right through it. And then for some reason I reached up and touched my hair. It was gone, on the right side of my head. My hair, gone. I was furious, and insulted. Why did they have to do *that?*

"I couldn't call my dad to pick me up, he'd ask too many questions, so I walked home, feeling wobbly inside. My mother could see in one look what had happened. My dad came home right after that and hit the ceiling. He tried to tell me I was grounded. I barely heard him. Nothing he was saying meant as much as what had happened to me."

Many other children were injured and shaken, but their courage had mattered. News photographers sent images from Birmingham, Alabama, around the world. Their photos showed young, nonviolent marchers being bitten by police dogs, clubbed in the head, and blasted by water cannons. Millions of people who read the paper the next day were outraged. Overnight, white leaders in Birmingham felt the intense pressure of national public scorn. Within weeks, an agreement was made between black and white leaders in Birmingham, ending legal segregation in the city. But the new rules didn't change the way many people felt. Carolyn, still shaken, spent much of her summer in the one place that always gave her peace—the church. She was just starting to feel like herself again on a pleasant Sunday morning in September:

"We had come to Sunday school that morning. My two little brothers, five and eight years old, were in class downstairs. I was delivering the attendance reports around the church. I dropped off a report downstairs and had just walked up to the second floor when I heard the phone ring in the church office. I picked it up and someone said, 'Three minutes.' I didn't know what it meant. I hung up and I had taken three or four steps into the sanctuary when the bomb went off. I thought for an instant it was thunder because it sort of rolled. Then all of the windows came crashing out. The building shook and there were screams everywhere. Everybody hit the floor and so did I. My first thought was for my brothers. I couldn't find them. I went in and out of the church. It turned out they had just started running. One was four blocks away; the other was three blocks in another direction.

"Soon the church was surrounded by whites passing by in cars. Maybe they didn't really understand how bad what had just happened was. I hope not. But they were singing this song, '2-4-6-8/ We don't want to integrate.' I was frightened. My parents never preached hatred, but I couldn't understand something like this."

Inside, four girls, all friends of Carolyn's, lay dead. Their names were Addie Mae Collins, Denise McNair, Cynthia Wesley, and Carole Robertson. Twenty others were injured. Until the day she left for college, Carolyn wondered if any place was safe in Birmingham.

## What Happened to Carolyn McKinstry?

She graduated from high school with honors, went to Fisk College in Georgia at seventeen, married, and became a mother. She taught school for several years. She was proud to talk with her students about what happened in Birmingham during her girlhood. At this writing, she trains new employees for a large communications company. Of her marches she says, "I haven't changed. I still feel proud that I participated. I'm proud of what we accomplished. Segregation was wrong."

*"A talk show host offered to lend a gun to anyone who would shoot my dad."*

# John Tinker: *Tinker v. Des Moines*

Des Moines, Iowa, 1965–1968

*The Vietnam War divided Americans in the 1960s and early 1970s. First the U.S. government sent military advisers to help one side of a civil war in Vietnam. Troops and high-tech weapons followed. It was like wading in quicksand: Every new step made it harder to get out and caused more and more people in the United States to oppose the war. By 1968, there were 520,000 American soldiers in Southeast Asia and huge protests at home.*

*John Tinker was part of a large Iowa family of war protesters. In 1965, John, fifteen, his thirteen-year-old sister, Mary Beth, and their friend, Chris Eckhardt, fifteen, wore armbands to school to protest the war. When they were expelled, they sued their school system, and the case went all the way to the U.S. Supreme Court. The decision in* Tinker v. Des Moines *still affects the rights of students to say what they like in school.*

*Mary Beth and John Tinker display the antiwar armbands that caused them to be dismissed from their schools and propelled their lawsuit into the U.S. Supreme Court.*

"Starting in 1961, when I was eleven, the Vietnam War became a big part of our family's dinner discussions. I read a lot about it and I heard speakers talk about it and I made up my mind. I opposed our involvement in Vietnam because it was a war. I didn't believe that there were good wars and bad wars. I was brought up to value human life and to see war as a defeat. It meant that better ways hadn't worked. Besides, we weren't defending ourselves. We were dropping bombs onto thatched roofs.

"I argued about the war with anyone who wanted to argue with me. Somebody at my school sizing me up might have said, 'He's wrong, but he's a good debater.' I had a handful of good friends but I wasn't popular. The popular kids couldn't risk their popularity by taking unpopular positions. I could.

"One weekend when I was a sophomore, I went with a church group to a protest march against the war in Washington, D.C. On the way back we decided to wear black armbands to school until Christmas as a way of supporting Senator Robert Kennedy's call for a Christmas truce. About a dozen students in the Des Moines school system did it, but I was the only one from North High. My sister Mary Beth, my eleven-year-old sister, Hope, and my eight-year-old brother, Paul, also decided to do it. So one night we bought black cloth and made armbands.

"Early on the morning of the first day we were going to protest, I was delivering newspapers on my paper route and noticed a story about it. I was amazed because we hadn't even started yet. It said that all the principals had gotten together and banned the wearing of armbands in the Des Moines school system. The story changed things for me: Now we weren't just protesting, we were committing an act of disobedience. These were things you talked out very carefully before you did them. I raced home and tried to call the others. But Chris Eckhardt [a friend who had been on the trip to Washington] and Mary Beth had already left for their schools with their armbands on. I didn't wear mine that first day because I still wanted to talk it over first.

"That night we met at Chris's house. Chris said he had gone straight to the office and presented himself. When he had refused to take off the armband, the vice-principal of his school had said, 'Do you want a busted nose?' When they called his mother, she said, 'I support what he's doing.' So they sent him home and told him not to come back with the armband on. They had told Mary Beth to take off her armband too, and she did, but they kicked her out anyway. We called the school board president for a meeting but he refused, saying it wasn't worth his time. After that, I felt real clear about what I was going to do the next day.

"I was really nervous before school the next morning. There was a story in the paper about Chris and Mary Beth being kicked out. They stayed home, but the other students dropped out of the armband protest, mainly because their parents didn't want to risk losing their jobs. Our parents were terrific—they supported us all the way.

"I put on a dark suit coat and a tie to show respect for the school, stuffed the armband in my coat pocket and walked out the door. I kept thinking, 'Will this day change my whole life?' I meant to put the armband on as I was walking, but I couldn't make myself do it. After home room I went into the bathroom and tried to pin it on, but my hands were shaking so hard I couldn't. I was fumbling with it when a friend of mine came in and helped me. Then I walked around with it on, trying to look normal, but I had to have looked pretty strange especially since I had never worn a suit coat to school before. But for some reason nobody said a thing about it. Finally I realized no one could see it against my dark coat. So I took it off and put the band on over my white shirt. Then it stood out real well.

"At lunch, as I sat with my friends, some students walked by and called me a 'Commie.' It made me feel nervous, because I wasn't used to being the center of attention. And I kept wondering . . . 'How come I haven't been kicked out of school yet?'

"Then an office secretary spotted the armband and reported me. I got called in to see the principal, Mr. Wetter. He said I was putting a black mark on my record, and that this could make it hard for me to get into college. We debated. He said wars are necessary sometimes. Finally I told him, look, I knew what I was doing and that if he had to kick me out of school then I would leave. He called my parents and my father came for me.

"Chris, Mary Beth and I stayed out for four days, until Christmas break. Paul and Hope kept going to school with their armbands on, because the grade school principals hadn't banned them. During the break there was a lot of publicity about our stand. Many people in Des Moines were angry at our family. On Christmas Eve, Mary Beth answered a phone call from someone who threatened to blow up our house. Someone flung red paint on our driveway. A radio talk show host offered to lend a gun to anyone who would shoot my dad. At night I would lie in my bed wondering, 'If someone throws a grenade through the window, what will I do? Dive into the closet? Put the mattress over my head?'

"Over the holiday break we had a big community meeting about what to do next. Lawyers from the Iowa Civil Liberties Union said we might be able to sue the school on the grounds that we had been denied our right to free speech under the First Amendment to the

## OLD ENOUGH TO FIGHT AND VOTE

The Vietnam War produced many changes in American life. One was the Twenty-sixth Amendment to the Constitution, passed in 1971, which lowered the voting age from twenty-one to eighteen. It reflected the widespread opinion that young men who were old enough to be drafted into the armed forces should be able to vote for or against officials who could lead their nation into war.

Constitution. We decided we'd go back to school without the armbands so we could keep studying, and we would sue the Des Moines school system. I wore black for the rest of the year.

"People called me 'Pinko' and 'Commie' all year long. A physics teacher told me he lowered my grade because of what he called 'my attitude.' A history teacher told me he raised my grade to make up for it. An English teacher said in class that maybe these protesters ought to be hung up by their thumbs. Some teachers gave me a chance to talk to their classes, to give my side of the Vietnam War. I welcomed these chances, but I was feeling weird at school."

In April 1966, their lawsuit against the Des Moines school system was heard. John, Mary Beth, and Chris testified in the federal district court in Des Moines. Their lawyers argued that the rule against armbands cut off their right to free speech. They also contended that the rule unfairly banned one form of expression—armbands—but allowed other expressions like wearing political campaign buttons or religious ornaments. The school system's lawyers countered that the school had the responsibility to maintain the health and safety of the students. They said the rule against the armbands was necessary to keep discipline, especially since a former student in one of the Des Moines high schools had been killed in Vietnam.

*Throughout America young antiwar demonstrators— like these in Chicago— found ways to protest.*

"The courtroom was filled with our supporters. Mary Beth, Chris and I were cross-examined by lawyers for both sides. The lawyer for the school board tried to prove that our parents had made us wear the armbands. We lost. The judge ruled that the schools could ban the armbands if they wanted to.

"We appealed the decision in the summer of '66, in St. Louis. It ended in a tie, 4–4, which meant that the lower court's ruling still stood. So we appealed for a hearing with the U.S. Supreme Court. I was driving around town when I heard on the car radio that the Supreme Court had decided to take the case. It didn't get argued until the fall of 1968, when I was a freshman at the University of Iowa. It came up so suddenly that I couldn't get to Washington, D.C., in time. The hearing was all over by the time my family picked me up at the airport.

"In the spring of 1969 it was announced that we won, by a 7–2 majority. The decision still affects students. The armband case made it clear that school officials can't just clamp down on kids for expressing their thoughts. They can tell you not to shout or fight or clap during class, but they can't keep a kid from expressing a thought based on the content of what they're saying. The Supreme Court basically just said, 'No, that's not the kind of society we have here.' "

## WHAT HAPPENED TO JOHN TINKER?

After a brief time in college he dropped out of school and decided to educate himself through reading and traveling. At this writing he lives in an old schoolhouse that he bought and fixed up, and he makes his living as a computer expert.

———◆◆◆◆———

*"I smelled funny smells on the grapes and vines."*

# Jessica Govea: Education of a Union Organizer

Bakersfield, California, late 1960s

*In 1965, California grape pickers made ninety cents an hour. Most were of Mexican heritage and were treated as inferiors by whites. Their average age at death was forty-nine. Migrant workers—those who traveled from field to field—lived in unheated shacks, without indoor plumbing or cooking stoves, segregated by race. Thousands of children worked in fields that had been sprayed with poisons to kill insects, and many died in accidents that could have been prevented. In the late 1960s, farmworkers formed a union and stood up to the growers who owned the fields. One of the first to work full-time for the Farm Workers Association was a girl still in her teens. But in her case, age didn't matter. Jessica Govea was already an experienced organizer.*

"I t was always dark when mother would wake me up. I'd pull on homemade pants and a long-sleeved shirt to protect my arms from scratches and bugs, splash water on my face and get in the car. Every day we went hoping we'd get work but not knowing for sure. The earlier you went, the better your chance, so it would still be dark when we'd get to the field.

## CESAR CHAVEZ

Cesar Chavez, shown here at his eighth-grade graduation, started life on a small farm in Arizona. But when he was ten his father lost the farm and the family became migrant workers in California, picking walnuts and beans and grapes, following the seasons. Sometimes they lived in tents, sometimes shacks. One neighborhood was called *Sal Si Puedes* (Get Out If You Can).

Chavez had attended thirty-seven different schools by the time he graduated from eighth grade. Most were segregated schools, where getting caught speaking Spanish meant being whacked hard across the knuckles with a ruler.

Chavez believed in nonviolent organizing, but he took brave and dramatic action. His tools were boycotts (organizing consumers not to buy grapes), picket lines (trying to get pickers not to work in a non-union grower's field), and strikes. Once he led marchers three hundred miles across California to attract attention to the cause. Another time he refused to eat for more than a month. "Because we have suffered," he declared, "we are not afraid to suffer. In order to survive we are ready to give up everything, even our lives, in our fight for social justice."

While we waited mother would give us breakfast—tacos made from tortillas, filled with eggs and pinto beans or potatoes.

"I worked every summer from the time I was four until I was about fifteen. The first time I picked was in a cotton field near Bakersfield, California. Adults carried sacks that would hold a hundred pounds of cotton. Mom made me a twenty-five-pound sack. I threw cotton bolls into it until it dragged behind me like a tail. Prunes were the worst: The foreman would shake the tree and knock them on the ground. Then we had to crawl around on our hands and knees and put them into buckets. The sweet fruit attracts wasps and we were scared to death of getting stung. Tray grapes were bad, too. You go down the row and cut bunches of grapes with sharp pruning clippers. Sometimes you got nicked by the clippers. Almost all tray grape pickers were children. There may have been child labor laws, but we kids worked because our families needed the income.

"My skin would itch and burn, but I didn't know why. I thought it was because it was hot. I smelled funny smells on the grapes and vines and on the ground. Often I could see them spraying pesticides on the plants that grew in the next field. They never sprayed us while we worked but our plants were covered with chemicals. The thing I hated most, though, was that there was no toilet. I just had to find a place and hope no one could see. It was embarrassing.

"I worked hard. I was like my mother, disciplined and fast. I had one treat to look forward to: Every day on the way home we would stop at a gas station and my mom would buy me an ice-cold bottle of Nehi orange pop."

When Jessica was seven, labor organizers Fred Ross and Cesar Chavez formed the Community Service Organization (CSO) in her hometown of Bakersfield. Bakersfield was a center for farm labor, and it attracted many poor Mexicans and Mexican-Americans. CSO set out to help them find places to live, medical care, food, and legal aid. CSO also encouraged them to register to vote. Jessica's father was a well-respected leader in the Mexican-American community, so Chavez looked him up right away. Jessica says:

"I could tell Cesar Chavez was important by the way others respected him, but there was nothing about him that made you afraid of him. It didn't matter that I was young, he sat down and talked with me. And when he did I knew that he really cared about what I was saying, and about me. It came through in his eyes, and in his face.

"I went door-to-door with my father when he worked for CSO and listened to him talk with people. My father never talked down to people. He listened carefully and spoke respectfully. People told him stories of how they had been discriminated against in jobs, hospitals, schools, public offices. He had no room in his heart for injustice. I learned a lot about organizing just from listening to these conversations.

"I had similar problems in my own life. At my school, we Mexican-Americans were punished when we spoke Spanish, even though that was the language we spoke at home. We were stood in a corner, or we got smacked. My father was asking people to join together through CSO to try to make some changes. To protest. To register to vote. To become strong by acting together. It all made sense to me.

"I became his assistant when I turned nine. I helped him produce leaflets, one sheet at a time on a machine with purple ink. 'Register to vote,' they would say, or 'come to a meeting.' Then I learned to type them myself. I started speaking before large crowds when I was very young. I recited patriotic poems at Mexican holiday celebrations. Some were ten or twenty minutes long, and I could deliver them from memory and with great expression.

*A young migrant child picks onions.*

*Children of farmworkers joined the fight for better pay and working conditions.*

"I grew more and more confident and independent. A bunch of farmworker kids and other working-class kids formed 'Junior CSO.' We had our own officers and meetings. I was president. Our first campaign was for a new park. When I was in eighth grade my best friend, Virginia, got run over by a speeding truck while she was taking her little brothers and sisters to a park, three miles away, that could only be reached by crossing a dangerous road. She just had time to throw the children aside but she couldn't save herself. We drew up a petition to convince county officials to make a park closer to us and went around door-to-door and asked people to sign.

"The lessons I had learned with my father came back to help me. I was always very clear about why I was at someone's door. I knew how to listen patiently and to express my own view. I knew how to discuss an issue and come to an agreement. Basically, I knew how to practice democracy. I knew that the most successful actions are those in which you figure out a way for everybody to make a contribution. One old man was especially mean to us. He kept saying, 'I'm not gonna sign anything . . . Get away from me.' I made him my personal project. And I signed him up, though it took a long time. Four years after Virginia's death, the county supervisors passed a resolution to make a park. They took all the credit—which was fine—but we Junior CSO'ers did it.

"In the middle 60's Cesar Chavez left CSO to organize a new labor union for farmworkers. Our family supported him. We knew for ourselves what it meant to work in the fields—the long hours, the lousy conditions, the poor pay. People sometimes met in my backyard when they were afraid to be seen meeting with Cesar at their homes. They feared they would be 'blacklisted,' which meant that no grower would hire them.

They felt safe talking with him in our home. Many important plans were made in a little circle of chairs in our backyard.

"One night after I graduated from high school, Cesar invited my dad to a meeting. He couldn't go, so I represented our family. We gathered in a little house about thirty miles out of Bakersfield. They were going to organize a union for farmworkers. The conversation so excited me that I started volunteering right away in the small office they set up, but I wanted to do more. I told my father, 'Dad, I want to go work full-time with Cesar.' At first he said no—college was his dream for me—but my mind was made up. For a while there was a lot of tension around home. Finally he agreed, but he said just for a year. A year turned into sixteen. After I started, it didn't take long for my mom and dad to support me.

"I moved to Delano, California, and joined the staff of the National Farm Workers Association [later renamed the United Farm Workers]. We urged workers to strike—not to pick table grapes until they got better pay and working conditions. I was still in my teens but I had a lot of work and responsibility. I started every morning at a field, carrying signs and marching in a picket line, urging the pickers who showed up to join us and not work in the fields that day. Then I worked in the service center, where we helped families of farmworkers. One of my first jobs was to act as a translator for a family whose toddler had been killed by the pesticides. She had inhaled them from her dad's clothes by hugging him when he got home from work.

"That life wasn't easy. Room and board often meant sleeping on someone's floor or in the basement, and food sometimes meant nothing. I got paid five dollars a week. But I believed in what I was doing, and I was good at what I did. The lessons I had learned as a girl had prepared me well."

## WHAT HAPPENED TO JESSICA GOVEA?

She worked for the United Farm Workers for sixteen years and became one of the group's key leaders. "Our union wasn't about high tech or computers," she recalls. "It started as a small group of dedicated people with a very clear message. We turned it into a lot of people with a similar message." Twenty-six growers ended up signing contracts with the union. At this writing Jessica still teaches workers, community groups, and college students how to organize.

### FRUITS OF VICTORY

By 1970, almost all California grape growers had signed contracts with the United Farm Workers. Among other things, farmworkers won:

- Higher wages
- A health clinic
- Health benefits
- A credit union
- A community center
- A cooperative gas station

## MOTHS TO MICROCHIPS

The first automatic computer, born in 1943, was nicknamed Mark L. Mark. It was fifty-one feet long. The moths that flew around inside it could foul it up for days. Getting them out was called "debugging" the computer. The next computer was faster, but it still weighed thirty tons. The invention of transistors—small wafers of sandy material on which electrical current could flow without burning out or using miles of wire—made it possible to move great quantities of information on small machines. In 1971, engineers developed the microchip, which allowed the computer to run on fingernail-size chips. In 1975, the year Bill Gates turned nineteen, the first desktop computers were being developed. He was ready to write and sell the software needed to operate the millions of personal computers that would soon enter homes and offices.

*"I knew more [about computers] than he did for the first day, but only for that first day."*—Bill Gates's math teacher

# Bill Gates: Another Revolution

Seattle, Washington, 1968

*As the Vietnam War turned college campuses into battlegrounds, and as racial tension caused American cities to erupt in flames, one freckle-faced Seattle boy with thick glasses barely seemed to notice. Instead, he took the first steps to build a different revolution that would also change the world.*

Bill Gates liked his parents at a time when others were rebelling against theirs. He was a short boy with big feet who worried so much that his little toe was crooked that he spent hours trying to straighten it. He was intensely competitive. When he thought or

*Bill Gates, in a photo from his high school yearbook. The caption reads* WHO IS THIS MAN?

listened intently, he folded his hands in his lap and rocked back and forth. He snapped at his classmates and instructors when they couldn't understand what he meant. He was so good in math and science that his elementary school teachers ran out of things to teach him. They urged his parents to send him to an expensive private school in Seattle called Lakeside Prep. That was no problem for the wealthy Gates family.

In the spring of 1968, when the United States was about to put an astronaut on the moon, Lakeside's teachers decided their students needed to know about computers. In those years, computers were huge machines stuffed with tubes that cost millions of dollars. Even Lakeside couldn't afford a computer, so parents raised three thousand dollars through a raffle to rent student time on a computer in downtown Seattle. They also bought a Teletype machine that allowed users to send messages back and forth to the computer.

Twelve-year-old Bill Gates first saw what a computer could do on a warm spring day when his eighth-grade math class visited Lakeside's computer room. Bill sat down at the Teletype machine, and, with advice from a teacher, pecked out a few instructions. He was amazed when the computer soon wrote him back the correct answers. He tried again. It worked again. For Bill, it was like falling head over heels in love. Though he couldn't see it, the object of his passion was about the size and shape of a refrigerator. It was called the PDP-10, and it sat in an office miles away.

Bill and a handful of classmates began to hole up in Lakeside's computer room most of the day and deep into the night, ordering out for pizza, reading books about computers, and typing instructions called programs to make the computer do what they wanted. They tried to win games. The first program was a tic-tac-toe game. Then it was Monopoly. Soon they knew much more than their teachers about computers.

But they began to get in trouble at Lakeside, cutting classes and not turning in homework. Worse yet, they used up of all the school's computer time in just a few weeks. Luckily for him, Bill's parents supported his passion. They were glad that something absorbed his intellect.

That fall, Lakeside school officials made a deal with a new company in Seattle that offered cheaper rates for the students to use a computer that was much more powerful than the PDP-10. Bill Gates, his fifteen-year-old friend Paul Allen, and a few others formed the Lakeside Programmers Group and dedicated themselves to finding ways to use computer skills in the real world. They envisioned a day when nearly everyone would have a small personal computer, and they wanted to get rich writing the programs that made them operate. Their round-the-clock experiments brought the system crashing down again and again. When the company tried to secure it, the kids foiled the computer's security system like house thieves picking a lock.

Instead of getting mad, the company's executives hired the Lakeside students to fix the weaknesses in the system. They offered a beautiful deal: all the free time they wanted at the computer. "It was when we got free time . . . that we really got into computers," Gates later said. "I mean, then it became hardcore." Worried that the machine was simply inhaling their son, Bill's parents ordered him to stop working on computers for a while. And so he did, for most of a year.

He came back with hurricane force. The Lakeside Programmers found computers on a university campus, and they got even more free time. It was there that they began to sell their services. Bill's father, a lawyer, gave him legal advice about contracts and deals. Making money meant a lot to Bill. He later recalled, "I was the guy who said, 'Let's call the real world and try to sell something to it.' " A company hired them to write a program to computerize company payrolls. They agreed, but this time Lakeside Programmers wanted more than just free time. Bill insisted that every time the company sold a program, the group would get a percentage of the money. They made twenty thousand dollars.

Bill Gates and Paul Allen found new ways to sell their talent. They started their own company, called Traf-O-Data, and produced a small computer to help cities measure how automobile traffic flowed. Another company hired them to find the bugs in their computer system. They even made a few thousand dollars computerizing Lakeside Prep's class scheduling.

By the time Bill Gates graduated from Lakeside Prep at seventeen, he was a world-class expert in computer programming. His senior yearbook photo shows him stretched out on a table in the computer room with a telephone in his hand and a knitted cap pulled over his eyes. The caption says WHO IS THIS MAN? The world would soon find out.

## WHAT HAPPENED TO BILL GATES?

He went to Harvard but dropped out at the age of nineteen when Paul Allen noticed a magazine article describing the first personal computers. They formed a company called Microsoft and began to write software programs for the new computers. As this is written, Microsoft is the world's most profitable company, and Bill Gates, now married and a father, is the richest person in the world. Paul Allen also became a multimillionaire.

### TRY IT FOR YOURSELF

American scientists worked hard to develop computers for military applications during World War II. In 1946, when the war was over, a few civilians got a first peek at ENIAC, which was ten feet tall and stuffed with eighteen thousand tubes. Reporters were skeptical as they watched a scientist prepare to demonstrate it. "Watch closely," said Dr. Arthur Burks, "you may miss it." He then told ENIAC to multiply 97,367 by itself five thousand times and pushed a button. The answer came in "less than the blink of an eye," creating a room full of believers.

*"What am I doing in New Hampshire playing soccer?"*

# Arn Chorn: Starting All Over

Cambodia and New Hampshire, 1970s

*The Vietnam War destroyed the homes and shattered the families of many in Vietnam, Cambodia, Thailand, Laos, and other nations of Southeast Asia. Hundreds of thousands of refugees found their way to the United States in the 1970s and 1980s. Like immigrants before them, they struggled to learn English and adjust to a confusing new life. Arn Chorn was a quiet, musical boy of eight when soldiers from a brutal army called the Khmer Rouge took control of Cambodia in 1975. They enslaved him and fed him so little that he survived mainly on frogs and other animals he could catch. Four years later, when Vietnamese soldiers arrived to take on the Khmer Rouge, Arn was given a machine gun and forced into combat. A year later, so sick of killing that he was willing to risk his own life, he deserted. Arn Chorn's long journey to the United States began with a single step backward into the jungle.*

*Arn Chorn's official Khmer Rouge identification photo. It says he is sixteen, though he was really much younger. The Khmer Rouge boosted the ages in such photos to defend themselves against charges that they used children as soldiers.*

"In a war you have to shoot or be shot. Sometimes I didn't know whether I was shooting at a Vietnamese or a Cambodian. I just shot. We were so deep in the jungle we could barely see each other. When I found out I had killed someone I didn't want to think about what I had done. I would say, 'No, that couldn't have been my bullet.' Finally there came a moment when I couldn't take it anymore. I had seen enough death. I decided to escape.

"One night, when it was very dark, I simply slipped away into the trees. I took my gun and my hammock. For clothing I had only my black Khmer Rouge outfit, so badly torn it was almost like being naked. I had no shoes.

"I lived in the jungle for six months. Most nights I tied my hammock up between two limbs and slept in the trees. I looked for dry places in the jungle, but so did other animals. Sometimes I would wake to feel a snake crawling across me. Most Cambodian snakes are small and neurotoxic: when they bite you, you die. I made myself be still, and they would pass over me. It was the monkeys that helped me survive. You can hear them miles away. They scream from the tall trees and throw food at each other. A lot of it would hit the ground and I would get it.

*The Khmer Rouge issued guns to their boy soldiers that were almost as big as the children themselves. The first few times Arn Chorn shot his, the impact knocked him backward into the dust.*

"I just tried to keep going, following streams, walking in the evening away from the sound of guns. I would tell myself, 'You will see your mother in another mile. You will see your brother, Arn Chorn. Keep going.' And then one day I came to a river. I sat on the bank and thought for a while before I decided to cross. But once I was there, I didn't feel safe under an open sky. For two days I crouched in the field, stuffing myself on corn and sleeping between the rows. On the third day I stood up. A soldier came upon me, and I dropped my gun. He picked me up and carried me in to a refugee camp. I didn't know it, but I was in Thailand.

"Two years later an American man named Peter Pond who was working in the camp got permission to take me and two other Cambodian boys to the United States. I went to live in a big house in a small town in New Hampshire with Peter and his wife. They adopted me.

"I had terrible nightmares almost every night. I didn't know where my family was, or if they were even alive. I slept on my bedroom floor because I couldn't get used to a bed. I still didn't feel safe. It was very hard for me to believe that I no longer had to hunt for food. At night I would steal down to the refrigerator almost every hour and take food back to my room. I would put bananas under my pillow so I could eat in the safety of the night. I wanted to eat them by myself, like I used to. I would finish the banana and put the peel on the floor. When my new mother would come in in the morning she would see the peels and get angry. I didn't know to throw things in a trash container.

"School was terrible. Even though I couldn't speak English, they put me in ninth grade. I had never been to school before, except for a little time at a Buddhist monastery when I was very young. It was so hard to speak English, which was very frustrating, because there were so many things I wanted to say and ask. My English teacher kept wanting me to say 'TH.' Well, there *is* no 'TH' in Cambodian. She kept going, 'TH, TH, *pronounce* it!' Finally she asked one time too many and I spat in her face. She sent me to the principal. I was so angry I was shaking.

"For two years I failed every course in high school, but they let me and the two other Cambodian boys stay in school because we were so good at soccer. We took our anger out on the field. We got to the state championship twice, and we were the stars of the team.

"I was worried about my Cambodian family. I couldn't keep from thinking about the others who were suffering in Cambodia. I wanted to help them. I kept thinking, 'What am I doing in New Hampshire playing soccer?' Then one day my adopted dad said to me, 'If you really want to help more Cambodians come to this country, you have got to speak out.' So he helped me write a speech, one word at a time on a piece of paper. I memorized it, word by word. One Sunday I went to my father's church and I spoke it. It ended, 'I have many friends in refugee camps. Please help me. Thank you.'

"When I finished the people stood up and started clapping. I looked out at them and said to myself, 'Hey . . . this is all right. These people were really listening.' And I thought that even though I was young, I could move people if I could just learn enough English. I could help. The English teacher I spat on didn't give up on me. A year and a half after that first speech in church, I was able to write my own speeches and say anything I wanted."

## WHAT HAPPENED TO ARN CHORN?

He later found out that no other member of his family had survived the Khmer Rouge. He continued to learn English and to speak out for Cambodian refugees. In 1984, Arn and his friend Judith Thompson co-founded Children of War, a group that brought young people from war-torn countries together and gave them a chance to tell their stories to large audiences throughout the United States. He currently lives in Massachusetts, where he works with an organization that helps Cambodian immigrants adjust to life in the United States.

---

*"Now I see you* can *fill this gym."*—Warsaw High athletic director Ike Tallman

# Judi Warren and the Warsaw Tigers: Taking Center Stage

Warsaw, Indiana, 1976

*The 1972 Educational Amendments, passed by Congress, made new rules for schools that receive federal tax money. One section, known as Title IX, requires these schools to provide equal "access and opportunities" for women and girls in education. That meant sports, too, and it was a major change. Most schools had sports programs for boys but very little to offer girls. Basketball-crazy Indiana was typical: There was a huge high school boys' basketball tournament, but there was no post-season tournament at all for girls. Judi Warren was an exceptional basketball player who grew up in a small Indiana town during those years of change.*

## TITLE IX'S EFFECT

In 1971, the year before Title IX was enacted, only 7.5 percent of all high school athletes in the United States were girls. By 1996, it was 39 percent. Powerful, well-funded college programs developed, spawning two women's professional basketball leagues. When the 1999 U.S. Women's Soccer Team won the Women's World Cup, they played before a TV audience of forty million people and a live crowd of nearly eighty thousand. A few months later, more than seven hundred girls' soccer teams entered a Washington, D.C.–area soccer tournament, far more than expected. College coaches begged tournament sponsors to keep the numbers low, so they could have a better chance to scout players for scholarships. One teenage midfielder told a reporter, "You can feel the future just around the corner. I see a professional career as a distinct possibility."

Judi Warren, Cindy Ross, Lisa Vandermark, and Cathy Folk played basketball together all through seventh and eighth grade. "It got so my teammates were closer to me than my own family," Judi remembers. "We really understood each other. Any of us would do anything in the world to keep one of the others from going down."

When they entered high school they became the core of the Warsaw High girls' team, but very few knew about them. At Warsaw, basketball meant boys' basketball. While the boys played on Friday and Saturday nights before thousands of fans, the girls played their midweek games after school in front of a few loyal friends and family members. Socially, boy players were admired as heroes while girl athletes were scorned as "jocks." "We weren't the cheerleaders and high society girls all the other girls looked up to," Judi recalls. "And it wasn't cool to date a jock . . . At times it was discouraging but usually we just went out and had a good time."

The men who ran the sports programs at Warsaw seemed to feel the girls should be grateful they even had a team, since ticket and food sales at the boys' basketball games helped pay for the other sports programs. Judi, Cindy, Lisa, and Cathy saw it differently: Warsaw High was their school, too. Why couldn't they have uniforms? Why should they have to practice in a grade school at 7 P.M., while the boys practiced in the Warsaw gym right after school? The late practices meant that Judi, who lived in the country, rarely got home before ten. Most irritating of all, the Warsaw girls *did* better than the boys' team. Going into their senior year they had lost only four games since ninth grade.

The girls blamed their problems on the varsity boys' basketball coach. Ike Tallman was a tall, imposing man who wore dark, formal suits to school. He had once coached a team to the Indiana boys' championship, which only added to his heroic and intimidating stature. Still, the girls realized they would have to confront him if anything was going to change. One evening after school, their hearts pounding, Judi, Cindy, and Lisa stepped into Warsaw High's athletic office and placed a list of demands on Mr. Tallman's desk.

He studied the list for a moment—uniforms, laundry service, buses to games, cheerleaders, and equal access to the high school gym right after school—and then looked up. He didn't seem angry, just busy. He told them that when they could fill up the Warsaw gym, as the boys did, then they could share it. He said that he would have his secretary print them some tickets and they should see if they could sell them. Then he turned back to what he was doing. Lisa, who had written the list, was furious but somehow held her tongue. Cindy burst into tears. When the tickets arrived, the girls tried to sell them at their churches and among their friends, but attendance didn't increase much. It looked like things would never change.

But important changes *were* happening in Indiana. In 1972, the year Title IX was enacted, a South Bend girl had sued her school for the right to play on the boys' golf team, since the school had no team for girls. She won. Another Indiana schoolgirl won the right to play on the boys' baseball team. New sports programs for girls were springing up at schools throughout the state. Best of all, at the beginning of Judi's senior year, the Warsaw girls learned that the first Indiana girls' state basketball tournament would be held that March. It would mimic the boys' tournament, with all of Indiana's 359 high school girls' teams competing, no matter how big or small the school was. One loss and you were out. The event would take a whole month, with four separate weekend rounds—sectionals, regionals, semi-state, and the championship round in Indianapolis.

Though the odds of winning the tournament were slim, the Warsaw girls thought they had a chance. They had been playing together so long that they were like a single organism. No team had come within twelve points of beating them all season. They had almost forgotten what it felt like to lose.

The usual scattering of relatives and friends watched them win the sectional final against Plymouth High, 52–38. As proud champions, once again they asked Mr. Tallman for better uniforms and cheerleaders. He agreed to let the junior varsity cheerleaders accompany them to the next weekend's regional tournament in Goshen. When they won, becoming one of only sixteen teams left in the tournament, their schoolmates seemed to notice them for the first time. Posters covered the halls. People they barely knew stopped at their lockers to wish them luck. Fifteen hundred Warsaw fans traveled to Fort Wayne to watch them play in the semi-state round. And when they won again, qualifying for the Final Four in Indianapolis, there was high-voltage excitement in Warsaw.

A few afternoons later, the school held a send-off pep rally for them. Judi, Cindy, Lisa, Cathy, and their teammates walked nervously into the gym and sat down on a row of

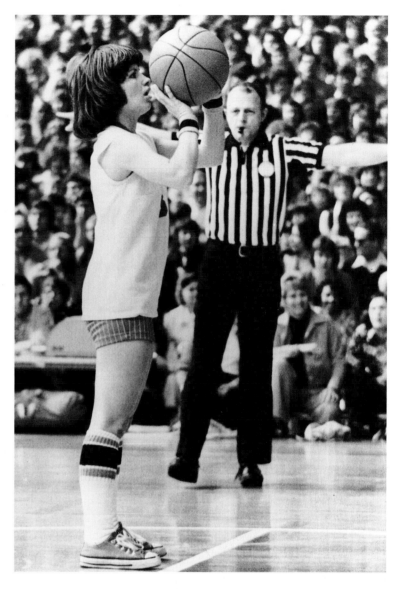

*Judi Warren shoots a free throw.*

*The pioneering 1976 Warsaw Tigers, Indiana's first high school girls' champions*

folding chairs that had been placed in the middle of the basketball court. They stared self-consciously at bleachers filled with their schoolmates.

After a few speeches and cheers, Mr. Tallman walked slowly across the polished floor and stood before the microphone. The gym fell silent. Looking directly at Lisa, he began. "Some of you have been after me to share this gym," he said, "and I said, 'No, not until you can fill it.' Well, I owe you girls an apology." He swept his hand in a slow arc around the room. "Because now I see you *can* fill this gym."

"After that," Cindy Ross recalls, "we got a whole lot of respect for him. It took a lot for the head coach of the Warsaw boys to say he was sorry to a team of girls in front of the whole school."

Warsaw faced East Chicago Roosevelt in the first game of the championship round. Roosevelt was a strong, big-city team led by freshman LaTaunya Pollard, who would later be named the outstanding woman collegiate player in the United States. Roosevelt jumped off to a quick eight-point lead, but Judi stole the ball repeatedly in the second quarter, threading her way through defenses and hooking passes over her head for easy baskets. Warsaw turned the game around and won by a big margin.

A few hours later they played Bloomfield High for the state championship. There were more than nine thousand people in the stands and a big prime-time TV audience. It is still remembered as the game that put girls' basketball on the map in Indiana. The contest was close until the final minute, when Judi once again took over, slashing through the defense to score, or pass for assists. Warsaw won 57–52.

When the last strands of the net had been snipped down, the girls climbed into a Winnebago van and headed home for some sleep. "I was hoping my parents would still be up to drive me home," Judi remembers. The van pulled into the school lot at 3 A.M. When

Judi drew her curtain back, she was looking at a police officer. When they opened the door, he said, "Better run, I don't think we can hold the crowd back any longer." Almost no one in Warsaw had gone to bed that night. Once again the gym at Warsaw was filled, this time well after midnight, and this time to celebrate Indiana's first girls' high school champions.

## WHAT HAPPENED TO JUDI WARREN?

She won a basketball scholarship to Franklin College and became a star player. At this writing, she is the head girls' basketball coach at Carmel High School, outside Indianapolis. Her players wear first-class uniforms. They share practice time on the main court with the boys and coordinate schedules so that both girls and boys get a chance to play on Friday and Saturday nights.

In 1996, Judi coached her team to the final game of the Indiana championship. Almost fifteen thousand fans attended the game, including almost all of Judi's old Warsaw teammates. Carmel lost by four points.

---

*"People would get up and leave, so they would not have to sit anywhere near me."*

# Ryan White: Going to School with AIDS

Kokomo, Indiana, 1984–1986

*Around 1980, Americans encountered a mysterious new disease that seemed to make it very hard for victims to recover even from simple colds and flu. Researchers could find no cure. It was named Acquired Immune Deficiency Syndrome, or AIDS. Later research found it to be a disease of the blood, caused by HIV, which stands for Human Immunodeficiency Virus. It attacks the body's immune system—weakening the body's ability to combat infections. The virus is transmitted through contact with the bodily fluids of an infected person or through medical products that contain blood.*

*An Indiana boy named Ryan White got AIDS in 1984, when he was thirteen. He suffered from hemophilia, which meant that his blood did not clot properly, and*

### SOME FACTS ABOUT HIV/AIDS

- You can't get it from hugging, coughing, sneezing, sweating, or through sharing food or eating utensils.
- You can't get it from toilet seats or drinking fountains.
- You can't get it from mosquitoes or other insects.
- It can be transmitted by having sex with an infected person, or by sharing needles or syringes with an infected person.
- It can also be transmitted through a transfusion of contaminated blood (which is why hospitals carefully monitor their blood supplies).

AIDS is a pandemic, or a worldwide health crisis. By 1997, AIDS had killed twenty-two million people, with many more millions infected. New medicines and treatments have slowed the virus in some parts of the world, but there is still no cure at this writing.

Some other important pandemics:

• The Justinian Plague. Plague is carried by a bacteria that lives inside rats and fleas. This epidemic arose near the Nile River and wiped out more than half the people in the world between A.D. 541 and 700.

• The Black Death. Another outbreak of plague killed one-fourth of the population of Europe between 1347 and 1352.

• Smallpox. Caused by a virus that spreads from human to human through the air. During the Middle Ages, smallpox wiped out hundreds of millions in Europe, Asia, and Africa, and then was carried to the New World by European explorers, where it killed millions of Native Americans.

• The Spanish flu. This flu killed twenty million people throughout the world in less than a year in 1918.

*he was infected with HIV from contaminated blood. Like many throughout history infected with serious diseases, Ryan found that once word got around, many people were afraid to be near him. He described what his life was like at school when he spoke before the Presidential Commission on AIDS in Washington, D.C., in 1988.*

"I came face to face with death at thirteen years old. I was diagnosed with AIDS: a killer . . . Given six months to live and the fighter that I am, I set high goals for myself. It was my decision to live a normal life, to go to school, be with my friends, and enjoy day to day activities. It was not going to be easy.

"The school I was going to said they had no guidelines for a person with AIDS . . . We began a series of court battles for nine months, while I was attending classes by telephone. Eventually, I won the right to attend school, but the prejudice was still there. Listening to medical facts was not enough. People wanted one hundred percent guarantees. There are no one hundred percent guarantees in life, but concessions were made by Mom and me to help ease the fear. We decided to meet them halfway. [This included]:

• Separate restrooms

• No gym

• Separate drinking fountains

• Disposable eating utensils and trays . . .

"Nevertheless, parents of twenty students started their own school. They were still not convinced. Because of the lack of education on AIDS, discrimination, fear, panic, and lies surrounded me.

1. I became the target of Ryan White jokes.

2. Lies [circulated] about me biting people

3. spitting on vegetables and cookies [and]

4. urinating on bathroom walls.

5. Some restaurants threw away my dishes.

6. My school locker was vandalized inside and folders were marked FAG and other obscenities.

"I was labeled a troublemaker, and my mom an unfit mother, and I was not welcome anywhere. People would get up and leave, so they would not have to sit anywhere near me. Even at church, people would not shake my hand.

"This brought in the news media, TV crews, interviews, and numerous public appearances. I became known as the AIDS boy. I received thousands of letters of support from all around the world, all because I wanted to go to school . . . It was difficult, at times, to handle, but I tried to ignore the injustice, because I knew the people [at school] were wrong. My family and I held no hatred for those people because we realized they were victims of their own ignorance. We had great faith that, with patience, understanding, and education, my family and I could be helpful in changing their minds and attitudes around.

"Financial hardships were rough on us, even though Mom had a good job at General Motors. The more I was sick, the more work she had to miss. Bills became impossible to pay. My sister, Andrea, was a championship roller skater who had to sacrifice too. There was no money for her lessons and travel. AIDS can destroy a family if you let it, but luckily for my sister and me, Mom taught us to keep going. Don't give up, be proud of who you are, and never feel sorry for yourself . . .

"At the end of the [1986–1987] school year my family and I decided to move to Cicero, Indiana. We did a lot of hoping and praying that the community would welcome us, and they did. For the first time in three years, we feel we have a home, a supportive school, and lots of friends. I am a normal happy teenager again. I have a learner's permit. I attend sports functions and dances. My studies are important to me . . . I'm just one of the kids, and all because the students of Hamilton Heights High

*Fourteen-year-old Ryan White walks into a middle school in Clinton, Indiana. School officials had told him he could not enter the building because he had AIDS, but the Whites obtained a judge's order that overruled the school.*

School listened to the facts, educated their parents, and believed in me. I believe in myself as I look forward to graduating from Hamilton Heights High School in 1991."

## WHAT HAPPENED TO RYAN WHITE?

Ryan died on April 8, 1990. He became well known throughout the world for his courage and positive attitude. The Ryan White Foundation was established in his name to "increase awareness of personal, family, and community issues related to HIV and AIDS."

*The AIDS Memorial Quilt on display in Washington, D.C., in 1992. Each three-by-six-foot panel commemorates a person lost to AIDS. The quilt covers an area larger than eleven football fields.*

◆—◆»×◆—◆

*"It started with seven kids, right around my kitchen table."*

# Kory Johnson: An Environmentalist for Life

Maryville, Arizona, 1990s

*In 1988, nine-year-old Kory Johnson's older sister Amy died from heart problems after a lifetime of serious illness. Amy's problems were probably caused by well water, contaminated by industrial cleaners, that her mother had drunk while pregnant. Months later, Kory started Children for a Safe Environment, and she has been organizing to keep polluters out of poor neighborhoods ever since. Her success has made her a speaker at youth conferences throughout the country. In 1998, at the age of nineteen, Kory Johnson won the $100,000 Goldman Environmental Prize, recognizing a decade of work on behalf of the environment.*

"I grew up watching Amy. Often I was in her hospital room. When she could come home, she was always hooked up to oxygen. Night after night I heard my mom go in her room to make sure the oxygen was working. Even though we had separate bedrooms, we often ended up sleeping together. We did everything together.

"She died on Valentine's Day, 1988. Not long afterwards, the Centers for Disease Control named our neighborhood a 'cancer cluster,' meaning that there was an unusual concentration of people with cancer there. It fit, too. Many children in our neighborhood had cancer and leukemia. My grandmother had it, and my mother, [and] many of her high school classmates.

"I couldn't accept Amy's death; I would go in her room and smell her clothes. My mom sent me to a bereavement group for kids who had lost siblings. A lot of them were from our neighborhood. We kids started talking. We decided we liked meeting every month, but we didn't like crying. We decided to start a group to find out why so many kids were dying. We called ourselves Children for a Safe Environment [CSE]. It started with seven kids, right around my kitchen table.

"Right when our group started, a company called ENSCO—Environmental Systems Company—applied for permits to put three hazardous waste incinerators into our community. They wanted to dump all the toxic wastes produced in the whole state there, and bring in more from out of state. Ours is just the kind of community dirty industry normally targets: poor people, minorities—I'm Mexican-American on my mother's side and Oglala-Sioux on my father's—not well educated [and] needing jobs. They promised everyone jobs and took the graduating class of a nearby school to Disneyland. A whole lot of people got excited. But we weren't excited. If this happened, trucks full of contaminated waste would be driving by all day long right in front of the grade school."

For the next two and a half years, Kory led CSE through a series of hearings and campaigns to oppose the incinerators. They wrote letters to public officials, testified at public hearings, and organized protests, demonstrations, and art projects, sometimes on their own and sometimes working with the adult-led environmental group Greenpeace Action.

"Right away we could see we had to learn about hazardous wastes. Whenever we'd go to a public meeting, reporters would ask us, 'Are you really concerned, or are your parents making you do this?' We made phone calls all over the U.S. and ordered educational materials. We taught ourselves. We'd make lemonade stands to raise money to send someone— often me—to conferences to get information. I learned not to waste my time going to information meetings organized by industry, but that it was important to attend public hearings where you can find out what the issue is, who controls it and what is being proposed. I learned to follow

the dollars, and how to find out whether my political representatives had accepted campaign money from the industries proposing the project.

"I learned to write good letters, to stage skits, to talk in sound bites at public meetings. I always mentioned my sister when I spoke, and if it made them cry, fine, because I don't want anyone to lose someone like Amy. Most of all I learned to organize, to use everybody I could. Some kids would say, 'My mom will let me play at your house, Kory, but I can't go to any more protests with you.' I'd say, 'Fine, can we make some signs together while you're here?' Our rule was that any action was fair, as long as we didn't commit acts of violence or destroy property.

"We did all sorts of things. Once, we and two other groups hauled a bed onto the lawn of the state capital. We carried briefcases and got in the bed two at a time and passed money back and forth. One [person] was industry and the other was our government. We said we wouldn't move the bed off the lawn until industry got out of bed with government. It went on for days and attracted bigger and bigger crowds. Reporters loved it—after a while *they* got in the bed. We made a sign-up sheet, and CSE's membership went from 7 to 359 [from] that one event.

"We developed creative ways to do press releases. We did a protest on Halloween, and put candy in the press packs. We organized a candlelight rally one night at the state capital, with no adults allowed to participate. Kids came one by one to a microphone to express their concerns, and every news outlet around covered it. One of the girls in our group—Amanda King—noticed that ENSCO had spelled the word 'Environmental' wrong on their stationery. They left out the second 'N.' We called a reporter and they did a huge article making fun of the company and playing up the fact that a kid had discovered the spelling error.

"My mother and I were both often in the news, and not everyone liked it. One teacher told me, 'If you keep this up, Kory, there's not a college in the world that will accept you.' Other teachers would sort of whisper, 'Keep up the good work, Kory, here's ten dollars for your organization.' It bothered me that they felt they had to whisper.

"Finally, as a result of the protests, the State of Arizona paid ENSCO forty-four million dollars to leave. They backed out. In his speech, the Governor said that if he hadn't taken the action, his sons wouldn't have let him come home. It made us kids feel good.

"After that, people around the country started calling me, asking me to speak, to help them organize, to take part in their Earth Day [events]. Sometimes my mother and I would go without good food to send a package of information across the country by overnight express.

"All through my high school years I kept on organizing. I was a cheerleader, and a dance team leader, and did a lot of other school things, but I was determined that young people should have a safe place to live, no matter how rich or poor they were, or what race they were. We fought a scheme to bring forty-five freight cars of DDT-contaminated dirt from California to be dumped in our neighborhood. That time I got arrested for carrying a sign that said, 'Save the Children.' The police grabbed me and put me into a Jeep and took me downtown and made me go to court. My mother was frantic. It got on the news, and school officials found out and said I couldn't be a cheerleader anymore. It was right before a big football game. The players were great—they said that if I wasn't on the field when the game started they would put their helmets down and walk off. Soon after that, my mother got a call saying everything was all right—I could cheer after all.

"I really get tired sometimes, burned out, but I'm not going to quit. We're talking about our future. If we kids don't do something, it's going to be worse. Older people tell me of all the places they could swim when they were young that are closed now, and of the birds and animals they saw that are rare now. My mom went to the same school I did. She said when she went there, there was only one kid in the school who had asthma. Now the nurse has three desk drawers filled with inhalers.

"I would advise kids to get going. Learn about issues, find out who runs your communities, propose good projects of your own. Talk from the heart. Find teachers or other adults to help. Insist on classes that teach more about the environment than the need to recycle and not litter. Get real, practical information. I get really excited when I go to youth conferences of environmentalists. There are a lot of kids willing to work.

"Some of my friends who have come and gone from CSE wonder why I've kept going. I watched my sister die. Ten years later, anytime there's a truck on the freeway, I'm wondering what's in it. And anytime I see a smokestack pouring, I'm wondering what's in the smoke. All kids deserve a safe place to live, rich or poor. I'm in this for life."

## What Happened to Kory Johnson?

After considering offers from several colleges, Kory enrolled at Arizona State University, where she is majoring in psychology. She plans to become a psychologist to help children who have lost siblings.

# Linking Up in the Twenty-first Century

Most mornings fifteen-year-old Mary Fister, coffee cup steaming on the desk before her, has logged on to her family's personal computer by 7 A.M. Typically, she is greeted by at least twenty e-mail messages from around the world. "Usually they arrive from the east overnight and from this hemisphere in the afternoon," she says. As an active member of Nation One, a global network of young people working for social justice, Mary plans events and organizes activities with colleagues in Madagascar, Mexico, Australia, Greece, Canada, and the United States. Often there are several messages from Dakar, Senegal, where Mary is raising funds for a computer lab in a school with fifteen hundred students. "It'll be available to the whole community," she says. "It's a way to help people in one specific place gain access to the Internet and all it has to offer."

Like the boys who sailed with Columbus, Mary is part of a voyage that is shrinking the world by connecting strangers from distant places. "As long as they're on-line," she says, "there is no one in the world we can't talk to, and very little we can't find or learn."

Indeed, young Americans have much to celebrate at the beginning of the twenty-first century. Most have adequate shelter and enough food. With such deadly childhood diseases as polio, tuberculosis, and measles controlled by vaccines, Americans now live nearly thirty years longer than they did in 1900. Laws prohibit child labor. Education is now a right, for both boys and girls. Slavery and racial segregation are forbidden by law. Girls have more opportunities than ever. American society is becoming increasingly diverse, with immigrants from around the world bringing with them their foods, dances, songs, languages, and customs.

But uncertainties and challenges remain. Children are growing up in smaller families, often living with one parent, often removed from the wisdom of elders. A large gap remains between rich and poor. Civil rights laws have not eliminated intolerance. We've only begun to understand how human activities affect the environment. And, looking ahead, some wonder: Will we be able to control technology or will it come to control us?

But the future has never been clear. "What's wrong with uncertainty?" Mary Fister asks. "If everything were predictable, this would be a boring place." Linked to young activists around the world, she feels hopeful about the future. "All in all," she says, "especially if you're above the poverty line, this is a very good time to be young."

# Acknowledgments

I want to thank the many people who helped me research, illustrate, and edit this book.

These historians, librarians, archivists, journalists, documentary filmmakers, and educators suggested subjects and helped me find material: John Noble Wilford, Carla Rahn Phillips, William Keegan, Laura Guadazmo, Jim Baker, Alfred F. Young, Ursula Lamb, Anne Kaplan, Howard Zinn, Wayne Coleman, Johnathan Stayer, Albert Nofi, Alfred Padula, Joel Rubin, Richard Strassberg, Ray Routhier, Cathy Nelson, Rutherford Withus, Steve Zeitlin, Amanda Dargan, William Ferris, Hal Cannon, Patricia Roy, Duncan Todd, Beth Miller, Charles Blockson, Catherine Gurry, Kim Harris, Reggie Harris, Bev Grant, Sally Rogers, Dick McDonough, Steve Grossman, Dan Simberloff, David Wilcove, Stephanie Philbrook, Peter Gribben, Susan Campbell Bertoletti, Fred Gray, Mike Ringring, Steve Thornton, Jeff Yip, Michael Finley, Michael Uys, and Georgia Barnhill.

Huge thanks to Cassandra Fitzherbert and her staff at the University of Southern Maine Interlibrary Loan Department for helping me order materials from around the world. Thanks and admiration to master sleuth Paul D'Alessandro of the Portland, Maine, Public Library. He finds material hidden to all other eyes.

Thanks to Shoshana Hoose, Hannah Hoose, Cheryl Nolan, Tina Groeger, Lena Groeger, The Bookies of the Cambridge, Massachusetts, Public Library, Chuck Wills, Elaine Chubb, and Howard Zinn for reading the manuscript.

For letting me interview them, thanks to Carolyn McKinstry, Judi Warren, Phoebe DeHart, Arn Chorn, Colin Pringle, Jessica Govea, Joe Nuxhall, Anna Meyer, Nona Peagler, John Tinker, Kory Johnson, Senator Gaylord Nelson, Harley "Doc" Holladay, and Mary Fister.

Thanks to Alfred Padula and Ricardo Cabezas for translating material from Spanish to English.

Grateful thanks to my wonderful editor, Melanie Kroupa, for five years of creative partnership on this project. Thanks, too, to her history-loving assistant Sharon McBride. Thanks to the countless people who work at historical societies, museums, and archives for helping us find images to illustrate the book, and to Marty Levick, Melanie Kroupa, and Sharon McBride for painstaking and productive image research.

Above all, thanks to Shoshana, Hannah, and Ruby Hoose, for helping and supporting me in so many ways. I hope I didn't miss too much while I was writing.

# Sources

These are some of the materials I read to research this book. Those marked with asterisks were written especially for young readers. I wish to thank those who kindly gave permission to use previously published material.

## SURVEYS OF UNITED STATES HISTORY

Bremmer, Robert H., ed. *Children and Youth in America: A Documentary History.* Cambridge, Massachusetts: Harvard University Press, 1971. A series mostly about health and social programs for children from colonial times on.

Colbert, David. *Eyewitness to America.* New York: Pantheon, 1997.

*Hakim, Joy. *A History of Us.* New York: Oxford University Press, 1993–97. A ten-volume series about U.S. history, written for young readers.

Takaki, Ronald. *A Different Mirror: A History of Multicultural America.* Boston: Little, Brown, 1993.

Zinn, Howard. *A People's History of the United States.* New York: HarperPerennial, 1990.

## BOOKS AND ARTICLES

### Part One. "¡Tierra!": When Two Worlds Met

Fuson, Robert H. *The Log of Christopher Columbus.* Camden, Maine: International Marine Publishing Co., 1987. Columbus's actual words, translated from Spanish.

Keegan, William F. *The People Who Discovered Columbus.* Gainesville: University of Florida Press, 1992.

Morison, Samuel Eliot. *Admiral of the Ocean Sea: A Life of Christopher Columbus.* Two volumes. Boston: Little, Brown, 1942.

### Part Two. Strangers in Paradise: The British Colonies

*Bulla, Clyde Robert. *John Billington, Friend of Squanto.* New York: Thomas Crowell, 1956.

Demos, John. *The Unredeemed Captive.* New York: Vintage, 1994.

*Fritz, Jean. *The Double Life of Pocahontas.* New York: G. P. Putnam's Sons, 1983.

Mason, Julian D., Jr., ed. *The Poems of Phillis Wheatley.* Chapel Hill: University of North Carolina Press, 1989.

Pinckney, Eliza Lucas. *The Letterbook of Eliza Lucas Pinckney, 1739–62.* Chapel Hill: University of North Carolina Press, 1972.

Smith, Captain John. *The Complete Works of Captain John Smith, 1580–1631.* Edited by Philip L. Barboron. Chapel Hill: University of North Carolina Press, 1986.

*Tom Savage: A Story of Colonial Virginia.* Filmstrip. Chicago: Britannica Books, 1962.

Vassa, Gustavas. *The Interesting Narrative Life of Olaudah Equiano, or Gustavus Vassa the African, Written by Himself.* First published in 1789. Many editions have been published since.

## Part Three. Breaking Away: The American Revolution

*Davis, Burke. *Black Heroes of the American Revolution.* Foreword by Edward W. Brooke. San Diego: Harcourt Brace Jovanovich, 1976, 1991.

*Douty, Esther M. *Forten the Sailmaker.* Chicago: Rand McNally, 1968.

Ellet, Elizabeth. *Women of the American Revolution.* New York: Baker and Scribner, 1849.

Fleming, Thomas. *Liberty! The American Revolution.* New York: Viking Penguin, 1997.

Fox, Ebenezer. *The Adventures of Ebenezer Fox in the Revolutionary War.* Boston: C. Fox, 1847.

Franklin, Benjamin. *The Autobiography of Benjamin Franklin.* Boston: Bedford Books of St. Martin's Press, 1993.

*Kent, Zachary. *Encyclopedia of Presidents: John Quincy Adams.* Chicago: Children's Press, 1987.

*Roop, Peter, and Connie Roop. *Buttons for General Washington.* Minneapolis: Carolrhoda Books, 1986.

*Scheer, George F., ed. *Private Yankee Doodle.* Boston: Little, Brown, 1962. This edition of Joseph Plumb Martin's story retains the original language of Martin's 1830 manuscript.

Winslow, Anna Green. *Diary of Anna Green Winslow, a Boston School Girl of 1771.* Boston: Houghton Mifflin, 1894.

Zobel, Hiller B. *The Boston Massacre.* New York: W. W. Norton, 1970.

## Part Four. Learning to Be a Nation

Cameron, E. H. *Samuel Slater, Father of American Manufacturers.* Portland, Maine: The Bond Wheelright Company, 1960.

*Curtis, Anna L. *Stories of the Underground Railroad.* New York: The Island Workshop Press Co-op, Inc., 1941.

Douglass, Frederick. *Narrative of the Life of Frederick Douglass.* Boston, 1845.

Holland, Ruth. *Mill Child.* New York: Crowell-Collier Press, 1970.

Jay, Allen. *The Autobiography of Allen Jay.* Philadelphia: The John C. Winston Co., 1910. From the Allen Jay Papers, Friends Collection, Earlham College, Richmond, Indiana. Excerpted by permission of Earlham College.

*Jones, Rebecca C. *The Biggest (and Best) Flag That Ever Flew.* Centreville, Maryland: Tidewater Publishers, 1988.

*Kaneko, Hisakazu. *Manjiro: The Man Who Discovered America.* Boston: Houghton Mifflin, 1956.

Meyers, Madeline. *The Cherokee Nation: Life Before the Tears.* Lowell, Massachusetts: Discovery Enterprises, 1994.

Moorhead, Alan. *The Fatal Impact.* Sydney, Australia: Mead and Beckett, 1987.

*Murphy, Jim. *Gone a-Whaling.* New York: Clarion Books, 1998.

Selden, Bernice. *The Mill Girls.* New York: Atheneum, 1983.

Smith, Captain John. *A Sketch of the Cherokee and Choctaw Indians, 1837–38.*

Still, William. *The Underground Railroad.* Chicago: The Johnson Publishing Company, 1970.

Tilton, George Fred. *Cap'n George Fred.* Garden City, New York: Doubleday, 1927.

Tucker, Barbara M. *Samuel Slater and the Origins of the American Textile Industry, 1790–1860.* Ithaca, New York: Cornell University Press, 1984.

## Part Five. One Nation or Two? The Civil War

*Abernethy, Byron, ed. *Private Elisha Stockwell, Jr., Sees the Civil War.* Norman: University of Oklahoma Press, 1958.

Andrews, Eliza Frances. *The Wartime Journal of a Georgia Girl.* New York: D. Appleton and Co., 1908.

Bates, Ralph O. *Billy and Dick: From Andersonville Prison to the White House.* Santa Cruz, California: Sentinel Publishing Co., 1910.

*Berry, Carrie. *Diary: August 1864–January 1866.* Civil War Manuscript 29f, Atlanta History Center Library. Archives/ Atlanta, Georgia. Excerpted by courtesy of the Atlanta History Center.

Bircher, William. *A Drummer Boy's Diary.* St. Paul, Minnesota, St. Paul Book and Stationery Company, 1889.

Davis, Kenneth C. *Don't Know Much About the Civil War.* New York: William Morrow, 1996.

*Hall, Gordon Langley. *Vinnie Ream: The Story of the Girl Who Sculpted Lincoln.* New York: Holt, Rinehart and Winston, 1963.

*Murphy, Jim. *The Boys' War.* New York: Clarion Books, 1990.

Quarles, Benjamin. *The Negro in the Civil War.* New York: Russell and Russell, 1953.

Taylor, Susie King. *A Black Woman's Civil War Memoirs.* Princeton, New Jersey: Markus Wiener Publications, 1995.

## Part Six. Elbow Room: The West

Abbott, E. C., and Helena Huntington Smith. *We Pointed Them North.* New York and Toronto: Farrar and Rinehart, Inc., 1939. Excerpted by permission of the University of Oklahoma Press.

"The Alamo's Only Survivor." Newspaper article in the *San Antonio Daily Express,* May 19, 1907.

Denby, Charles. *Indignant Heart.* Detroit: Wayne State University Press, 1989.

De Voto, Bernard. *The Journals of Lewis and Clark.* Boston: Houghton Mifflin, 1953.

Holt, Hamilton. *The Lives of Undistinguished Americans.* New York: Routledge, 1990.

Kingston, Maxine Hong. *China Men.* New York: Knopf, 1980.

*Madsen, Susan Arrington. *I Walked to Zion: True Stories of Young Pioneers on the Mormon Trail.* Salt Lake City, Utah: Deseret Book Co., 1994. Excerpts from *The History of Mary (Goble) Pay,* published by permission of the Church of Jesus Christ of Latter-day Saints.

Simmons, Leo C. *The Autobiography of a Hopi Indian.* New Haven, Connecticut: Yale University Press, 1942. Excerpted by permission of Yale University Press.

Utley, Robert. *The Lance and the Shield.* New York: Ballantine Books, 1993.

Visscher, William Lightfoot. *The Pony Express, a Thrilling and Truthful History.* Golden, Colorado: Outbooks, 1980 (from a 1908 original).

## Part Seven. Shifting Gears in a New Century

*Bartoletti, Susan. *Growing Up in Coal Country.* Boston: Houghton Mifflin, 1996.

Cohen, Rose. *Out of the Shadow.* New York: George H. Doran Co., 1998.

Dargan, Amanda, and Steven Zeitlin. *City Play.* New Brunswick, New Jersey: Rutgers University Press, 1989.

Mofford, Juliet H. *Child Labor in America.* Carlisle, Massachusetts: Discovery Enterprises, Ltd., 1997.

*Nasaw, David. *Children of the City: At Work and at Play.* New York: Doubleday/Anchor, 1985.

Schermerhorn, Gene. *Letters to Phil.* New York: New York Bound, 1982.

Shuldiner, David, ed. *Connecticut Speaks for Itself: Firsthand Accounts of Life in the Nutmeg State.* Middletown: Connecticut Humanities Council, 1996. Excerpted by permission of the Connecticut Humanities Council.

Stein, Leo, ed. *Out of the Sweatshop.* New York: Quadrangle/ The New York Times Book Co., 1977.

Thayer, John B. *The Sinking of the S.S.* Titanic. Self-published in 1940.

## Part Eight. Hard Times: Wars, Depression, and Dust

DeHart, Phoebe Eaton. *Chronicles of a Western Family.* Copyright © 1993 by Phoebe Eaton DeHart. Excerpts used by permission of the author.

Dunnigan, James F., and Albert A. Nofi. *Dirty Little Secrets of World War II.* New York: William Morrow, 1994.

Harries, Meirion, and Susie Harries. *The Last Days of Innocence: America at War, 1917–1918.* New York: Vintage Books, 1997.

## Part Nine. Times That Kept a-Changin'

Bates, Daisy. *The Long Shadow of Little Rock.* New York: David McKay, 1962.

Branch, Taylor. *Parting the Waters.* New York: Simon and Schuster, 1988.

Erickson, Wallace. *Hard Drive.* New York: John Wiley & Sons, 1992.

Hoose, Phillip. *Hoosiers: The Fabulous Basketball Life of Indiana.* New York: Vintage Books, 1986.

*Levine, Ellen. *Freedom's Children.* New York: G. P. Putnam's Sons, 1993.

*Rochelle, Belinda. *Witness to Freedom.* New York: Penguin Books, 1993.

Seabrook, John. "Getting Wired: E-mail from Bill." Article in *The New Yorker,* January 10, 1994.

White, Ryan. Remarks to the Presidential Council on AIDS, March 1988.

# Index

Howland, John, 28
Hoxie, Richard, 127
Hubbard, Elizabeth, 32
Human Immunodeficiency Virus (HIV), 243
human rights, 125
Hunter, Maj. Gen. David, 117
Hunter, Ned, 107

# I

immigrants
  in American society, 161, 250
  Cambodian, 237–239
  German, 192–195
  Jewish, 165–168
  prejudice against, 191
Incas, 10
Indiana, basketball in, 239–243
Indians. *See also specific tribes*
  bounty on, 35
  captives of, 33–35
  Cherokees, 85–87
  Comanches, 135
  Creeks, 85, 86
  Hopis, vi, 155–159
  Mohawks, 33, 34
  naming of, 7
  Seminoles, 85, 86
  Shoshones, vi, 130, 132
  Sioux, 129, 157, 158
  Utes, 140, 143
  in West, 155
Indian schools, 155–159
Indies, trade routes to, 2
indigo, 37–38
Industrial Revolution, 74. *See also* child labor; factory workers
influenza, Spanish, 195, 244
integration
  of Little Rock, Ark., schools, 218–220
  of Montgomery, Ala., buses, 214–217
internment camps, for Japanese-Americans, 206–207
inventions
  attitudes toward, 235

impact of, in nineteenth and twentieth centuries, 161
Iowa City, 139
Iowa Civil Liberties Union, 227

# J

Jackson, Pres. Andrew, 87
Jackson, "Contraband," 104–105
James I, King, 25, 29
Jamestown colony, 15, 16, 17
  English boys at, 20
  orphans sent to, 23–24
  promotion of, 19
Japan
  in nineteenth century, 87–90
  war declared on, 202
Japanese-Americans, and World War II, 205–208
Jarrett, Vernon, 184
Jay, Allen, 97–100
Jay, John, 59
Jefferson, Pres. Thomas, 36, 45, 129, 130
*Jersey* (prison ship), 67
Jews, immigration of, 165
Jim Crow laws, 214, 220
*John Howland* (whaling ship), 88
Johns, Barbara, 213
Johnson, John Henry, 118, 119
Johnson, Kory, 246–249
Johnson, Pres. Lyndon, 225
Jones, Cleon, 202
Justinian Plague, 244

# K

Kansas, dust storms in, 196–198
Keetley, J. H., 144
Kennedy, Pres. John F., 225
Kennedy, Sen. Robert F., 226
Key, Francis Scott, 73, 81
Khmer Rouge, 237–239
Kickapoo Indian Reservation, and railroads' land sales, 139
King, Amanda, 248
King, Dick, 112–116
King, Edward, 118, 119

King, Dr. Martin Luther, Jr., vi, 213, 215, 217, 220, 221, 222

# L

labor, slave, 97. *See also* child labor; unionization
*La Hogue* (British ship), 77, 78
Lakeside Programmers Group, 235–236
Lane, Ralph, 22
Langston, Dicey, 62, 64
languages
  Cherokee written, 85–86
  difficulty learning English, for immigrants, 238–239
  Spanish, 231
  Taino, 8
Laos, 237
Larcom, Lucy, 82–84
Lee, Clarence, 198
Lee, Gen. Robert E., 126
Lee Chew, 146–150
Lewis, Meriwether, vii, 130–133, 134
Liberty Bond rallies, 193
liberty tea, 48
Lincoln, Mary, 126
Lincoln, Pres. Abraham, 97, 112, 115–116, 117, 143, 171
  bust sculpted of, 124–127
  death of, 126
Lincoln, Tad, 125
Lincoln, Willie, 125, 126
Little Big Horn, battle of, 158
Little Rock, Ark., schools, integration of, 218–220
Little Rock Nine, 218, 219, 220
"lobsterbacks," 50, 51
Long, Milton, 179, 180
Longfellow, Henry Wadsworth, 60
Louis XVI, King, 58
Louisiana Purchase, 130
Lowell, Mass., 82, 83, 84
Loyalists, 62
Lucas, Eliza, 36–38
Ludington, Col. Henry, 60
Ludington, Sybil, 60–61

# M

Macy's department store, 163
Manjiro, 87–90
Manzanar Relocation Center, 206
maps
  Eunice Williams's journey, 34
  fifteenth-century world, xii–1
  John Smith's New England, 26
  John Smith's Virginia, 20
  Lewis and Clark's route, 131
  Sybil Ludington's night ride, 61
marriage, interracial, 18
Martin, Joseph Plumb, 53–57
Mason-Dixon Line, 185
Massachusetts Bay Colony, 25, 29
Massery, Hazel Bryan, 219
Mather, Cotton, 32, 33, 42
Mather, Increase, 33
Matoaka. *See* Pocahontas
Maverick, Samuel, 50, 51, 53
*Mayflower* (ship), 25, 26
McAleenan, Boots, 177
McKendra, Fatima, 220
McKinstry, Carolyn, 220–224
McNair, Denise, 224
McNeil, Margaret, 141
Melville, Herman, 90
Memorial Quilt, AIDS, 246
Mexican-Americans
  as migrant workers, 229, 230
  as Spanish speakers, and school systems, 231
Mexico, 134, 135–137
Meyer, Anna, 208, 210, 211
microchips, 234
Microsoft, 236
migrant workers, 229–233
Miliauskas, Joseph, 168–171
militiamen, in Revolutionary War, 53, 60
mill girls, 82–84
mills. *See* cotton mills
Mills, Clark, 125, 126, 127
mines
  breaker boys in, 168–171
  child labor in, 72
  coal, 170

# Picture Credits

*Every effort has been made to trace the copyright holders, and we apologize for any unintentional omissions.*
*We would be pleased to insert the appropriate acknowledgment in any subsequent edition of this book.*

Alabama Department of Archives and History, Montgomery, Alabama, 109

Courtesy, American Antiquarian Society, 33, 35, 39, 40, 42, 44, 46–47, 49, 55, 69, 72–73, 84, 98

Arents Collections, The New York Public Library, Astor, Lenox and Tilden Foundations, 24

Courtesy of the Atlanta History Center, 120

Alice Austen Collection, Staten Island Historical Society, 177

Baker Library, Harvard Business School, 83, 139

Courtesy of the James Ford Bell Library, University of Minnesota, 4, 6, 11, 12, 19, 20, 26

Boston Athenaeum, 41, 94

Courtesy of the Trustees of the Boston Public Library, 82

Margaret Bourke-White/LIFE Magazine © Time Inc., 190

*Boy and Girl Tramps of America*, by Thomas Minehan, Farrar and Rinehart, 201

Brown Brothers, 166

California Historical Society, North Baker Research Library, Broadside Collection, FN-31871, 148

The Center for American History, The University of Texas at Austin, 134, 136

Courtesy of the Charleston Museum, Charleston, South Carolina, 37 top, 37 bottom

*Child Life in Colonial Days*, by Alice Morse Earle, reprinted by Omnigraphics, 48

Courtesy, Arn Chorn-Pond, 237

Courtesy, Cincinnati Reds, 209, 211

ClassMates.Com Yearbook Archives, 234

Clements Library, University of Michigan, 63

Corbis, 111, 165, 181, 189, 212–213, 219, 225, 228, 245

Courtesy, Phoebe Eaton DeHart, 198

The Denver Public Library, Western History Collection, 133, 140, 156, 157

The Denver Public Library, Western History Collection, painting by Karl Bodmer, 128–129

Courtesy, George Eastman House, 163

Courtesy, Harold Feinstein, 250–251

Courtesy, Lois Thayer Frazier, 180

The Goldman Environmental Foundation, 247

The Granger Collection, New York, 164, 192

Courtesy of the Harvard Map Collection, xii–1

Hawaii State Archives, 147

Courtesy, Will Heyman/The Nature Conservancy, 248

The Historical Society of Pennsylvania (HSP), watercolor of James Forten, from the Leon Gardiner Collection, 65

Courtesy of the Houghton Library, Harvard University, 8

Courtesy of the Illinois State Historical Library, 175

Courtesy, Indiana High School Athletic Association, 241, 242

Courtesy, Terry Grimmesey Janzen, 205

Kansas State Historical Society, 144, 152, 196

The Library Company of Philadelphia, 100, 102, 116

Library of Congress, iii, iv, vii, 3, 15, 16, 17, 43, 51, 52, 54, 96, 104, 107, 108, 110, 113, 123, 124, 153, 160, 169, 170, 172, 176, 185, 186, 188, 197, 199, 204

Paul Margolies © 1996 NAMES Project Foundation, 246

Courtesy, Martha's Vineyard Historical Society, 91

Courtesy of Massachusetts Archives, 25, 70

Courtesy of the Massachusetts Historical Society, 57, 118, 119

Don McCullen/Contact Press Images, 238

Courtesy, Carolyn Maull McKinstry, 221

Courtesy of *Montgomery Advertiser*, Montgomery, Alabama, 214

Charles Moore/Black Star, 223

National Archives, 95, 141, 206, 207

Courtesy of the National Woman's Party, Sewall-Belmont House, Washington, D.C., 183

Nebraska State Historical Society, Solomon D. Butcher Collection, 142

Collection of the New-York Historical Society, 67

New York State Historical Association, Cooperstown, 193

Old Dartmouth Historical Society–New Bedford Whaling Museum, 92, 93

Outbooks, 143

Courtesy, Peabody Essex Museum, Salem, Massachusetts, 29, 30, 31

Courtesy, Anna Petrovich, 210

Courtesy of the Pilgrim Society, Plymouth, Massachusetts, 27

Walter P. Reuther Library, Wayne State University, 230, 231, 232

Rosenbach Museum & Library, Philadelphia, Pennsylvania, 87, 89

St. Joseph Museum, St. Joseph, Missouri, 145

Courtesy of the Scituate Historical Society, 77

Slater Mill Historic Site, Pawtucket, Rhode Island, 75

Sophia Smith Collection, Smith College, 99

Spencer Museum of Art, The University of Kansas. Gift of Marion Palfi, 217

The Star-Spangled Banner Flag House, Baltimore, Maryland, 79

State Historical Society of North Dakota, i, 158

Stock Montage, Inc., 178

Texas State Library and Archives Commission, 137

Courtesy, Jessica Govea Thorboume, 229

*Titanic: A Survivor's Story & The Sinking of the S.S.* Titanic. Courtesy, Academy Chicago Publishers, 178

Union Pacific Museum Collection, 149

United States Postal Service, 60

United States Treasury, 130

Courtesy of the Veterans of Underage Military Service, 202

*We Pointed Them North: Recollections of a Cowpuncher*, by E. C. "Teddy Blue" Abbott and Helena Huntington Smith, reprinted by permission of the University of Oklahoma Press, 151 top, 151 bottom

Western History Collections, University of Oklahoma Library, 86, 159